# Authenticity Is a Feeling

## My Life in PME-ART

by Jacob Wren

With contributions from Caroline Dubois, Richard Ducharme, Claudia Fancello, Marie Claire Forté, Adam Kinner, Sylvie Lachance, Nadia Ross, Yves Sheriff, Kathrin Tiedemann, and Ashlea Watkin

With an afterword by Kathrin Tiedemann

BOOK*HUG, TORONTO | 2018

FIRST EDITION



Cover and inside cover images: The "Monster Book" from *Adventures can be found anywhere, même dans la mélancolie* at the Université du Québec à Chicoutimi in Saguenay. Photo: Marie Claire Forté

The production of this book was made possible through the generous assistance of the Canada Council for the Arts and the Ontario Arts Council. BookThug also acknowledges the support of the Government of Canada through the Canada Book Fund and the Government of Ontario through the Ontario Book Publishing Tax Credit and the Ontario Book Fund.

Book*hug acknowledges the land on which it operates. For thousands of years it has been the traditional land of the Huron-Wendat, the Seneca, and most recently, the Mississaugas of the Credit River. Today, this meeting place is still the home to many Indigenous people from across Turtle Island and we are grateful to have the opportunity to work on this land.



LIBRARY AND ARCHIVES CANADA CATALOGUING IN PUBLICATION

Wren, Jacob, author

Authenticity is a feeling : my life in PME-ART / by Jacob Wren ; with contributions from Caroline Dubois, Richard Ducharme, Claudia Fancello, Marie Claire Forté, Adam Kinner, Sylvie Lachance, Nadia Ross, Yves Sheriff, Kathrin Tiedemann and Ashlea Watkin ; with an afterword by Kathrin Tiedemann.

Issued in print and electronic formats.
ISBN 978-1-77166-389-2 (softcover)
ISBN 978-1-77166-387-8 (HTML)
ISBN 978-1-77166-388-5 (PDF)
ISBN 978-1-77166-386-1 (Kindle)

1. Wren, Jacob. 2. Performance artists–Québec (Province)–Biography. 3. Performance art–Québec (Province). 4. Performance art–Philosophy. 5. Autobiographies. I. Title.

PN2308.W74A3 2018 700.92 C2018-900353-7 C2018-900354-5

PRINTED IN CANADA

Authenticity Is a Feeling
My Life in PME-ART

# Table of Contents

It is in that narrow passage from representation to less deliberate acting, with its space for improvisation and spontaneity, that live art treads, along with the terms 'happening' and 'performance.' It is also that tenuous limit where life and art approach one another. As one breaks away from representation, from fiction, a space opens up for the unpredictable, and therefore living, since life is synonymous with the unpredictable and risk.
– Renato Cohen, *Performance como Linguagem*

Perhaps authenticity is not a grasping for a foundational claim of origin/ality, but it is a reaching – with depth and breadth – inward and outward, an extensional mobility, a centrifugitive movement and dilation that seeks escape and refuge, creating sonic spaces in which one can inhabit that are, at the same time, the public zones in and through which contact occurs.
– Ashon T. Crawley, *Blackpentecostal Breath: The Aesthetics of Possibility*

I simply want to say that representation itself is suffering a deep crisis. This means – and this is probably the biggest quality of the contemporary era – that because of this crisis, human dimensions become very important. The quality of the result is very relative. It is important now that an object – and not just an object, it could be a gesture, a performance, etc. – is based on the human gesture behind it. We are facing the moment when notions such as style, fashion, language...have completely lost their significance. It becomes ridiculous to discuss such issues, as for example the European intellectuals in the fifties who spent a lot of time discussing figurative and abstract painting, what is their relationship, etc. From my point of view I live in the era of total absence, irrelevance of these kinds of criteria. What is relevant now is human presence, with its statement, its body, with its ethical being.
– Viktor Misiano, *Interpol: The Art Exhibition Which Divided East and West*

Introduction:

# Can't leave interdisciplinary performance alone the game needs me

This is my version of some of the things we made and some of the things that happened in and around the things we've made and performed together. The work of PME-ART has always been highly collaborative. Therefore, there are many different versions of these stories, many different ways of telling them. Some of these stories could also be told by Sylvie, Richard, Mathieu, Martin, Tracy, Julie-Andrée, Alex, Benoît, Simone, Samuel, Gaëtan, Laure, Jean-Pierre, Caroline, Claudia, Adam, Marie Claire, Nadège, Ashlea, etc. Each would have their own ways of describing events, placing emphasis on aspects of the work and process that are completely different from what I have chosen to describe. (When I finished a first draft of this book we sent it to everyone, asking for their comments. So now some of their perspectives have been included as well.) The work of PME-ART has been highly collaborative – we sometimes describe it as pseudo-collective – but I now find myself, it seems I now choose, to write this book (mostly) alone. It is a book to mark our twentieth anniversary and only three of us have lasted the full twenty years (Sylvie, Richard, and myself). I will try my best not to do the pleasures and difficulties of the past twenty years a disservice, but with every sentence I can't help but think that there are also so many other ways of telling these stories.

\+ + + +

When people ask me about PME-ART I do my best to describe it accurately and, at the same time, I often find myself describing it in wildly differing ways. It is a bilingual French/English interdisciplinary performance company based in Montreal. However, I am the co-artistic director and I basically don't speak French and understand only a little. The work is based on the paradox and vulnerability of being yourself in a performance situation. Already here my perspective most likely differs (slightly or greatly) from many of our co-conspirators, since I'm the one who first set us on this course. I have always been interested in what it means to stand in front of a room full of people, often strangers, who are watching you, and to do so with as little armouring as possible, not hiding the fact that the situation is potentially unnerving or even nerve-racking, being as vulnerable as possible without turning vulnerability into any kind of drama or crutch. I often say that I personally find performing to be humiliating, and do my best, while performing, not to conceal this aspect of my experience. I often wonder why I have spent the past thirty years of my life obsessively working on this particular question and practice. Perhaps it is only because it is a kind of impossible undertaking, always leaving me artistically destabilized and therefore always leaving me wanting more.

*Destabilizing* is another word we often use to describe the work of PME-ART. Vulnerable, intimate, destabilizing, direct. Unafraid to speak directly to the themes and questions we find ourselves exploring. Bringing imperfection into the performance space. These are all words and phrases I have used over and over again in artist talks and grant applications. They are the sentences I repeat to give those who have never seen our work some sense of what it might be like and, more importantly, of some of the impulses that lie behind it. I often worry these explanations have supplanted the work itself, especially in my own intimate understanding of it, that there is some feeling, perhaps the most important one, regarding how and why I am doing it that these explanations don't even begin to touch. If explanations could suffice there would be no need to perform.

\+ + + +

What exactly did we want so badly to destabilize? And is it still the same thing or things I might want to see destabilized today? In the late eighties, when I was starting out, I would watch theatre in Toronto. I was a teenager interested in art. I also felt extremely alienated (this unfortunately hasn't changed much). I had the feeling, the hope, that live theatre might be a place to partly break this sense of alienation. That the communal experience of being in a room with others, of watching something all together, might be a way of being together that was also art and also somehow more live, immediate, intimate, and collaborative than anything one could experience on television or in the movies. I didn't exactly see this as a reality but more as a possibility or desire. I also didn't have many, or any, friends.

I went to the theatre and what I saw hinted at my desires but mainly felt like their frustrating opposite. If in conventional theatre you had costumes, characters, acting, scripted narrative, piped-in music, and artifice, instead I wanted people dressed in their normal clothing, being themselves, walking a tightrope between structure and spontaneity, music we loved played on vinyl, CDs, or with instruments, anything and everything that might bring us just a little bit closer to authenticity or reality. There was a kind of theatre that already existed and a kind of theatre that didn't yet exist, might never exist, and I knew which side I was on.

+ + + +

This is the way I most often tell the story of my formative years, but there is another side to the story that I talk about considerably less. The reason I, at times, conceal this other side is nothing for me to be proud of. Like many artists, I prefer the mythology of the figure who invents himself. But once again, there were many, many other players directly and indirectly involved in my so-called self-invention. There were shows I saw by international artists like Robert Wilson, the Wooster Group, and Needcompany. There was a small theatre community I was quickly becoming a part of with groups like DNA Theatre, the Augusta Company, Da Da Kamera, Mammalian Diving Reflex, STO Union, and so many others. An entire book could easily be written about this period, Toronto in the nineties, and the community of artists who were all searching for new ways of using the stage, for confronting the audience more directly, trying to update theatre and bring it into dialogue with our contemporary world. So many artists who influenced how and why I was asking myself these questions. An entire book could be written about this period, but this is not that book and I don't think I could be the one to write it. I've erased so much of that time in my memory of it. Over and over again I have wanted to start again, clearing away the past in an attempt to find out what may or may not be possible now and in the future.

+ + + +

The title of this introduction is "Can't leave interdisciplinary performance alone the game needs me" and, though it is often a terrible idea to explain a joke, this particular joke might have a kind of explanation. It is of course a play on the well-known Jay-Z line: "Can't leave rap alone the game needs me." But while millions of people love and follow hip hop, and it is possible to imagine a fan base who might be disappointed if Jay-Z stopped making music, it is difficult for me to imagine anything similar pertaining to the more marginal field of interdisciplinary performance. Hip hop is a living popular art form, with a well-documented, well-loved history and millions of artists competing to bring this vital history into the present. Interdisciplinary performance is something else.

My performance work began as a kind of anti-theatre, as a desire to change theatre and see theatre change. But theatre didn't change, the struggle of always working against an unchanging status quo became exhausting and counterproductive, and therefore gradually my work transformed into something else, a game that also doesn't need me but not the game I was previously pushing so ineffectually against.

\+ + + +

I am writing this book for PME-ART's twentieth anniversary and literally cannot believe we have been doing it this long. I often say I don't necessarily relate to people who make art, performance, or literature, but I do relate to people who make art, performance, and literature who think of quitting every fifteen seconds. Those are really my people. I call us the boy-who-cried-wolf set, since we always announce we're quitting but never do, and therefore no one believes us anymore. It seems to me that anyone who works in the arts today and doesn't have serious, ongoing doubts as to the validity or efficacy of the situation is not facing all of the current, inherent problems and questions with open eyes.

I have been making performances and literature for almost thirty years and, despite or perhaps because of my incessant doubts, I apparently have not quit. I constantly wonder what keeps me going. In one sense I feel that when you're an artist the only way to keep going is to believe you have no choice. Believing one has no choice is also a form of privilege. I also receive more than my fair share of praise for my work and this encouragement must be a factor in how and why I continue. But if I look back over the last twenty years, it becomes clear to me that the most significant factor keeping me in the game are Sylvie and Richard.

Something else I often say: all the artists I admire are such a strange combination of completely open and completely stubborn. I cannot think of two people I have met who are more stubborn and more open, more sincere and more baffling, more consequent and more playful than Sylvie and Richard. Sylvie Lachance and Richard Ducharme. Lachance meaning luck and Ducharme meaning charm. Luck and charm.

+ + + +

My performance work has been a search for authenticity, but I don't think authenticity is something that exists. A work of art cannot be authentic, it can only feel authentic for certain people at certain times. Which is to say that, for me, authenticity is a feeling and about what we feel. In much the same way one might feel sad or feel joy, one can feel something to be authentic. It is a word that suggests engagement and connection. If you feel that Beyoncé is authentic and I don't, this simply means that for you Beyoncé is authentic and for me less so. It doesn't necessarily mean anything about Beyoncé. However, what works of art we feel to be authentic can also tell us a great deal about how we see things, what we value, and can at times also potentially change how we see and feel about the world that surrounds us.

A good conversation is a conversation in which one might change one's mind. I am a ridiculously stubborn person and in fact change my thinking rarely. Yet, at the same time, I am constantly searching for ways to push myself toward openness, for situations and conditions where some shift as to how I see the world might become possible. This is my dream for art, a dream that so often feels like empty idealism, since the vast majority of my art-viewing experiences do little more than make me feel empty. My greatest fear as an artist is making empty work while not knowing I am doing so. When something is rare, I suppose that also makes it precious. (I don't like this way of thinking because it reminds me too much of capitalism. I prefer a world view based on plenitude as opposed to one based on scarcity.) The most intense experiences I've had making and viewing art continue to resonate and return to me. Why do I continuously focus on the anxiety that they are so few and far between?

\+ + + +

The work of PME-ART is highly collaborative and is also very much about collaboration, about people working together, trying to negotiate what is meaningful to them, where and how they disagree, and how such agreements and disagreements might be evocatively conveyed. Collaboration is definitely not easy. As a teenager in Toronto I would see many one-person shows and think the reason there is only one person onstage has little to do with art and much to do with economics. I would see many shows where the people onstage felt like employees primarily doing what they had been told. Instead I wanted to see people onstage doing what they wanted to do, and felt that this wanting should include active, alive ways of working together.

However, looking back over the past twenty years, I also have to admit that I'm not completely sure collaboration is the place for me. It seems I am temperamentally ill-suited for it. Twenty years of doing something I'm ill-suited for and justifying it to myself through compelling artistic results. (This book is in many ways the story of this struggle.) Because though collaboration has never felt good, I still believe in it. Perhaps I believe in it even more because I find it so difficult. Perhaps I believe in it too much. We are all here on this planet, in our various societies and communities, and like it or not we must find ways to work together. The fact that it is often not easy makes it all that much more necessary.

I sometimes wonder if over the years I have over-relied on the metaphor of the collaborative process as microcosm for various global-political realities. It must be a way for me to feel that what

I'm doing is more important than it actually is. I think this might be true of all art. Art is a place where the artist feels what they are doing is more important than it actually is. I sincerely wonder if we'll make it another twenty years.

Part One:

# 10 Years of PME

[1998-2008]

One:

# Prehistory

[1996-1998]

The last performance I made before leaving Toronto was *I Cut, You Bleed*, a show about hurting people unintentionally. (Created and performed in collaboration with Joey Meyer, Denise Mireau, Jennifer Moore, Clinton Walker, Christofer Williamson, and Tracy Wright.) I was young, somewhat younger than my actual age, and not especially self-aware. When I hurt people now I generally know I am doing so. The way we worked on *I Cut, You Bleed* was a kind of revelation for me. Instead of making a show all at once, we created it in small parts, showing each work-in-progress as we went along. I look at the list of these smaller parts, a short list of titles, and it's like looking back into my younger self: *The Physicality of Cynicism, The Deafening Noise of Tupperware, Nightmarehead, a connoisseur of despair*. I had already been making work for about eight years, since I was seventeen, and yet this was the first time it had occurred to me that I could find my own way to develop work, that I didn't have to make shows the same way everyone else made them. That not only the content of the work could be different, but I could also change everything: the process, the presentation cycle, how work accumulated and organically shifted over time. It was as if I was suddenly realizing that, in some artistic sense, the workers could own the means of production, though I of course owned nothing, was only a guest at various festivals and venues.

I met Sylvie in 1996 when we presented *The Deafening Noise of Tupperware* at the Rhubarb! Festival. She was running a festival in Montreal called Les 20 jours du théâtre à risque (the translation I've always preferred is 20 Days of Theatrical Risk) and she had come to see work in English Canada. I had only ever performed in Toronto, and the idea that we could take our show to a festival in Montreal seemed almost impossible to me. I now almost can't remember just how impossible it felt. All the things I once wanted so much that I could barely even believe they were possible, and that now I unthinkingly take for granted. (I am writing this on a plane to Europe. Over the next month we will perform in: Birmingham, Manchester, Bordeaux, Munich, and Cardiff.) I believe Sylvie and I talked for many hours that night, or maybe it was some other night shortly thereafter. She was fascinated by our show but also unconvinced. I don't remember if I sensed this at the time or it was something I only learned later.

I'm trying to remember but I remember almost nothing, though it was one of the most important first meetings of my life. The way Sylvie was talking about art – I was listening, trying to follow, she had so many strong opinions and with each one I thought, or had to ask myself: this is something new, this is something I haven't heard before, or is it. I remember how many times I had been told, as a critique of my young work, that everything had been done, that there was nothing new under the sun, and if I thought I was doing something new, which I did (or maybe I didn't but certainly had the desire to create something I'd never seen before)...but if I thought I was doing something new then I was most likely wrong. Talking to Sylvie was the first time I'd heard so many ideas about theatre and performance that weren't instantly recognizable, that I couldn't immediately place. I was also having difficulty understanding her Québécois accent.

+ + + +

Much later, Sylvie told me that the first time she saw my work she was really not sure it was good. But as she was about to dismiss it, she thought of an observation she'd often had about presenters: that when there was something new in art, when they saw something that might be truly new, they often didn't like it at first. They would dismiss it, using an always similar series of arguments: that we had all done stuff like that, all tried our hand at failed experiments when we were younger (or that our youthful experiments were better). That it was amateur, not professional, too chaotic. That it looks like things that were done in the sixties, seventies, and eighties, and those who don't know history are doomed to repeat it. That the artists don't know what they're doing. That of course it's important for art to be provocative, it's important be provoked, but this work isn't really doing that, fails to provoke them enough. That they of course like to be disturbed, but this work isn't really all that disturbing. And yet they would make all of these points with a lot of anger in their voices, with a strong surge of frustration. Saying that the work makes no impression on them but sounding angry and upset as they said it. Sylvie found herself thinking some or all of these things about *The Deafening Noise of Tupperware*, and therefore wondered if she was seeing something that was in fact new.

It is flattering to my artistic ego to think I was, or am, doing something new. When I was starting out that was still definitely my overwhelming goal, and in many ways it still is, though it is now a goal I treat with the utmost suspicion. The idea of an avant-garde, of a modernist break, now seems to me connected to notions of progress that from, for example, an environmental perspective, are extremely misguided, perhaps even suicidal. I now also see there is something settler colonialist about it all, about saying this is new territory and, in doing so, implicitly erasing everything already there. Things do not move only forward. They go in circles, like the seasons. In art, when you feel you have made a breakthrough, when you feel you are making something new, you are most likely also coming around again to things that have been done before. At the same time, one cannot step in the same river twice, and doing something that has been done before, but doing it now, with a different emphasis, in a different historical moment, with somewhat different questions, assumptions, desires, and hopes – can also (in some sense) be said to be new. Of course, capitalism thrives on novelty – the bright sticker saying "New and Improved" – and I continue to have such a strong desire to be and become anti-capitalist. Though I am also constantly aware of just how close innovation in art is to innovation in capitalism.

It all seems so strange to me – in one sense every time we begin a process I am aiming for a breakthrough, hoping to surprise myself and make something that doesn't particularly remind me of anything I've seen, or if it does remind me of something else, if it does remind me of some other work, or some particular aspect of my own previous work, I still want it to do so in a surprising way. And yet on the other hand I no longer believe in any of these things, they seem to me only like some youthful fantasies that my current understanding of the world can no longer support. What's important, it now seems to me, must be something else: to make work that doesn't feel empty, that raises striking questions, where the content and form are inseparable. But also to deal with the collaborative process in an honest and human way, and for the integrity with which the work has been made to come across as we perform it.

I am still working on all of the same artistic questions I started with, and often wonder if they are now only bad habits, or if the fact that I'm still working on them displays a certain degree of necessary commitment and fidelity to my earliest artistic impulses. At the same time, I'm also working on a more recent set of questions, many of which almost completely contradict the earlier ones, and most often I make no attempt to resolve these contradictions. Everything I do brings me into paradox, and the paradoxes only deepen over time.

Nonetheless, as a matter of principle, I remain fiercely against those who say that everything has been done, even if I am gradually becoming one of them. Because how do they – how do we – know. There is always a certain energy and curiosity in believing that anything might still happen. As well, saying things go in circles has a different emphasis than saying everything has been done, since every time you come around again, the things you do are both the same but also, somehow, desperately not the same at all. Yet now it is still 1996 and therefore, at age twenty-five, I very much believe it is possible and important to make something completely new in art.

\+ + + +

We were invited to Les 20 jours du théâtre à risque and performed in Montreal later the same year. This was the premiere of *I Cut, You Bleed*, the first time we'd taken all the separate parts and put them together. Because the premiere was in Montreal, I added a new text, which was translated into French, and Christofer Williamson then memorized and spoke:

> French is the most beautiful language. Anything you might want to say automatically sounds better when spoken in

French. One sentence in English equals at least two sentences in French. Everything is not only longer, but also more beautiful.

French is the language we use to clarify and illuminate sentiment. Its delicacy reveals what the rough-hewn edges of English do not.

Language destroys what it creates, is inhuman, makes true intimacy impossible, separates us more ferociously than the crumbled stone edifice of the Berlin Wall. But within the humble clemency of the French tongue, all is forgiven.

Politics is a disciple of language. Legal documents form a literature within which it is possible to destroy people's lives in a much more concrete manner than the great romantic poets had even imagined. But every word one writes has consequences. And it is no coincidence that so many of the great works of literature and philosophy were originally formulated in French.

And when Europe becomes the most violent bloodbath that the millennium has yet to experience, as seems likely within the next hundred years, it is even more likely that the epitaph for the millions of mutilated and dead will be written within the supple intonations and tonalities of the ancient yet incalculable French language.

Personally I do not speak, read, or understand a single word of French. I am speaking only hypothetically.

Near the end of his life Rainer Maria Rilke switched from German to French for the following reason: in German there is no word for absence which also implies presence and fulfilment. In German, absence is only emptiness...

The pinnacle of *I Cut, You Bleed* was our interaction with an installation by the artist John Dickson. Three large bags of water hung from the ceiling, and we opened small holes in them, catching the streams of water first with pint glasses and then later with large metal bowls. As the other members of the cast filled a seemingly unlimited supply of pint glasses with falling water, clinking the glasses together as they traded places under the streams, I wandered around the stage with a microphone interviewing them one after another. I think it was probably the last time I created such a purely visual, poetic stage image, since I was steadily drifting toward an artistic point of view in which poetic stage images were unnecessary or even corrupt. I was starting to want something more stripped away, to the point, unadorned. I don't quite remember, but I believe the interviews were about hurting people unintentionally: have you ever hurt someone without meaning to, why do you think you did so, how did they react, etc. Every night the answers were different, and as they answered they also had to concentrate on catching the stream of water, of watching their glass fill toward the rim, of waiting for someone to rescue them, to clink and switch places, before the contents of their glass overflowed onto the stage. I don't know if I thought of it at the time, or if it is only something that occurs to me in retrospect: that this scene has something to do with tears.

\+ + + +

When the run ended I had to return to Toronto, but made it back to Montreal for the end of the festival (which, as its name suggests, lasted twenty days). I had a specific reason for returning: I wanted to meet Sven Åge Birkeland and Knut Ove Arntzen. That year Les 20 jours du théâtre à risque had been part of an exchange with Norway. Norwegian artists Finn Iunker and Lisbeth J. Bodd had come to Montreal to stage a reading of Finn's play *The Answering Machine*. For the second part of the exchange, Quebec artists Carole Nadeau and Gilles Arteau were supposed to go to Bergen to stage a Norwegian translation of a text by Gilles. Sven and Knut Ove had gone to Quebec City to meet with Gilles about the project, but Gilles had for some reason stood them up. (Sylvie tells me she later learned the reason was a significant crisis in his professional life: the artist-run centre he had founded was closing down.) When Sven and Knut Ove returned to Montreal they were furious, they had travelled all the way from Norway to meet him and he hadn't bothered to show up. They were thinking of cancelling the second part of the exchange. Quick on her feet, Sylvie said that if they didn't want Gilles to be part of the project then she had another writer in mind and that other writer was me. I had never been to Europe. I don't think I had ever even met anyone who had been to Norway, and I had certainly never met anyone who ran a theatre in Europe (Sven ran the BIT Teatergarasjen in Bergen).

At that time I was strongly feeling that my possibilities for making and presenting work in Toronto were running out. My work was getting steadily more experimental and Toronto theatre was getting steadily more conservative. People who liked my work were starting to feel they could no longer present it, that it would alienate viewers and funders alike, that it was a risk for them. (The name of Sylvie's festival in Montreal was starting to seem more important to me every day.) A new conservative, provincial government – Mike Harris's "Common Sense Revolution" – was cutting everything, and therefore arts funding cuts could, at times, feel like the least of our worries. I remember reading that Harris had said: let them keep protesting until all the grass in front of City Hall has been completely stomped away. He didn't care, protests or no protests he intended to cut. I remember complaining about the situation to a playwright I knew, and him carefully explaining to me that 'hard times are good for artists.' It was only years later I read a similar sentiment expressed in a different way by Roger Fry:

> And here we touch on a curious economic accident, the importance of which as a determining condition of art production has never been properly emphasized. In modern life, great works of art generally have been, and I suspect, almost must be, produced in defiance of the tastes and predilections of society at large. The artist, therefore, except in those cases where he possesses inherited means, must be able to live and function on an extremely small sum. He must exist almost as sparrows do, by picking up the crumbs that fall from the rich man's table. What wonder, then, that periods of artistic creation and impotence are as hard to predict or account for as the weather itself! And yet there is a certain irony in the fact that every

> civilization is ultimately judged by what of spiritual value it has contributed to the human patrimony. It is only at each present moment that this appears to be of so little consequence as to be negligible.

As I was sitting on the train, on my way to Montreal to meet Sven and Knut Ove for the first time, I wondered about my situation: if I could no longer continue to make and present work in Toronto, was it really possible that I could begin to do so in Europe. I believe at that time, in my mind, the answer was probably not. I found it hard to imagine anything more far-fetched.

\+ + + +

One of my strongest, but at the same time most banal, memories from this time is of getting on the plane to Norway in 1997. I don't think I've ever told even Sylvie this, but getting on that plane somehow brought an end to one of the worst periods of my life. This was a period that lasted several years, a time in which I had a headache more or less twenty-four hours a day, my throat hurt constantly, and, in many ways, everything else, all my muscles, head to toe, hurt as well. Years of seeing doctors, chronic fatigue and fibromyalgia specialists, osteopaths and sacreo-cranial practitioners, starting Feldenkrais and Alexander Technique. I remember lying in the bath and repeating over and over to myself: my throat is going to heal, my back is going to heal, my hip is going to heal, with the idea that I could get on top of the problem through positive thinking. I hadn't completely stopped working – for example, we had just performed in Montreal – but was nonetheless working less and less, wondering if doing less or doing nothing might be some sort of solution.

I remember staring out the window as the plane took off, wondering if when I got there I would be too sick to work. But somehow this first trip to Europe snapped me out of it. I was in basically the same amount of pain, and still am to this day, but slowly it seemed possible to get everything done anyway. I still don't really know the exact nature of my health problems, or what kind of life this is where I mainly try to ignore them, but Norway was the place I first realized it might be possible.

+ + + +

Marie Nerland picked us up at he airport. Marie visited Montreal recently and when I met her for coffee I had the thought – a thought I've had more than a few times before – that she was the very first person I met in Europe. Bergen looks a bit like a town from a storybook: small clapboard houses, winding paths and hills surrounding a small lake, never-ending rain (I was told Norwegians call it 'the shower'). The BIT Teatergarasjen was located in a former garage, a cavernous space that had barely been renovated for maximum coolness. The show that had ended just before we arrived was called *Everybody Goes to Disco, from Moscow to San Francisco* – by the Macedonian company Montažstroj – which I thought was pretty much the best title for a show ever. I was there with Carole Nadeau to stage a reading of the Norwegian translation of the text they had commissioned me to write: *Unrehearsed Beauty*. And to participate in the conference TheatreTextContext, which I was told was about innovative approaches to making text for experimental theatre. The example given was Gertrude Stein's *Dr. Faustus Lights the Lights*, which had recently been staged by Robert Wilson. For *Unrehearsed Beauty* I had the idea to write a text that could be used in absolutely any way, as described in the subtitle: *A series of theatrical proposals – to be repeated, discarded, performed simultaneously and/or recombined in any and all of the many possible combinations – all vaguely relating to the topic of the author's considerable moral ambivalence. (Numbers 1-49 in a continuing series.)*

I had started as a playwright but didn't want to be a playwright anymore, didn't want to put words in other people's mouths, wanted instead to create situations that provided everyone involved with maximum autonomy. It somehow seemed more ethical to me if performers said and did things they could take full responsibility for. At the conference, Finn Iunker, who basically still wanted to be a playwright, said that he particularly didn't like the term. As an example of why he found it inaccurate, he asked the room: have you ever heard of a shipwright? He preferred the term *theatre worker*, someone who makes something, someone who builds theatre piece by piece. TheatreTextContext was the first time I had been around so many people who explicitly wanted to see theatre change. But over the course of the conference I came to understand something I hadn't understood before, that simply because we all wanted to see theatre change didn't mean we were searching for even remotely the same things.

\+ + + +

Knut Ove Arntzen is a theorist who teaches at the University of Bergen. His influence on Norwegian and international theatre has been considerable. One of the terms that Knut Ove coined, and introduced me to during that first visit to Bergen, was post-mainstream. If I understand it correctly, it has to do with the fact that there were many companies making successful large-scale, experimental work in the eighties; this was the work he referred to as the experimental mainstream (for example, some of the same companies I had seen growing up in Toronto: the Wooster Group, Needcompany, etc.). These were shows for large stages and large audiences, that played at international festivals and often combined challenging ways of approaching dance and theatre with spectacular stagings and performer virtuosity. The work that came after, that was still just emerging in the mid-nineties, and that I was apparently a part of, was what he referred to as post-mainstream. This work was often smaller or ambient, privileging an engaged amateurism over clear virtuosity, and was often made by groups or collectives as opposed to one genius director or choreographer.

The term *post-mainstream* continued to follow me around for many years. When we performed in Zagreb, at the Eurokaz Festival, it was one of the key words in the program, along with the term *iconoclastic*. Then, much later, we were invited to Tokyo to perform at the Tokyo Post-Mainstream Performing Arts Festival, run by Hiromi Maruoka, who had picked up the term when she performed at Eurokaz with the Japanese company Gekidan Kaitaisha. A term that had travelled from Norway to Croatia to

Japan, and then with me back to Canada. There was a moment when I even thought post-mainstream might succeed and become a key performance-related art historical term or movement – like postmodernism, surrealism, conceptual art, or relational aesthetics – but it seems within the kinds of performance worlds I inhabit that no single term can ever fully stick, no name for it ever become dominant. Years later there was Hans-Thies Lehmann's book *Postdramatic Theatre*, named for a category that, it seems to me, encapsulated both the experimental mainstream and the post-mainstream and, in Germany at least, this term might now be the one most widely used.

I was in Europe for the first time with a desire to place my work within some larger international context, and I was finding it, but as I was discovering it bit by bit I was also discovering how deep my dissatisfaction with theatre and the world were. Post-mainstream was an idea that more or less described what I was trying to do – and it was even a term that I liked, I actually liked the sound of it – but, like that old joke about not wanting to be part of any club that would have me as a member, I couldn't quite imagine how all this new information could someday become a part of my artistic life. There was now a term that accurately described what I did, but how did that help me or what else did it suggest? I wanted it just as strongly as I didn't.

+ + + +

(Sylvie says that after TheatreTextContext in Norway, many discussions were taking place among our European friends. We also attended the next TheatreTextContext meeting organized by the Belgian theatre company Dito'Dito, during the Kunstenfestivaldesarts in Brussels in 1998. Among other things, we discussed how "theatre was obsessed with the past" [as the playwright Paul Pourveur put it] and raised the question of doing new scripts instead of always doing classic or repertory texts. At that meeting, the Flemish theatre companies who were influenced or inspired by the Dutch group Maatschappij Discordia brought up questions of non-acting and non-rehearsing. Instead of rehearsing, why not have a process that focused predominantly on reading and discussing the script? This would be a way to develop a show without ever fixing anything, allowing the eventual performance to be more open, unset and alive. However, when we finally saw shows created using these methods, we realized they were still very much based on a script, albeit allowing for some improvisation and enlightened overstaging. We also realized that the acting in these shows was quite prominent, even over-the-top, in comparison to the North American style – a style more influenced by performance art, the stand-up comic tradition of speaking directly to the audience, as well as physical and experimental theatre traditions in Quebec, and even more, experimental theatre in Toronto, where all these devices were explored and developed to an impressive extent, as in the work of the Augusta Company.

Sylvie goes on to say that in 1998 we were getting ready to create something from scratch, not based on a script at all. Of taking our own content, developed through reflection and sharp dramaturgical work. This content would be made collaboratively with the artists engaged in the show, who would be speaking for themselves directly to the audience – the whole thing in a form shaped by our discoveries, by research into other art forms, and by each of our varied backgrounds. We were therefore more open than the "Discordians" to rehearsal as a way to write the show together – instead of using or even making a script – to rehearsal as a way of identifying the basics of what we could do in a performance situation. All these discussions influenced what we wanted to do with our work from then on, and with our first show, *En français comme en anglais, it's easy to criticize*. The feeling of having a breakthrough after doing what we did came partly from these earlier experiences and thoughts.)

+ + + +

One or two days before our staged reading of the Norwegian translation of *Unrehearsed Beauty*, Mads Ousdal decided to drop out of the project. The BIT Teatergarasjen had hired three actors from the Theatre Academy, and as we rehearsed I felt everything was going well, until we were told that Mads was leaving. Later, there was some speculation as to why he quit: that the work was too experimental, that he was worried it would make him look bad, that he was famous, or at least his father was a famous actor, but we weren't treating him like he was famous, we were treating him like a normal collaborator. At any rate, we needed a solution and the solution was that I would play Mads's role. (I was originally not supposed to perform at all.) Goril Mauseth and Elin Sogn would speak their already-memorized text in Norwegian translation and I would read the words I had written in English, since there was no time for me to memorize the text (and I obviously wasn't able to read or speak Norwegian).

Carole created *Unrehearsed Beauty* with the audience sitting on the stage at small café tables, transforming it all into a more intimate space. Goril, Elin, and I would alternate between sitting at different tables, speaking our text in a quiet casual manner directly to the two or three audience members who surrounded us, and standing up, addressing the entire room. The show ended with the three of us sitting side by side in the normal audience seating, watching the actual audience, who were still all seated onstage, listening as Leonard Cohen's "Avalanche" played on a record player at 78 instead of 33⅓, Leonard's chipmunk voice bringing another off-kilter aspect of Canada into Norway. Afterwards, I was surprised to learn one of the aspects people liked most was how they interpreted my being onstage with the two Norwegians, and the mixing of our respective languages, as a kind of thematic staging of the artistic collaboration between Canada and Norway. This was of course the furthest thing from my mind – I was only filling in for a performer who had quit, but in doing so it seems the thematic territory had shifted more than we thought.

+ + + +

I sometimes think of these two coincidences that in many ways got me started (or, more accurately, got me started for a second time, since I had already been making work for almost ten years in Toronto). If Gilles had shown up for the meeting in Quebec City, it is likely he would have gone to Norway instead of me. If Mads had stayed in the project, it is likely those who saw it would have understood the work differently, and my role within the project would have felt considerably less prominent. Twice someone dropped out and each time I stepped in to replace them. If these replacements hadn't happened, it is a distinct possibility I would have never gotten off the ground in Europe, or it would have all happened much later, or more gradually, or in some different way.

I don't know if I should think of such occurrences as luck, chance, or opportunism. In a way they are examples of what I have always tried to do: take something negative or unexpected and turn it around so it might resemble a possibility. Anything that goes wrong might be also a chance for something nice to happen. At the very least it is unexpected, and therefore can shift us, even slightly, out of our routines and routine ways of thinking. I'm not sure I exactly like what I'm writing here. It feels to me too much like a motivational speech, an inspirational message, all that bullshit that can so easily devolve into capitalism insisting the individual must make the best of each and every situation, whatever hardships arise along the way. But if there's anything I still like about performance, it's that the unexpected might happen at any time, live in front of an audience or at any point during the process. It is a place where surprises can most productively occur, and it is still somewhat shocking to me that most shows are set up to ensure they so rarely do.

Two:

# En français comme en anglais, it's easy to criticize

(1998–2002)

Created/Performed by:
Martin Bélanger, Alexandra Rockingham Gill, Benoît Lachambre, Julie Andrée T., Tracy Wright, and Jacob Wren

We performed it in:
Montreal, Tangente/Les 20 jours du théâtre à risque • Montreal, Nouvelle Scène-Festival de théâtre des Amériques • Bergen, BIT Teatergarasjen • Prague, Divadlo Archa • Dresden, Projekttheater • Quebec City, Mois Multi Festival • Toronto, The Theatre Centre • Lisbon, Culturgest • Cognac, L'Avant-Scène • Brighton, Gardner Arts Centre • Mont-Saint-Aignan, Centre d'art et d'essai • Manchester, The Green Room • London, ICA • Cardiff, Chapter Arts Centre • Zagreb, Eurokaz Festival • Berlin, Podewil • New York, P.S. 122 • Hamburg, Kampnagel • Stockholm, Kulturhuset • Ghent, Nieuwpoorttheater • Montreal, Usine C

If we could make work in Norwegian, I saw no reason why it wasn't also possible to do so in French. I spoke almost no French, but certainly understood more than I understood Norwegian (actually, this was by no means clear). But how exactly did it all start and does it even matter how. It started in crisis. It started with Les 20 jours du théâtre à risque losing its funding while, at the same time, I felt there was no way for me to continue making work in Toronto. We had both come to the end of something, maybe to the end of our respective ropes, and decided to make a project together. Later, Sylvie told me that part of her decision had to do with how she felt the *I Cut, You Bleed* we performed in Montreal was so much stronger than the earlier version she had seen in Toronto. And when she told me this, something I had always tried to do began to take on the quality of a mission. To never consider any work finished, always keep making it better, while remaining careful not to do anything that might make it worse. (Sometimes I would joke: if the show isn't ready for opening night, maybe we can still get it ready for closing.)

One of the first ideas must have been a collaboration between two anglophones from Toronto and two francophones from Montreal. The relationship between the two cities seemed like a kind of energy to me. I remember going to the first rehearsal. On the smokestack above the building in giant block letters was spray-painted the word OUI. This was just a few years after the 1995 referendum, and OUI meant a yes vote for separating from Canada, for an independent Quebec. It is so hard for me to remember how I saw such questions back then, on my first day working in Montreal, and not to view it all through the lens of having lived here for over fifteen years. But I'm almost certain I had the feeling then that if I had lived in Quebec during the referendum I would have also voted OUI. (And maybe I would even vote yes today, depending on the circumstances.) At the same time, mainly because I didn't speak French, that spray-painted OUI made me feel almost painfully unwelcome.

\+ + + +

There's a story about one of the early rehearsals that has often been repeated. I had brought a pile of books, and was flipping through one particular book, looking for a passage I wanted to start the process with. But I just couldn't seem to find the quote. What's worse, the more I searched the more certain I became that I would find it at any moment. Much later I think I understood what had happened. I believe the quote I was looking for was in the book *Serpent* by Nicholas Mosley, but in my nervousness I was instead searching for it in *The Pugilist at Rest* by Thom Jones. Looking back, the passage I had wanted to begin with was most likely as follows:

> Now it is here that there is an ambiguity in the story even as told by Josephus. It was apparently agreed by the people in the cave that Josephus, as the leading citizen, should himself arrange the drawing of lots to see who should be killed by whom in the suicide pact; and it is also apparent that the drawing of lots and the killing went on until there were just two men left alive in the cave – and one of them was Josephus. In one of the versions of the story that have survived Josephus comments about his own survival – 'Shall we put it down to providence, or simply luck' – and in another he says about himself – 'He counted the numbers cunningly and so deceived them all.' It is not known which of these two versions is the more authentic: but in any case, might they not be complementary? The fact was that after a time there were just two men left alive in the cave; and Josephus put it to the other man yet again – Shall we now surrender to the Romans? And the other man said Yes.
>
> This is the story of why Josephus has been so much hated for centuries – as being someone who, after he had done such fighting as seemed necessary, not only preferred what was traditionally called dishonour to death, but seemed openly to be somewhat mocking of the tradition about honour. And he lived to a successful old age in Italy.
>
> It is true, is it not, that any society, if it is to hold together, has to have ideals which members of the society are ready to die for? What other sort of forces can hold a society together?

> And it is true, is it not, that if in such circumstances an individual chooses to live, then he will naturally be seen as a traitor by those who choose to die?
>
> All this is dependent, of course, on the belief that society is the unit that has to hold together.
>
> But then, if the members of a society are dead, what is it that holds together?
>
> If anything is to live, is it not individuals that do so?

But there was another part that I never did find, that I must have simply imagined or made up, about how Josephus loved life so much, he just wanted to live so fucking much, that he was willing to do anything to keep on living, to keep relishing his great love for life. And this overwhelming love and relish he had for life was a virtue, a virtue that we might say is far more important than any other morals or scruples one might have in such a situation. And also, because he wanted to live so much, he lived to tell the story, become a historian, which is the only reason we today know about the history of the Jews during this time (i.e., the first century CE and the First Jewish–Roman War, including the Siege of Masada). I so clearly remember reading the line "that bastard loved life so much," even though I have never been able to find it in any book.

You can imagine it didn't make an amazing early impression, the image of me endlessly searching through the pages of *The Pugilist at Rest*, announcing that I would find what I was looking for in just one more moment, but never actually finding it. I didn't do it on purpose, but there is a way in which this inefficient uncertainty destabilized my role as head of the group, a destabilization that was in many ways at the heart of the project all the way through. At the same time, if I had found the above passage, I'm not sure the others would have been particularly impressed.

Later I remember Sylvie saying that this idea that I took from Josephus, the idea that there was joy and energy in simply being alive, joy and energy in the simple fact that life is an "ongoing concern," for her seemed like a too obvious one in Quebec, where people already placed a high value on the pleasures of life and on enjoying themselves. For me it was something new, an idea that had previously seemed utterly counterintuitive to my endlessly depressed mind. I thought I was making a breakthrough, and for myself I suppose I was. But there was a sense in which I had come to Quebec to accidentally tell people something they already culturally understood so much better than I ever would. The questionable phenomenon of art telling people things they already know is something I might have first become aware of around this time. And how, paradoxically, sometimes an epiphany is simply hearing something you already know in a new way, almost as if for the first time.

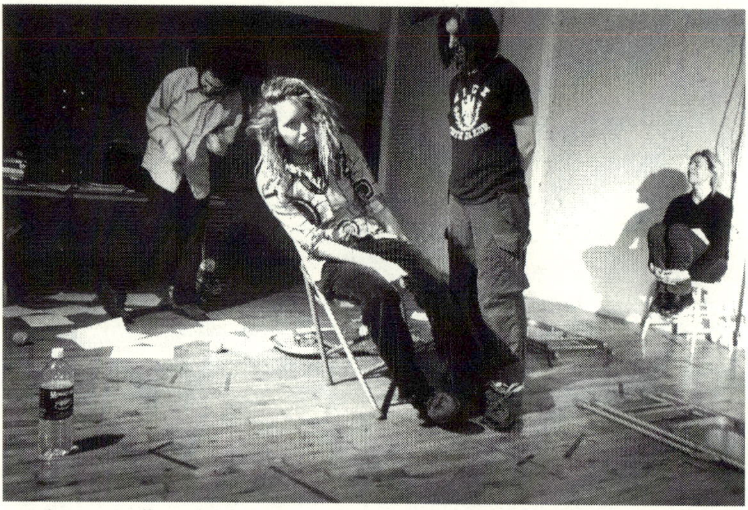

Jacob Wren, Julie Andrée T., Tracy Wright, and Alexandra Rockingham Gill in *En français comme en anglais, it's easy to criticize*. Photo: Sébastien Fournier

Rehearsals were not easy, like five people all pulling in different directions. Tracy Wright and Alexandra Rockingham Gill (Alex) had come with me from Toronto. In Montreal, Julie Andrée T. and Benoît Lachambre (both of whom I had previously seen perform) had joined us. Tracy was an actor, Alex a filmmaker, Julie Andrée a performance artist, and Benoît a choreographer. There was a drawing I did around this time that placed *En français comme en anglais, it's easy to criticize* in the centre of a Bermuda Triangle between dance, theatre, and performance art. (Or, as Richard had joked: it's a combination of non-dance, non-theatre, and non-performance.)

I am wondering what's the best way to speak about the tensions and artistic semi-conflicts that filled the time of that process, which in the middle of it all seemed almost too stressful and difficult to navigate, but in retrospect I now realize was incredibly productive. I don't think I would be willing to put myself in such a contentious situation again today, and worry that my work now suffers from this reluctance I can only call experience. At the same time, it of course wasn't that bad, and in my memory of things I have the not uncommon tendency to focus on the most negative aspects. (Not just in my memory, often also in the present.)

I remember Benoît insisting that dance didn't just concern movement, that everything was dance, and he wanted his practice to reflect that, not just be a series of choreographed gestures. I also remember Benoît insisting that he couldn't stand work that was always frontal, when the audience sat in front and passively watched, that he preferred something more immersive, where the audience was within or all around.

I remember Julie Andrée saying that for her own work she didn't rehearse, she preferred a situation in which the performance gained intensity because the performer both knew and didn't know exactly what was going to happen. I also remember Julie Andrée saying that she thought we should be making a durational performance, something that lasted twelve or twenty-four hours. (About fourteen years later we did make a durational version of *The DJ Who Gave Too Much Information*. But back then I couldn't relate to the idea, or I could see what was interesting about it but didn't feel like doing it myself. From the point of view of my artistic trajectory, her suggestion was very much ahead of its time.)

I remember Alex talking about depth, questioning what might make a work of art feel deep. She had never performed onstage before. When I was in Norway I had met Willy Thomas from the Belgium theatre company Dito'Dito. I complained to him that I didn't know any performers I felt I could work with in Toronto who would understand what I was trying to do in a way they could effectively contribute to it, and Willy said he thought they didn't need to be performers; what he had done in Brussels was simply find some non-performer friends who were willing and then start making things together. So when I got back to Toronto I started looking around, wondering who might be willing. Alex had cast me in her experimental film *Leda and the Swan* and it made sense to me that in return I could also ask her to perform in something I did.

And Tracy, who I had already been working with for over ten years in Toronto, must have been asking herself why the divisive opinions of all these new people seemed to weigh so much more heavily on the process, seemed to influence it so much more, than her own thoughts on these questions, which had been built up in parallel with mine during the time we were creating and performing, both apart and together, in the Toronto scene. I can now understand the ways in which it must have felt unfair.

I was being hit by so many new thoughts, so many new kinds of thoughts, so much information. But in a sense I didn't even realize there was anything new, I was just trying to roll with it, listen to and respond to each thing and discussion as it occurred. I had wanted a new challenge and this was it.

+ + + +

At the time, I would have said *En français comme en anglais, it's easy to criticize* was about two things: criticism and translation. I thought it was fascinating to have not one but two themes, somewhat unrelated to one another, so they could conflict, interweave, bounce off and question each other. I also had an idea for a kind of game: we would translate each other back and forth, from English to French and back again, but as we did so each could use their translation as an opportunity to criticize what had just been said. This was a game I of course couldn't participate in, but I also thought it was striking that someone could translate what I said, criticize me as they were doing so, and I wouldn't understand enough French to even realize what was happening (if they were clever about it and slipped in their criticisms stealthily enough). A kind of subterfuge where you could secretly yet openly criticize the person allegedly in charge.

But was I in charge? It must have been around this time I came up with the term *pseudo-collective* to describe what we were doing. (Sylvie says I was already using the term during *I Cut, You Bleed*.) We were trying to work in a collective way, but I had a distinctly different role within the group, as someone who brought everyone together and came up with the initial ideas. It is now clearer to me that this idea of a pseudo-collective is rife with difficulties, and the longer I try to make it happen, the more I realize just how problematic it might be. At its worst, it could represent a particular kind of lack of transparency around power, and how power is actually taking place within the group.

In Norway I'd heard a great deal about the Norwegian artist collective Baktruppen, who I was told were a real collective who made all decisions about their work together, with no one in a leadership position. I unfortunately never saw a Baktruppen show but I heard about so many: a show where they made traditional Norwegian moonshine for the audience and while it was brewing washed each other's feet and then sucked on each other's toes (or maybe I'm misremembering it and these were actually two different shows). A show that took place out in a field, where they turned their backs on the audience and instead performed for the cows. The show they had just performed when I first went to Norway was called *Good Good Very Good*, a title that immediately resonated with me though I didn't know why. I met many members of Baktruppen over the years and, because I wanted to learn more about how to work collectively, would do my best to pester them with questions. One time there was an answer that really stuck with me: I was told that all the way through the process Baktruppen was democratic and collective, but right at the very end, a few days before the premiere, two of the members (I now can't remember which ones) took over and made all the final decisions. And that's the way it had always been with Baktruppen. It's unfair of me to recount this story, I wasn't there, never sat through a Baktruppen process, but it was something that really stuck with me and influenced my ongoing thinking around artistic collectives.

All of this was in my mind as I attempted to propose and navigate the idea of a pseudo-collective. I wanted the best of both worlds: the fullness of everyone's ideas, autonomy, and contributions mixed with the guidance of a single clear artistic vision. But who gets to decide when it's going to be more collective and when it's going to be less so? The answer was basically that I did. Even the fact that I'm writing this book alone, and not in collaboration with all the others (albeit with some of their comments included), displays the desire to take hold of the story, and the work, from my own perspective, something that might, at times, be an artistic virtue, while at other times might be seen as a severe ethical shortcoming. During each process, when anyone questioned my decisions, I hope I've always done my best to make sure their questions significantly affected the overall process and work, that everyone had as much individual and collective say as possible over what we were all making together. But all those we've worked with over the years might very well not completely agree that this was the case. At times I could have done better.

+ + + +

Criticism and translation. I wanted to get at the entire spectrum of criticism: from a newspaper review of a performance all the way to how some small criticism of a friend might unexpectedly change the dynamic of the friendship. I was also thinking about the current (at the time) situation of the left, where it felt we could only criticize capitalism but it was extremely difficult to do anything about it. How did all these aspects connect, conflict, and relate?

There was a part of the show we called "the conversation" in which we all sat in a semicircle at the front of the stage and attempted to have a real conversation in real time. In a way it echoed the part of *I Cut, You Bleed* when I interviewed the others as they caught endless streams of water in pint glasses. But I was wondering how we could take it further, make a conversation onstage feel more like a conversation that would happen somewhere out in the world.

And, in a sense, the way it went further was that we simply didn't agree on anything, or at least not very much, not even that it was a good idea to attempt to have a real conversation live in front of an audience. There were awkward pauses, people talking around and past each other, disagreeing about how the question was phrased (I would often start us off with a question) or if it was even a topic worth discussing. When I was younger I had been repeatedly told that there was no theatre without conflict, and I had questioned it, wondering if this connection between theatre and conflict was only the artistic version of a misguided social Darwinism. But here we had conflict onstage that was also so deeply anti-theatrical, we weren't disagreeing toward some larger dramatic effect, we were just disagreeing in a casual, everyday manner that wasn't immediately or obviously compelling but, for me while doing it, made time stutter and go more slowly. This felt real to me in the sense that it wasn't something I could have predicted, had little to do with my desires or intentions (I was hoping to have a constructive, productive discussion), and was almost impossible to manage, corral, improve upon through effort or control. It simply was what it was, however much I tried to push or pull to make it something else. It felt more real, what I had allegedly been searching for all along, but I had absolutely no idea if it was something I might actually want to watch. Of course, I wasn't going to be sitting in the audience watching it. I would instead be onstage in the midst of it all, and whatever I might learn I had to do my best to learn from that compromised position.

+ + + +

A few nights before the premiere Sylvie and I went for dinner at a Vietnamese restaurant. We talked about it all for a while and both agreed that we had tried something, tried our best, an honest, thorough attempt, but it still wasn't coming together. There were some good aspects to it, some beautiful moments and strong thoughts, but what we had created was essentially an ambitious, incoherent mess. I felt nothing was working, that it was people who didn't particularly like each other each trying to make their own show, leading to greater and greater onstage fragmentation, nothing ever cohering. Later, I would come to see all of these traits as virtues. That the performers were embodying their autonomy, that we weren't steamrolling over our differences and all acting the same way, which was often the standard in so much dance and theatre.

(Sylvie remembers this differently. She says that during this period I made significant changes to the structure of the show, changes that were considerable improvements. That before these changes the show might have been an incoherent mess, but after the changes it was all starting to work. She says that night at the Vietnamese restaurant was the night she learned the English word *baffled*, and that means we were both baffled by what we had made. But she says she was also excited by this feeling of not knowing, by the exhilarating feeling of: what is it?

Sylvie also says I should give more of a sense of how and why we considered this moment to be a breakthrough. How we were both proud of the proposal and anxious about its fragility. Time was framed in a special way within the show; it was scattered as if the show were not relying on any disciplinary rules. A non-acting inseparable from the weird personas created naturally by the performers; brief texts both funny and intellectual, very blunt, playing around the themes of criticism and translation; little dances lasting too long for a theatre show. Sometimes nothing happened onstage but a presence. We were not looking to fulfil the spectator's expectations: no bravura – which is what crowds usually like most – yet at the same time acknowledging that the audience shares real time and space with us. Walking a fine line that is constantly being redrawn. On the verge of not being theatre anymore. Feeling we were at the limit of what we could do and wondering what else we could do after this.)

I now think that night in the Vietnamese restaurant I had lost perspective, could not see the forest for the trees. I've always thought it was one of the small tragedies of making shows that, after a long, intensive process in which one continuously becomes more submerged in the work, right before the premiere you have the least perspective, just when you need it the most.

And yet, at the premiere, it was anything but a failure. It wasn't exactly a success either. At least not yet. Over the course of the run the word I heard most frequently was *refreshing*. We had made something refreshing, different from what people were used to, unexpected, meaning they weren't quite sure how to take it. I also didn't know. Of everything I had made so far, it was the furthest away from my initial intentions, and of course that was because I didn't make it, it was really something we had all made together, almost in spite of ourselves. (If you are now dying of curiosity as to what the show was actually like, you can jump to page 273 and read the *rough blueprint toward an eventual (never to be written) script*, which will give you at least some initial idea, and then, at your leisure, return to continue this chapter, starting with the next paragraph.)

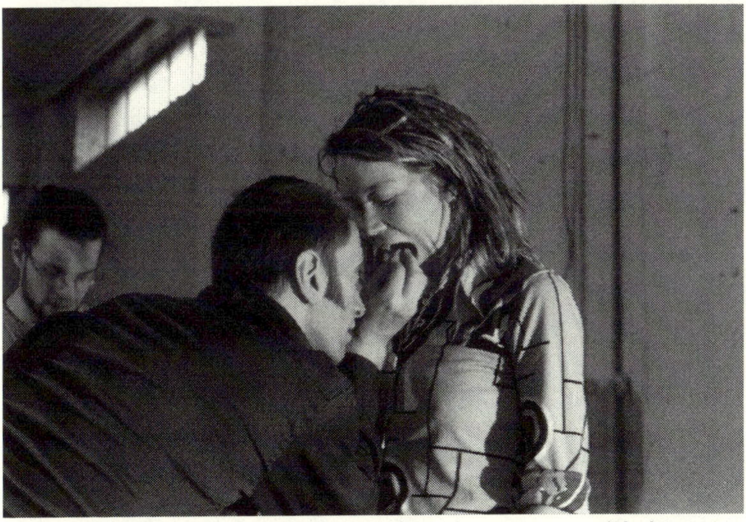

Benoît Lachambre and Julie Andrée T. in *En français comme en anglais, it's easy to criticize.* Photo: Catherine-Mélina Bisaillon

Sylvie had organized the two-week run so that the second week coincided with CINARS, the biennial performing arts market in Montreal. PME attended CINARS as an "observer," and on the convention floor Sylvie worked to get international presenters to come see our show. As word began to spread, slowly they came. One of the reasons they did so is because Gordana Vnuk, who would later invite us to Zagreb, was also on the CINARS floor, telling everyone she knew to come see us. Sylvie had met Gordana a few years before. When they first met they'd had a long session where they compared notes on what it was like to run their respective festivals. Sylvie had outlined all the endless difficulties of running Les 20 jours du théâtre à risque – funding problems, ungrateful or demanding artists, venues that cancelled on them, etc. Gordana apparently responded, "Yes, I have all those problems at Eurokaz too. Plus, when we're organizing the festival, we have to go down into the basement because airplanes are dropping bombs on our building." Gordana never minced words.

There was an incident I didn't witness, only heard about later, in which Don Shipley, who at the time ran the World Stage Festival in Toronto, was telling some other presenters that our show was a failure, that it didn't work, and they shouldn't bother to go see it, when Sylvie interrupted him, saying he was completely wrong, that we were making groundbreaking work and they absolutely had to come. There were a number of stories like this, which for me took on probably more symbolic resonance than they should have. Don represented Toronto, where I was banging my head against the wall and where, it felt to me, my work would most likely never be accepted, and Sylvie represented Montreal, where I was starting to hope that someday it might.

Because European presenters were now coming, and some of them were expressing interest, Sylvie knew it was time to start organizing a tour. I remember a night when Sylvie was listing all the theatres that had expressed interest – in Bergen, Prague, Lisbon, Zagreb, Cognac, etc. – and both Tracy and I were extremely skeptical. Neither of us really believed that the show was going to tour Europe – maybe one or two places but not so many – and I'm sure we hurt Sylvie's feelings by expressing so much doubt. However, as time would prove, Sylvie was completely right and we were very much in the wrong.

I also remember Sylvie saying repeatedly, as more and more excitement started to gather around the work, that: "We should not become victims of general approbation." We should not let success make us think that everything is okay now, we're great, there's no need to continue questioning ourselves or that we've got it all figured out. But I was definitely surprised by it all. Just two weeks earlier I had felt certain that I was rapidly approaching my artistic Waterloo and now more and more people were telling me we had made something unexpected and groundbreaking. Also, presenters from Europe were interested. This had been my goal for years. Despite Sylvie's admonishments not to become a victim of general approbation, I believe that was one of the many moments in my life I've become overly confused by my own swelled head.

+ + + +

Something else Sylvie would often say around that time: "The purpose of a tour is to put the artists in crisis." But before we could fly off into crisis, there was a problem. Benoît wasn't available for most of the tour. He wanted to do the dates he was available for and have someone else do the rest, and for a long time we considered this option, but the extra plane tickets to fly Benoît out and someone else in, several times over a period of six weeks, didn't seem economically feasible. At the same time, there was the question of whether we could even replace him. He had made the show along with the rest of us, it was his work too, so was it ethically all right to do it with someone else. This was the beginning of something I have often wondered about: to what extent are or aren't collaborators and performers replaceable. In capitalism, it is almost a truism that everyone can be replaced. And I have seen many shows where they had to replace a performer for a wide variety of reasons. It's not a particularly nice feeling to replace someone. And in PME, where we are performing as ourselves, and making work based on our own desires, experiences and understandings of the world, it is an even more prickly dilemma.

But it seems we had no choice, so Martin Bélanger – who was suggested to us by Benoît – joined the project. (Sylvie reminds me it was our agent, Menno Plukker, who said replacing Benoît was a necessity if we wanted to tour. We worked with Menno for about four years before eventually parting ways.) It was amazing to me how quickly Martin remade Benoît's part to suit his own questions and ways of being. The version with Martin premiered at Festival de théâtre des Amériques, and it already seemed like he had been part of it all along (which probably also has something to do with Martin's particular brilliance). The question of to what extent are people replaceable also entered the show, becoming one of our themes. But the fact that it worked so well only made me question it further. Clearly it was something you could do, but did that also mean it was something you should do. What did it mean in a show in which we were being ourselves that these selves could so easily be replaced. One thing it meant is that the show wasn't only us, it was also a structure, a series of sections, topics, and actions, carefully organized in a specific order, which of course anyone could do, and what's more, it was also possible for them to bring their full selves to these tasks, and even change the words and tasks as necessary. It was possible, but I must have not really liked the idea – it felt too much like replacing someone at a job, and I've always wanted PME to feel like the people onstage were the opposite of employees. At any rate, we didn't replace anyone onstage again for another sixteen years. (Sylvie says this isn't true. Because of a scheduling conflict, we replaced Tracy with Shannon Cochrane for the final Montreal remount of *En français comme en anglais, it's easy to criticize* in 2002 and again for *Unrehearsed Beauty-Le Génie des autres* in Norway in 2003.)

+ + + +

The purpose of a tour is to put the artists in crisis. First there was the small tour: Bergen, Prague, and Dresden.

In Prague we had a problem that has continued to haunt me, in one form or another, for the entirety of my artistic life. At the top of the poster for the show (a poster made by the Projekttheater Dresden) was my name in big letters, and if I remember correctly, no other names were mentioned, or they were much smaller. The others understandably felt that we'd all made the show together, and therefore should all get equal credit, as had been the case in Montreal. We had a meeting about it that for me was quite tense. There is a real, ongoing problem with who gets credit and how in the performing arts. The title of our 2008 show, *Individualism*

*Was a Mistake,* encompasses my feelings on the issue. If we take a common yet hypothetical example from contemporary dance: the group engages in a process where they all improvise and generate material, then the choreographer selects and shapes the material, and in doing so gets full authorship credit for the work. This has never seemed completely right to me, because the people who create and perform the work feel equally important, and their contribution should be more fully recognized. We have continuously pushed against this way of thinking, yet are still most often working in a system in which my name is the only one that matters. (And I fear writing this book will even further contribute to the problem.) At any rate, since Prague in 1999 we have done everything in our power to ensure everyone's name is on all promotional material in the same size font, and that everyone is given proper credit. This has not been easy, and sometimes they just go with my name anyway. In fact, it is continuously surprising to me how difficult this simple act of artistic fairness is to achieve – so if you're reading this and you run a festival or venue, please take some time to consider how important it is that artists working collaboratively get the proper credit for what they have worked so hard on, in some sense for their entire lives.

+ + + +

Right after Prague the schedule was tight, and I had to leave immediately after the show. Detlef Julius Skowronek, the presenter who invited us to Dresden, picked me up and we drove all night. We were stopped at the border, and the very young, apparently drunk, border guard, with what looked to me like a machine gun, made us take every single item out of the trunk. I was asleep when this happened, and sleepily getting out of the car I must have made a sudden move, because he yelled at me in German, and there was at least a split second I thought he was reaching for his gun, but Detlef intervened. When we got back in the car, having repacked all our props, it crossed my mind that there would have been something perversely appropriate about getting shot by a drunk border guard during my first ever attempt to go on tour. My punishment for appearing all alone across the top of the poster in Prague.

+ + + +

Between the short tour and the long tour we performed in Quebec City and Toronto.

At Mois Multi in Quebec City I experienced another side of Quebec, as an audience member moved his chair onstage, lit up a cigarette (perhaps to demonstrate that, unlike in Toronto, people still knew how to enjoy life here), and heckled me by yelling, "Hey, Ontario," several times over the course of the performance. Afterwards, with Sylvie translating, he said that he did like the show, wondered if I was influenced by Guy Debord, said Debord was good but didn't have all the answers, we shouldn't treat him like a God, and also wondered why the show was so slow, but then thought maybe that was just my style. (I hadn't particularly noticed the show was slow, but later think I knew what he meant.)

When we performed at the Theatre Centre in Toronto, I felt a new kind of hometown enthusiasm for my work. Perhaps they liked it better because I was now doing things in Montreal, and there was a feeling (real or imagined) that I had found a kind of freedom and energy that was never possible before, when I was working only in Toronto. We also got a review in the *Globe and Mail*, one line of which will forever be etched into my memory: "If this show is trying to be bad on purpose, then it's flawless." He was trying to be scathing, but in a way he summed up the paradoxical glee of the work better than I ever could.

+ + + +

Then there was what we called the long tour: Lisbon, Cognac, Brighton, Mont-Saint-Aignan (near Rouen), Manchester, London, Cardiff, and Zagreb. For Europe I'd had an idea: since parts of the show involved translating between English and French, why not add a third translator into the language of each country we were visiting. (Sylvie says this idea actually came from Ondřej Hrab, who ran the Archa Theatre in Prague.) What's more, I thought it would be good to ask the presenter who had invited us to be that translator. Together we would find local equivalents:

for example, when Martin spoke about the rivalry between Montreal and Toronto, Sven would extend it by mentioning the similar rivalry between Bergen and Oslo. (And when Sven performed with us in Stockholm, the rivalry was between the Norwegians and the Swedes.) One of the things that surprised me on these first tours was showing up at each venue and having the presenter apologize because they had an audience problem, meaning mainly, I suppose, they had difficulty finding audiences for work people were unfamiliar with. I had always imagined that in Europe it was easier to find audiences for difficult and challenging work, but it seems things were changing, that those days were at least partly over. We often had good audiences; therefore I also learned that the presenters were simply bracing us for the worst, so we wouldn't be too disappointed if it wasn't a full house. Nonetheless, touring was making something clear: art was in crisis everywhere.

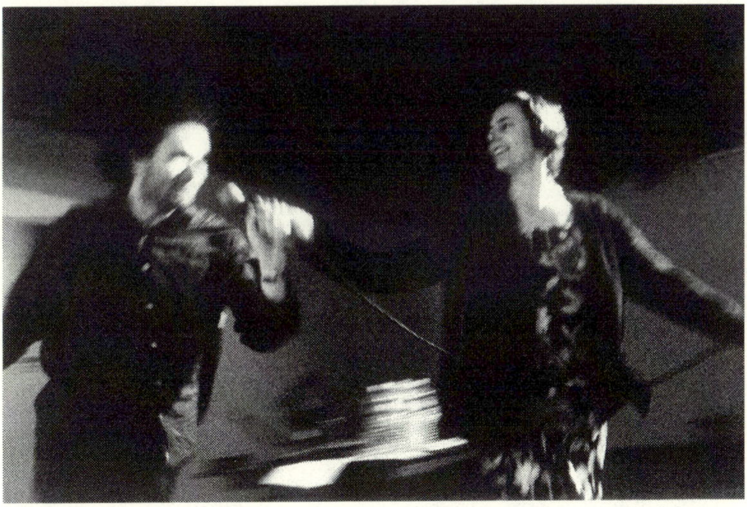

Jacob Wren and Alexandra Rockingham Gill in *En français comme en anglais, it's easy to criticize* at Nouvelle Scène-Festival de théâtre des Amériques in Montreal. Photo: Sébastien Fournier

At the very end of the long tour, at Eurokaz in Zagreb, we performed on my birthday. There was the idea to have a birthday cake onstage, and that during "the conversation," while we were talking, we would also eat cake. As we were talking and eating, I heard a voice from the audience, maybe from the front row: "Jacob, it's not your birthday. You're lying, Jacob. It's not your birthday." In a way this echoed something that had followed us since the beginning of the show: when you are being yourself, when you are trying to bring more of this reality into the performance situation, so many people think that because it is still theatre, taking place onstage, everything you're saying must not be true. Or at least they come expecting fiction, and when it's so unclear how the things you're saying match or don't match this expectation, they can easily become suspicious.

"You're lying, Jacob. It's not your birthday. You're lying." The voice in the audience belonged to Florian Feigl, from the German performance group Showcase Beat le Mot, who along with Baktruppen, Goat Island, Gob Squad, and many others, was a group that PME was often compared to around that time. We knew Florian, we had seen Showcase's show *Burn Cities Burn* the night before, and it was true, there were many similarities. I don't know how drunk Florian was that night but he had definitely been drinking. (At one point I had seen him leave the show and return with an armful of beer.) "You're lying, it's not your birthday." I stood up and took out my driver's licence, showing the audience that it clearly stated I was born on June 23, but of course it was much too small for anyone to read (it was a large theatre, I think there were about three hundred people there). "You're lying, Jacob. It's not your birthday."

It seemed to me that Florian was just starting to pick up steam, that he wasn't going to stop anytime soon, so without even thinking I jumped off the stage and started wrestling with him, in what was probably the most awkward public display of incompetent wrestling in the history of experimental theatre, since neither of us had any idea how to wrestle. Then Florian started kissing me. All of this couldn't have lasted longer than a minute or two, after which I stood up, climbed back onstage, and we finished the show. For years afterwards, when Tracy or Martin wanted to mock me, or mock the idea that everything we were doing was "real," they would imitate Florian's thick German accent: "You're lying, Jacob. It's not your birthday." (And it actually was my birthday.) But this shorthand for how when you put something onstage it becomes representation, artifice, somehow less true, makes a point that I have never really been able to agree with. I guess, in a way, I'm some sort of ideologue for the value of attempting to put reality onstage, even (or especially) if it proves impossible. Even if no one believes you.

+ + + +

It was fascinating to me that Gordana was so instrumental in getting us to Europe, but then, when we performed at Eurokaz, seemed almost disappointed in what we presented. (After the wrestling incident she looked me in the eyes and said, "Are you happy now?" As if all I had ever wanted was for something crazy to happen.) This might be unfair, but I felt she was looking for the next artistic movement, the next thing that would revolutionize theatre, that all the festivals would be lining up to program. She was hoping to call this movement Iconoclasm, and for her PME was part of its second wave. As she wrote in her editorial for Eurokaz's fifteenth anniversary:

> Eurokaz has shown in the last few years that this theatre language [Iconoclasm] has left a trace and influenced many young artists. We can call groups like PME, Showcase beat le mot, L&O, Gob Squad, and Fanny & Alexander the *second generation* of iconoclasts who bring the disregard for the usual categories of *good theatre* and *professional acting* to an extreme. Acting is absent from most of their productions. Performers are simply present onstage, their set-ups are structured incompetently and as if by dilettantes (I talk about these performers as *noble dilettantes*). The performances can be described as: *spending time, directing the void, intensity that doesn't say anything* (Heidegger), *passive theatricalization.*
>
> They also play with exhausted styles and eradicated signs, and it all speaks against the laws of the theatre market...

Perhaps when she put us all together in Eurokaz, it became clearer to her that we weren't popular or spectacular enough, that we weren't going to take over in the way she had hoped. (What she was looking for did in some way happen with the conceptual dance wave of the nineties.)

(Reading an earlier draft of this book, Kathrin Tiedemann comments: "I can maybe add a few things to the post-mainstream and the iconoclastic theatre. The latter term was coined by Romeo Castellucci's company Societas Rafaello Sanzio, going back to their early work in the eighties, especially *Santa Sofia - Khmer Theatro*, which was accompanied by a manifesto against false representations of reality, proposing instead the power of images and visuality onstage. Later they even published a book about their iconoclastic theatre. Gordana borrowed the term from them and developed it into her own more general approach, with different generations of iconoclastic theatre, Societas Rafaello Sanzio being the first generation. It's definitely true that Gordana had hoped for a broader success of her concept - and it's also true that this failed, as nobody, especially in the European circle, picked up on it. This is where the post-mainstream comes in. Knut Ove was defining post-mainstream also in a kind of geopolitical sense: in the centre of the mainstream he identified the Dutch and Flemish wave - Rosas, Jan Fabre, Needcompany, etc. - opposed to Baktruppen and theatre from smaller countries on the periphery that were not connected to the rich and powerful circuit of presenters. Gordana used this idea to try to push groups from the former Yugoslavia. She was very much attacking the IETM [Informal European Theatre Meeting] politics and left all the usual networks, becoming quite isolated. Probably you have heard all this already. She never liked or understood the pop aspect of many of the works of younger groups like Showcase Beat le Mot and She She Pop, not to mention the following generations coming out of the Gießen School of Applied Theatre Studies. Which is what your quote from Gordana's Kampnagel book is basically referring to.")

(Sylvie reminds me that after we had toured and seen many shows in Europe, we were starting to feel that the Europeans would never fully recognize what was artistically valuable in the North American approach to non-acting. As well, our need for a greater freedom from theatre canons and rules seemed destabilizing for them. On one hand, we were sympathetic to Gordana's fight to open up Central European presenters to current breakthroughs in theatre. On the other hand, we felt we would never make some of the things that were most important to us clear to the establishment theatre, in Europe or in North America.)

I now find myself wondering if the larger point was that, at the end of the twentieth century, art movements were no longer nearly as easy to incite. All the isms had been played out and it didn't seem people were especially hungry for more. (One theory is that the twentieth century drive toward artistic movements and isms was concurrent with a will toward political ones - socialism, communism, fascism - and when those were stamped out the will for artistic movements disappeared as well.)

I don't know, I have also always had some vague desire to be part of a movement, part of something larger in art. But perhaps I'm not enough of a believer to actually join. As the Czech poet Vladimir Holan writes: "We who do not believe are always expecting something." And in a way I do think I've always expected that, at some point, my work would have been swept up and along in some zeitgeist or wave. Maybe if I had been born in 1945, and was twenty in 1965, it might have happened. But it didn't happen in Zagreb with Iconoclasm. And the term *post-mainstream* never took on a full life of its own (though there was definitely a moment when I thought it might). When we performed at Festival de théâtre des Amériques, I was also told we were part of a movement that was happening in France called No Theatre, but that seemed short-lived as well. And Postdramatic Theatre encompasses things that are both similar to and completely different from what we're doing. Maybe I'm too idiosyncratic, can't seem to join something even when the joining is good, or when it's in my best interest to do so, or when it would make me feel less artistically lonely. Individualism is a mistake.

\+ + + +

We were scheduled to perform in New York City, at P.S. 122, on September 20, 2001. After 9/11 happened, Richard phoned Mark

Russell at P.S. 122, asking him how he was doing. Mark said that in fact all he was doing was sitting in the office staring at the walls. Richard replied, "I suppose that means you don't want us to come, that our show is cancelled" (which would have been understandable). But Mark said no, on the contrary, it meant that it was even more important for us to come and perform. To bring some energy and questioning into the situation. Arriving in New York, what I remember most is newspaper headlines reading TERROR SEX. Apparently, at least according to certain sensationalistic accounts, with the fear of another attack in the air, people were hooking up like crazy, the fear sending them into each other's arms.

During "the conversation" we spoke about the Twin Towers, and after the show people told me it was the first time they had heard the event spoken about publicly, live, since the attack. It had caught them off guard, set them off balance, since it came when they were least expecting it, right in the middle of our show. If *En français comme en anglais, it's easy to criticize* was partly about how the left could only criticize capitalism or the government - and it was much more difficult, at times seemingly impossible, to actually effect change - then the planes crashing into the towers felt like an example of just how extreme an action is required to truly shake things up. These were the days before I fully understood what was happening, all I knew was that *something* had happened, and already it felt like the biggest world historical shift during my lifetime so far.

I had been to New York when I was younger, but not often enough to have a stable point of reference against which to compare. Nonetheless, New York felt so quiet to me during that visit, like the calm before the storm (I guess everyone was at home having terror sex). And it clarified another aspect of having an unscripted conversation directly in the middle of our show: that the show wasn't just its own little bubble - world events could more easily enter it and be incorporated. I knew I didn't want to make shows in which we spoke about current events, about whatever happened to be in the news that particular week, but I did want to make work that was more in and of the world, so that while watching it you felt an implicit awareness of socio-political realities, sometimes more explicitly and sometimes less so, that the world outside the show fully exists, and we are all in this world together.

\+ + + +

In Stockholm, when we arrived, Claes Karlsson also told us that they had an audience problem at Kulturhuset. By this point I had heard it all before, and knew to take it with a grain of salt, though it is also true my heart sank each and every time I heard these words, as I imagined travelling all this way to perform for only a handful of people. But instead something very different happened. In New York, we had gotten a glowing review in the *Village Voice*. Brian Parks had written:

> God bless Canada. First it gave the world the manifold joys of *Hockey Night in Canada*. Now it's presented us with *En français comme en anglais, it's easy to criticize*, a captivating performance piece by Jacob Wren and PME, mounted at P.S. 122. Toronto-Quebec kissing cousins of ERS and Collapsable Giraffe, but more somber and purposeful, the five-member group has created a collage that's part dance, part social critique, part heady fucking around.
>
> Four tables supporting stereo equipment anchor the dimly lit stage. Lacking a conventional plot, the piece comprises a sequence of moments that appear random but have their own internal logic. Performers Martin Bélanger and Tracy Wright discuss theorist Gilles Deleuze on one side of the stage; on the other, two women (Julie Andrée T. and Alexandra Rockingham Gill) dance together silently. Bélanger disappears, but later speaks in French over a walkie-talkie illuminated by a spotlight. Wren runs repeatedly between the front and back of the stage, delivering a monologue on how the World Trade Center attack has confused his piece's critique of bourgeois comfort. The ensemble stops for a group discussion of the work. Wright confronts Wren, complaining that the last thing the world needs is another boy genius. The group breaks into dance, sometimes ecstatic, sometimes gently coordinated. Andrée T. has a particu-

> larly compelling presence – her sullenness only makes her movement more fascinating.
>
> Alternately hypnotic and amusing, *En français* – like much postmodern work – interrogates the idea of the performance itself. But it never fails to *be* that performance, and a damn good one. "The real avant-garde is to be found in doing nothing," Wren observes, despairing of the action-driven, media-saturated world. He and his ensemble have happily ignored their own counsel.

Kulturhuset had taken the review and sent it to all the press in Stockholm. It was the first time in my life I had truly seen publicity work. We played to packed houses. It was also the first time I had experienced how the power and mystique of New York could be effective, since I believe one of the reasons the review worked so well was that it came from the *Village Voice*. Everyone in Stockholm had of course heard of the *Village Voice*. This was American cultural hegemony in action, with the slight difference that in this particular instance it was some Canadians who happened to benefit from it. It occurred to me that "if I can make it there, I'll make it anywhere" was more than just a line in a song.

\+ + + +

*En français comme en anglais, it's easy to criticize* continued to tour on and off for the next four years. One of the things I remember most from those years is audience members telling me what we were doing was "not theatre." It took me a long time to more fully understand what was at stake for them with this particular complaint. In one way, I was still trying to change theatre, so my first reaction was always something like: it might not be traditional theatre but for me this is the theatre of now, of this contemporary moment, or of the future. But more and more I began to feel these kinds of arguments were a dead end. What did I care if we called it theatre or something else, what particular investment did I have in the word *theatre*, and why would I spend time arguing about it with people it seemed increasingly clear I was never going to convince.

It took me even longer to realize that my thinking around these questions had a great deal to do with the fact that I was an autodidact, that I hadn't invested my time studying any particular discipline, and was instead more interested in my autodidact's way of learning-through-doing, through trial and error, which for me was always based on trying to become more curious, opening things up – the possibility that theatre, or any art form, could be anything, regardless of what they had been in the past or were in the present. (Sylvie says being an autodidact is also about reading, research, seeing performances and exhibitions, etc.) I don't know this for a fact, since I've never experienced it myself, but it seems to me that so much training in the performing arts is based on the idea that there is a right way and a wrong way to do it, and we're going to teach you the right way. But I have always felt that there's no right way to make art, and art is a process of exploring what such a statement might mean.

I read over what I have so far and wonder if there should be more stories about Alex, Benoît, Julie-Andrée, Martin, and Tracy. It feels wrong that there aren't more, that I haven't found a way to more fully encompass each of their perspectives, but it also feels wrong to tell stories that aren't really mine. We were friends-in-work but, at the end of the day, perhaps not entirely friends. (Some of them were probably friends with each other to a greater extent than any of them were friends with me. One reason might be that the idea of a pseudo-collective means that in some sense I'm the boss. And in general no one wants to be friends with their boss.) I don't know. This all happened twenty years ago. My thinking now is different from my thinking back then. But also, my thinking now is different *because* of all the things that happened back then. I am rewriting history from the perspective of now, because non-fiction is always also a kind of fiction.

+ + + +

In 2009 I got an email from Chris Abraham and Christian Lapointe. They had been invited by the National Theatre School in Montreal to make a show for the school's fiftieth anniversary. It would be the first time the French side and the English side of the school had ever worked together on a full-scale production. Chris and Christian didn't know each other so well, and I think it's fair to say they are completely different people and very different artists, but after talking awhile they came up with the idea that they could collaborate on a project loosely based on *En français comme en anglais, it's easy to criticize,* inspired by the connection between the title of the show and the fact that the French and English sides of the school were now working together.

They wrote to ask my permission and, to be honest, my first instinct was to say no. I had dedicated my life to a different kind of theatre and it seemed clear to me that the National Theatre School production would recuperate what we had done, making it more normal, more theatre, more acceptable. Taking the aspects that worked for them and, most likely, jettisoning some or all of the aspects that were most important to me. But Sylvie and Richard carefully explained to me that I should say yes. It was important that an institution like the National Theatre School recognize our work, and even more that they would do so to celebrate their fiftieth anniversary. The argument that most convinced me was that saying yes would help PME in the long run, since like most small arts organizations, PME often struggles financially (to be honest, in this sense, I really don't know how we've survived this long), and in an ongoing way I feel that anything that helps PME is something I simply have to do.

The National Theatre School students worked on the show for two full years. I believe it was a difficult and important experience for practically all of them. They continuously translated everything from French to English and back again, creating a laborious and challenging process that brought so many of these questions into sharper focus. But I actually don't know. They wanted me to attend rehearsals, but for most of that period I was touring heavily in Europe with *An Anthology of Optimism* and the *HOSPITALITY/ HOSPITALITÉ* series. All I managed was to Skype with them once and to attend one rehearsal, both occasions that seemed to go well enough.

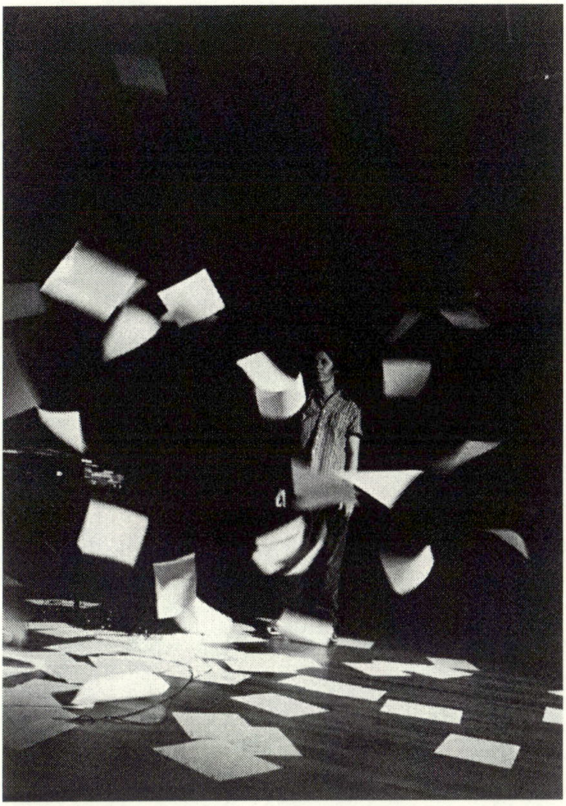

Tracy Wright in *En français comme en anglais, it's easy to criticize* at Nouvelle Scène-Festival de théâtre des Amériques in Montreal. Photo: Sébastien Fournier

Opening night, strangely, my parents travelled to Montreal to see the show. They had seen all the work I had brought to Toronto but had never come to Montreal to see something before. During the first section of the show, the cast came up the aisles to interview the audience. My father was sitting on the aisle, and gave cogent, intelligent answers to each question. I think, in my entire performing arts life, this is the moment that felt most like a dream, like I was actually dreaming. I was at the fiftieth-anniversary production of the National Theatre School, they were performing my words, and my father was sitting beside me also momentarily performing in the show. Since this production was not only *En français comme en anglais, it's easy to criticize*, but also contained texts from all periods of my writing and artistic life. My reaction to watching the show that night was basically to have a small nervous breakdown (something that, to varying degrees, happens to me anyway once or twice a year). About a week into my nervous breakdown, and halfway through the two-week run, I went onto my blog and posted this:

> Strange Gratitude
>
> You said to me that I saved the institution's anniversary. (Of course only a joke.) But I don't want to save the institution. I don't want to save anything.
>
> I think the institution is a factory for producing mediocrity and for maintaining the status quo (sometimes a little bit more adventurous, sometimes a little less, but never a compelling shift, never a hopeful curiosity, openness, or break.)
>
> I want to burn it to the ground but I'm too polite. And there would be no point since new institutions would quickly arise, the same or worse. And my burning to the ground skills aren't up to the task.
>
> I want things to change but the changes I desire are too much for reality. And the small shifts that do occur feel in not exactly the wrong (or right) direction.
>
> Why must everything be pumped up with false energy and enthusiasm? Where is the vulnerability? If we are insecure, why must we front? Why can't we walk onstage and perform in ways that show our insecurity? That are fragile? That show we are damaged, curious, unsure, and therefore human? Why can't our politicians do the same? (Because they would never win.)
>
> Is it only because we are always auditioning, for everything: for love, work, friendship, value, meaning, time, hope? I no longer know how to sort the fantasies that matter from the ones that don't.

What others find entertaining does not entertain me, but, then again, what does? If I feel that someone is trying to sell me something, especially themselves, I completely shut down.

And yet here they were trying to sell myself back to me at a reduced, yet more expensive, price. A commercialized, scrambled, overproduced version of myself I could barely recognize.

How to be if the world does not understand my aims, even when they try, and if equally I do not understand theirs? (And is there anything accurate in this sensation I had while watching, and later thinking about, what had occurred. Rarely am I accused of excessive gratitude.)

M. writes: "More problematic to me was to see them bursting from a kind of overconfidence that seemed to hide their own lack of self-assurance. While it gave an interesting look to the more political bits of your work, it also seemed to hinder the parts that are more revealing, full of self-doubt and honesty."

But it's easy to criticize. This, what I write here, is barely rational, not critique, an emotional language, a sad insanity, intensity.

Such insanity compels me to send this out into the world, fires me up to confess that watching that show, even once, made me feel completely suicidal, completely bereft. (But I'm always suicidal, so what is this sudden surge in intensity? Might there be something positive in it?)

I don't even know how to live in the days following the premiere, a night that feels like the complete betrayal of everything I have been trying to do for the past twenty-two years, of everything I desire, of everything I believe in. And I really don't say this against the people who made it, since, in many ways, I believe they genuinely did the best they

> could. I say this only against myself, for agreeing to it, for saying yes in the first place. For saying yes to a scenario I knew from the start would have this precise result.
>
> I fear my "yes" came mainly for cheap reasons: to promote my name, expand my brand. I have no high horse to get up on. And yet I'm on this galloping horse nonetheless. Henri Michaux writes: "It is when you gallop that your parasites are most alive."
>
> And if, actually, against my better judgment, I do eventually post this, it will be little more than another passive-aggressive act in a lifetime of the same. I apologize and, as always, feel sad. Sadness, confusion, and conflicted feelings.
>
> From this position what constructive politics could possibly emerge?

Part of me now regrets having posted this when it was all so fresh. I guess I just needed some sort of release. I believe it wasn't until much later that most of those involved in the show read my post, and when they did I'm sure a few feelings were hurt. But in this sense I feel it is important to point out that my poem is called "Strange Gratitude." The strange part is how negative my words are, but the gratitude has to do with meeting their hard work and artistic commitment by responding with how I honestly felt at the time, so there was some way our two perspectives might someday meet. With the calmness of hindsight, I now think what was so interesting about the event is how far apart we were to begin with, and the extent to which they came to meet me in the middle, and how for me, perhaps unfairly, the middle was still not nearly enough. I believe the National Theatre School's version of *En français comme en anglais, it's easy to criticize* was well-received as one of the most future-forward and groundbreaking productions the school has ever made. After the opening night I stayed to have a drink with them, and I was talking to one of the performers about their version of "the conversation," in which they sat onstage and answered questions that were beamed in via video from the lobby. I said this was my favourite part (which was true) because it was the only part I felt they weren't acting (hopefully I didn't say overacting), it was the only part I felt they approached really being themselves. "That's frightening," I think he replied, "that means that maybe you actually have a self."

## Three:

# Unrehearsed Beauty-Le Génie des autres

(2002–2004)

Created/Performed by:
Martin Bélanger, Alexandra Rockingham Gill, Simone Moir, Samuel Roy-Bois, Julie-Andrée T., Tracy Wright, and Jacob Wren

We performed it in:
Quebec City, Carrefour international de théâtre/Les Productions Recto-Verso • Montreal, MAI (Montréal, arts interculturels) • Hamburg, Kampnagel • Berlin, Prater-Volksbühne • Tokyo, Post Mainstream Performing Arts Festival • Cardiff, Chapter Arts Centre • Glasgow, CCA • Manchester, The Green Room • Bergen, BIT Teatergarasjen • Trondheim, Teaterhuset Avant Garden • Olso, Black Box • Prague, Divadlo Archa • Halifax, Khyber Centre for the Arts • Toronto, 7A*11D International Festival of Performance Art

Projects emerge from other projects. With *En français comme en anglais, it's easy to criticize,* we had taken the casual kind of theatre I had started in Toronto and made it even more casual, more unravelling, ramshackle, seemingly catch-as-catch-can. One unintended result of this shift was that it gave the audience a greater feeling that they could do it too. It generated a frequently stated desire to join in, get up onstage with us, or talk to us from their seats, especially during "the conversation." If we were just being ourselves, they also had selves they could be, so why couldn't they join in?

\+ + + +

Around the time we began touring, one of the most successful groups on the circuit was Forced Entertainment from Sheffield, U.K. Part of their mystique was being a six-person collective who had been working together for fifteen (now thirty) years. They had moved from London to Sheffield, the logic being that if they had stayed in London they'd have all been pulled in different directions, but in Sheffield there wasn't much happening (in the realm of experimental theatre), so all they had was each other. Moving to Sheffield was a way to stay together, and it worked. Shortly after I met them, I was invited to watch a week of their process for the show *Disco Relax*. One could say that Forced Entertainment are also a pseudo-collective, led by Tim Etchells, and therefore I went to Sheffield hoping to learn how their process was both similar to and different from the work we were doing at PME. They had been at it for fifteen years while we had just started recently.

I watched them work for an entire week and wasn't sure what to think. It didn't feel familiar at all, a completely different beast. I joined them in the middle of the process, never quite getting my bearings. They were working through a text Tim had written, twisting it backward and forward, while at the same time talking about lighting, constantly referring to past shows. That they couldn't do something because they had already done it before, or was what they were doing now different enough that it would still work? Their process was also British in ways I couldn't put my finger on; meaning, most likely, that they were so much rougher with each other than we would have been back in nice, overly polite Canada. (But working in Quebec was already starting to complicate my understanding of these dynamics, of what kind of dialogue during rehearsal was productive or counterproductive.) I say this with all respect, but what their process most reminded me of was a loving, but very dysfunctional, family.

This was all just as *En français comme en anglais, it's easy to criticize* was coming to a end, as we were trying to decide if PME would continue and, if so, what form it might take, what we would do next. That last night in Sheffield, when we all went for drinks, I asked them what I should do. Should the five of us in PME continue as a group, trying to further our collaborative method and grow closer, push steadily over time toward the artistic rewards of greater collective authorship and intensity? Or should we also find new people, become more open, more of an organic, shifting organism from which people come and go over time? The answer was instant and unanimous: everyone around the table said the more open option was the way to go. Since they had all been working together for so long, it might well have only been an instance of the grass looking greener on the other side, but at that moment it seemed like good advice from people who should know, and I took it as a kind of small truth. I now wonder, if they had recommended the opposite, would I also have done what they said, or was I only looking for confirmation of what I had wanted to do anyway.

Either way, when I returned to Montreal we began the search for new people, and Simone Moir (from Toronto) and Samuel Roy-Bois (from Montreal) both joined the process for *Unrehearsed Beauty-Le Génie des autres*. We were now seven. They were both visual artists. I had gone to high school briefly with Simone, and inviting her in was a continuation of the idea that it was valuable to find people you knew who weren't necessarily actors or performers. Samuel also played double bass, he started in bands but was now mainly free improv, and the fact that he both played music and made art felt important to me, since that was also what we were trying to do – put things together that didn't necessarily fit. There was also an idea we might play music in the show, so a strong rhythm section wouldn't hurt. I wonder what it was like for Simone and Samuel to join us, to try to integrate into the strange culture within PME that had slowly been building up over the past five years of working and touring. I'm sure, at first, the way into the group was by no means obvious.

By this time, a book of the text I had written for TheatreText-Context had been published, but I was thinking that our production of *Unrehearsed Beauty-Le Génie des autres* should definitely not be a staged version of that book. (At any rate, we had already done that in Bergen, albeit in Norwegian.) If *Unrehearsed Beauty* was a text that could be staged or used in any way, we would try to make the most of such freedom and openness, and in the end we spoke only one paragraph from the entire book (though other parts were used in less literal ways):

> Actors are also musicians. Therefore, the show should also be a band. First, find out who plays which instruments. If one of the performers does not already play an instrument, assign them one arbitrarily. At various intervals in the production, the performers can gather in the back corner of the stage, pick up their respective instruments, and perform a piece of amateur music. Rock 'n' roll is the amateur music par excellence. Music is quite possibly the most direct art form known to man. Quite infamously, Friedrich Nietzsche once wrote: "Mankind without music would have been a mistake." (This is the only Nietzsche quote I know off the top of my head.) When it is late at night, I turn on the radio and become lost. There is very good radio late at night. Perhaps I go into the washroom and vomit. I vomit because when I am alone listening to music is the time when I feel most human. At this particular point in history, to be a human being is a rather nauseating thing.

\+ + + +

Once again, the process was anything but easy. Thinking back, I suddenly feel me comparing Forced Entertainment to a dysfunctional family is pretty rich, the pot calling the kettle black. I wanted to work on the question of the public sphere, to what extent could the theatre space approach becoming some kind of public sphere over the course of two hours, how could we open up the question of who, in our society, had the right to speak and who didn't. I was reading David Levi Strauss's book *Between Dog and Wolf: Essays on Art & Politics*:

> If there is no public sphere, no place for private persons to assemble to discuss matters of public concern, things of common interest and importance, then there is no place for democracy to operate. The stakes involved have been forcefully articulated by the filmmaker Alexander Kluge:
>
> "The conception of a public sphere that is neither privately owned nor simply the classical type is of fundamental importance: the very conditions of politics depend on it. The public sphere is...what one might call the factory of politics – its site of production.
>
> "For these reasons, this use value, this product, which is the 'public sphere,' is the most fundamental product that exists. In terms of community, of what I have in common with other people, it is the basis for processes of social change."
>
> Kluge defines an "oppositional public sphere" as "a type of public sphere that is changing and expanding, increasing the possibilities for a public articulation of experience." He calls the creation of an oppositional public sphere something "that is just as important as direct action."

In a conventional theatre production the people onstage have the right to speak and those in the audience are only allowed to quietly watch. This is the contract you generally agree to when you buy a ticket and enter the space. But how could we open this up? What if we created a convention, or condition, in which the audience had the right to speak as well? Near the beginning of the show, Simone read this text:

> If a healthy society is to exist, we need places where we can gather and talk about what we want our society to be like.

> There are many reasons why our show here tonight cannot usefully be one of these places: we don't know each other, we don't live in the same community, we're only going to be in the same room together for the next hour and a half and then we'll probably never see each other again. But so many things seem impossible nowadays. And just because something's impossible doesn't mean you shouldn't try.

+ + + +

Before our premiere in Quebec City at the festival Le Carrefour international de théâtre we had a residency with Les Productions Recto-Verso at Méduse to finish making the show. The residency was in May and when halfway through I woke up, looked out the window, and saw at least five feet of snow on the ground, I thought maybe hell had frozen over. I was hoping for a pleasant, springtime sprint toward opening night but the weather clearly had other ideas. I hadn't known it was possible to have that much snow in late May, and still wish I could go back in time and return to my previous weather-related innocence.

There is one particular moment I remember from the Quebec City residency, a few days before we opened. We were sitting around the space, discussing how it should be set up. We had already decided to have a small stage in one corner, barely large enough for us all to cram onto it, two red paper lanterns hanging overhead at different heights, a microphone in the middle of the room surrounded by café tables and chairs. The audience could go to the bar in the lobby and bring their drinks back in with them. There was a red curtain that normally covered one wall, the wall behind one half of the small stage, and we were now discussing whether to let it completely cover the painted black brick, have it pulled away, or have it only half-cover the brick (which is what we decided in the end). But it seemed to me that we were discussing this curtain endlessly, everyone had a different opinion on the matter, and I didn't feel we were moving toward anything resembling consensus. Suddenly I began laughing hysterically, I was laughing and laughing, couldn't seem to stop. I fell off my chair onto the floor, I was laughing so hard. Here we were in Quebec City, two days away from having to perform for an actual audience (a Quebec City audience that I was particularly nervous about due to my previous experiences here). I remember feeling the show was basically a shambles, was almost completely shapeless. We could not really agree what it was about, or how to convey any of the themes, or even if this way of thinking about themes and art had anything to do with the piece we were making. It didn't have an ending, and I believe there were still no suggestions as to how we would end it. (I might be exaggerating, I'm not sure.) There was far too much material, no agreed upon way of editing it down, and no consensus as to which parts should stay and what, if anything, we might let go. And yet instead of concertedly applying ourselves to these very real and immediate artistic difficulties, we were endlessly debating whether a red curtain should be open or only half-open. Thinking about all this I could not stop laughing, had difficulty catching my breath. I believe anyone who has ever worked in a collective has had some sort of similar experience (which they may or may not have found funny at the time).

In Quebec City we decided we would perform the show predominantly in French, which meant in that first version I barely spoke, and often didn't know what was going on. The show alternated between us doing performance activities, playing songs, and opening up the microphone to the audience. That first night we had absolutely no idea what would happen: would anyone speak, what would they say, how would it be taken, would it develop at all over the course of the show and, if so, how. This really felt like what I had come to Montreal to do, what had felt impossible back in Toronto: to take a real artistic risk, make something in which I genuinely had no idea what would happen or how it would be received. It was also terrifying.

During the second performance, many people did go to the microphone to speak, and several of them also used the opportunity to verbally attack us. At the time I didn't know exactly what was being said, because I didn't understand the French, but later I was told it was things like our show was boring, or what we were doing might be alright if it had only cost five dollars, but there was no way it was worth the thirty-dollar ticket price. (How we dealt with, and felt about, theatre and festival ticket prices would continue to be an ongoing discussion within PME.) What I do remember is Julie-Andrée saying into a microphone: "We are losing control of the show." It honestly did feel that way. It wasn't until later I realized we hadn't actually been losing control of anything. People did go to the microphone to insult us and our work (Richard feels they were mainly Quebec City theatre people irritated that Carrefour had given us a co-production instead of them, made worse by the fact we were from Montreal and featured anglophones from Toronto), but they did so during the times the microphone was open, and then sat back down when it was our turn to perform. (Sylvie says that some Quebec performance artists also went to the microphone and said things like "Welcome to Quebec City," meaning that now we were experiencing the conservative local milieu that they had to work within all year round.) Thinking back to *En français comme en anglais, it's easy to criticize,* I was fascinated that we had now created something in which the audience could criticize us *during* the show, and yet the show could still continue basically as planned.

Marie Gignac, one of the co-artistic directors who had invited us, after that difficult second show, asked if we knew what a "Spanish hotel" is. Apparently it's a hotel where you have to bring everything yourself: towels, bed sheets, soap, food and drinks, etc. Marie said our show was like a Spanish hotel: the audience had to bring some of the content, bring their questions, insights and concerns, and the problem that night in Quebec City was we had "a talentless audience." At the end of each show, Martin said he would like to slow dance with an audience member, and as they did so, the rest of us stood on the small stage and played our best approximation of a slow song. I can't remember if it was then, or earlier in the show, when we were all singing and I shouted my only French line: "*Tout le monde ensemble.*" And every night, to my surprise, people understood my mediocre French pronunciation and sang along, a feeling that at least something about what we were doing was working, or at least had inspired a certain degree of goodwill. Every time we performed I felt we were starting to figure it out, learning through doing, understanding the resonances through listening to what the audience brought and adjusting accordingly.

(Yves Sheriff, who previously presented us at Usine C and was later on our board, remembers seeing *Unrehearsed Beauty-Le Génie des autres* in Quebec City. He had been hired by the CEAD [Centre des auteurs dramatiques] to accompany a few African dramaturges to the festival, one of them being William Sassine, a political writer from Guinea he had met previously in Limoges. William was a fine, sharp writer, witty and always saying clever words against the colonialist French with a sweet smile. He had a column in a newspaper in Conacry that was called *La Chronique à Sassine* – a French pun between his name and *assassin*, meaning something like the Cutthroat Chronicle. William sat quietly through the entire show, did not say a word. Only after, while they were walking, he simply said, with his Guinean French accent: "You Canadians, you're lucky to present plays like that. In Conacry you would be thrown in jail for putting a microphone in the audience.")

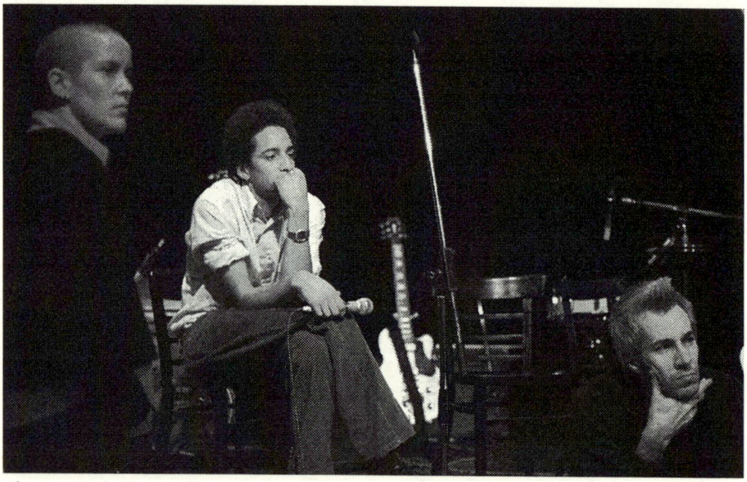

Simone Moir, Samuel Roy-Bois, and Martin Bélanger in *Unrehearsed Beauty-Le Génie des autres* at Le Carrefour international de théâtre in Quebec City. Photo: François Bergeron

Six months later we performed *Unrehearsed Beauty-Le Génie des autres* at the MAI (Montréal arts interculturels). I'd now had time to think about the work, and this new version had a clearer, more transparent structure. Which made me seriously reconsider something I had been trying to do throughout the entire process. Sylvie had encouraged me to work toward controlling the process less, letting it be less pseudo-collective and more simply collective, trying to let the energies of the group and their individual desires lead the project where it wanted to go. *En français comme en anglais, it's easy to criticize* had been somehow more collective than the previous work I had made in Toronto, as well as my first international success, and I genuinely did want to see if we could take working as a group further. But after Quebec City I felt the show still needed a great deal of attention, especially the overall structure, and at that moment it seemed to me it was only going to happen if I intervened.

This question has obviously confronted me consistently over the past twenty years: how collective should PME be and how could we understand the relationship between my attempts to guide the process and the far more important reality of everyone's individual and collaborative contribution. In a way, *Unrehearsed Beauty-Le Génie des autres* in Montreal was a moment when I felt I shouldn't have let it go for so long, I should have intervened sooner, tried to fix the structure as we went. I made the new changes in a panic, as if I were trying to save something before it was too late, and everyone agreed to them, wanting the show to improve quickly, before the Montreal audiences arrived. For me, the new structure made everything in Montreal so much clearer than it had been in Quebec City. But I still wonder if there was some more democratic way we could have done so, or if we could have achieved a similar result through different means, or if that would have simply required a different kind of group. There are very few artists who are deeply interested in collaboration, and I'm not certain I'm one of them, though there must be some reason I keep returning to it with a vengeance. It's as if I need to believe in something, and nothing else comes close. Most theatre directors have no problem telling others what to do, or changing everything on a whim, but I always work hoping there is some other way, or searching for it.

\+ + + +

In *Unrehearsed Beauty-Le Génie des autres* we also sang a few of my songs. One song in particular strikes me as connected to my concerns at the time:

Here's to a long life

You too will outlive your idealism
it is sad, it is cruel, but it's true
as under the rubric of realism
you renounce what you once tried to do

You'll get a job, in the evenings you'll be tired
and you'll often think fondly of the past
you'll only grind yourself down if you fight it
so my advice: enjoy it now while it lasts

Says one woman: "do you remember us in high school"
says the other: "please don't start, you'll make me cry"
we were beautiful and everybody said so
now with the mortgage and the kids I live a lie"

Says the first: "but now our lives are what we make them
back then we were tossed around like dice
I no longer have to pretend that I'm happy
no longer pretend that attention will suffice"

When it rains, it rains practically forever
and the sun might not come out before you die
you too will outlive your idealism
but until then keep on asking why

Why get a job, in the evenings you'll be tired
why often think fondly of what was
there's a rhythm to this life and if you fight it
you'll be defeated but at least you'll have a cause

The song was sung by Martin and Tracy, with Martin wearing a wig to play the other woman, as they went back and forth, singing the two characters in dialogue. (It strikes me that I always say we never play characters, but in this particular song we did.) Looking back, these lyrics feel representative of the sharp yet bland, somewhat self-aware, despair I was trying to break away from by being open to what the audience had to say.

One of my favourite things about *Unrehearsed Beauty-Le Génie des autres* was, each time we opened the microphone, even if no one said a word, you could feel such a distinct shift in the air in the room. I don't think I've ever, before or after, experienced an atmosphere like it, with everyone thinking: Could I go to the microphone? Should I? If I did so, what would I say? Would it matter to me or anyone else if I went and said something? How and/or why?

One night in Montreal two young men came and tried to take over the show with a Vox Pop survey of the entire audience. They took the microphone and asked each person why they weren't using this opportunity to speak. Once again, this was all in French so I didn't entirely follow, but everyone seemed to have an answer: that they didn't have anything to say or that they might go up later. For the ending, the two young men both joined us on the small stage and played along. My impression was they were considerably better musicians than us (except, of course, for Samuel).

Another night, someone told me that when the first person went to the microphone, they just naturally assumed this audience member was a performer as well, a plant we had placed in the audience. Then another one went and they assumed the same thing. By the end, they had convinced themselves that every single person in the room was part of the cast, and they were the only "real" audience who had come. In some sense they were right, though definitely not in the sense they meant.

+ + + +

Near the end of the Montreal run, we got a review in *Le Devoir* from Solange Lévesque:

> Jacob Wren and his crew do not choose the path of least resistance. Their performance is disconcerting and substantial, in that it is thought-provoking. It brings to mind Robert Gravel's experiments and his theory of non-acting, which the performers of PME adopt each in their own way in this latest work. The show walks a fine line, raising many questions: politics, for example, the quality of work and

of relationships between people, the ideas we have about beauty, and through a negative lens, the expectations we have when we go to the theatre.

Even before we take our seats, the double title – made of segments in English and French, not as translation but as complementary clues – suggests several trains of thought for the audience to consider: what is "unrehearsed" beauty? We might understand it as beauty that is not rehearsed, or not repetitive, beauty that escapes commodification and commercial logic. We might also understand it as beauty that presents itself without artifice, unmarked, as is. In fact, how do we conceive of beauty? And how does this conception influence the ways we relate to each other?

Wren is ferociously deadpan, practising extreme degrees of irony. He discourages those who have come as a passive audience, waiting to be fed something or looking for tame entertainment. Truthfully, the performance does not "unfold": it takes form before our very eyes through an accumulation of magmas – of silences, gestures and confidences, gradually, incrementally, like life offstage, without an immediately perceptible through line. And, as in life offstage, there is an invisible line that requires work to be perceived. We are not sure who the performers are until they go up onstage. They are distributed amongst us in the audience, sitting at tables, dressed as we are: they have no distinguishing qualities. Suddenly, one of them relays an anecdote at the microphone set up in the audience. And two others dance a little dance. A third takes a precarious position, off balance. Ah! They are the actors. The spectators are invited to come up and tell stories as well. A woman takes a chance and approaches the microphone. But is she a real audience member, or is she an actor? Who is who? In terms of beauty and of the material presented, are our expectations different if we know who is talking and what this person's function is? How do we become available to listen or not?

The systematic deconstruction of theatrical conventions

> characterizing this show takes on extraordinary proportions. We are forced to think about what we have named theatre. We listen to people tell their little stories, and we realize that the simplicity is fascinating. We already suspected that human beings are often much more perceptive than they tend to reveal. We gradually become certain that beauty resides largely in the way we listen carefully to a narrator, which is inextricably tied to the ways in which we consent to listen. Thoughts and images abound in the question mark-filled silences following the (false?) confessions, silences respected by Jacob Wren, smiling angelically with his eyes down before strumming a few guitar chords. They are quite beautiful, these others we know nothing about and about whom we hadn't imagined anything because we satisfy ourselves too often with snap judgments based on appearances; we didn't know they had such interesting things to say beyond banal facts.
>
> Jacob Wren and company's previous *En français comme en anglais, it's easy to criticize* was already rebelling against representation. *Unrehearsed Beauty-Le Génie des autres* seriously unsettles the expected functions and roles of performer and audience, as well as the interactivity of art and life.

This was the first time I can remember someone writing about something I had done in a manner that felt right. With *En français comme en anglais, it's easy to criticize,* it might be said that I'd slammed critics, and I now wondered if part of the reason was because I'd simply never had my work engaged with by a really good one. Having that review roughly translated by Sylvie, as she read it aloud to me, was one of the first moments I experienced my new life in Montreal as a real, startling change from my previous life in Toronto. It wasn't that Solange Lévesque particularly loved the show, more that she had taken the time and careful effort to genuinely attempt to understand what we were doing and why, and to put it into her own considered words.

One thing we were now doing, the more we continued to perform *Unrehearsed Beauty-Le Génie des autres,* was thanking each person after they had said something at the microphone. It felt simpler and stronger than any longer response we might give. This had something to do with realizing that people wanted an acknowledgement, that they had been heard. More consequent than any debate or response was the simple acknowledgement we had heard them. In a way, listening to a rough spoken translation of that review was one of the first times I'd felt heard, and it made me feel that continuing to work in Montreal was a good idea. Which now seems so strange to me, or at least yet another paradox in a long string of comical life paradoxes, since it was also a review in French that I couldn't read. All of this makes me believe that Solange Lévesque was a very special writer and critic (she's now retired), and such things do clearly make a difference in artists' lives. So I'd like to thank her now.

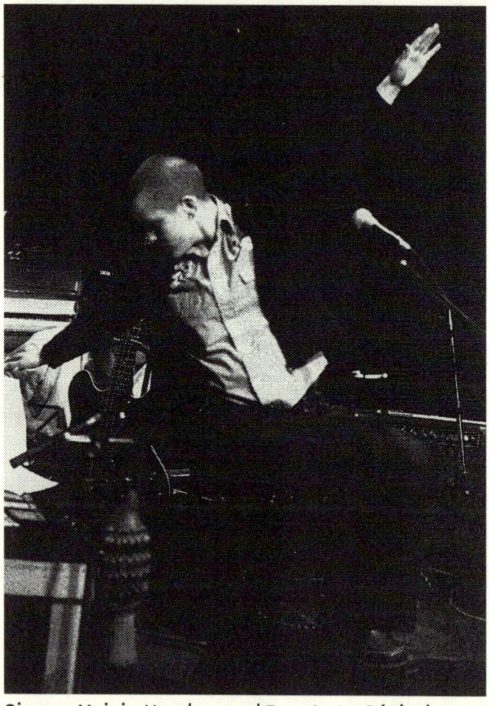

Simone Moir in *Unrehearsed Beauty-Le Génie des autres*. Photo: Unknown

Gordana Vnuk had become artistic director of Kampnagel in Hamburg. Kampnagel also co-produced *Unrehearsed Beauty-Le*

*Génie des autres* and therefore was the first stop of our tour. When we arrived, Simone started asking around to find out what was happening. She had the idea that in each city we could include some local event, include it in how we introduced the possibility that the microphone was open. We learned that activists were occupying an inner-city autonomous housing project called the Bambule, fighting with police to prevent imminent evictions. In the show we asked about this situation, and people got up to speak about it, sometimes in German, so that now none of us understood. I no longer remember many details of the protest itself, but I still remember the way it was spoken about, that it felt to me like something important for Hamburg, a fight worth fighting. Listening to so many get up and speak about the Bambule, in both English and German, half reminded me of our shows in New York when we spoke of 9/11, flashes of the outside world momentarily folding into our performance.

When we thought there would be a smaller audience we would put out fewer chairs, and when we thought more would come we'd put out more, but we always kept the extra chairs stacked against the wall just in case. On the final night in Hamburg it was 8 p.m., the time we were supposed to start, and we only had eight or maybe ten people. We had already taken away most of the chairs, and at eight-fifteen, just as we were about to start, more audience started to arrive. A few more people came and we put out a few more chairs, and then they kept coming, almost faster than we could get the chairs. There was a kind of comical panic to how quickly we were moving chairs. Apparently we'd had a convincing review in the *Hamburger Abendblatt*. I don't think anyone ever translated that review for me, so I don't even know what it said. At 8 p.m. I had been depressed, more than depressed, feeling we'd travelled all this way to once again perform for only a handful of people, and by eight-thirty there was a completely packed room and we were starting the show over thirty minutes late.

I believe that was also the night when an audience member, as we were all milling about after the show, picked up my guitar and walked straight out of the building with it. Our German technician saw this happen, followed him out, ended up chasing him ten blocks before returning, out of breath, but holding my guitar in front of him like the prize at the end of a race. I was so confused by what had happened that I didn't even manage to properly thank him. And the following year that same guitar was stolen for good when the PME office was broken into (they also got our computers).

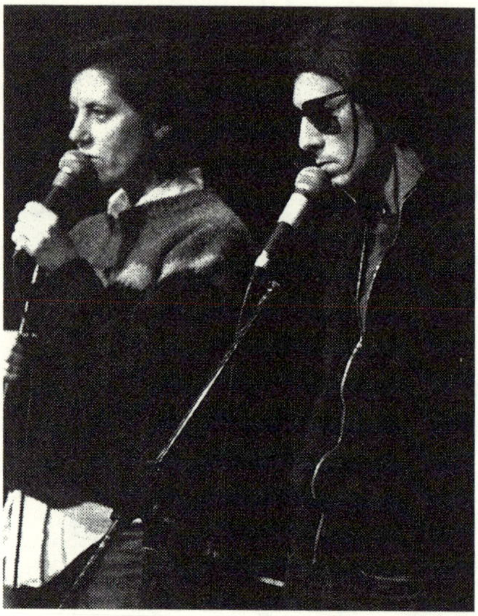

Tracy Wright and Martin Bélanger in *Unrehearsed Beauty-Le Génie des autres* at Le Carrefour international de théâtre in Quebec City. Photo: François Bergeron

After the opening in Hamburg, we all went for dinner in the Kampnagel restaurant and I sat next to Gordana. She once again seemed disappointed in me. She told me the work I was making wasn't strong enough. That I should be making work that was more bold and striking. That I should make work more like Romeo Castellucci and his company Societas Rafaello Sanzio. (When I later told Sven this story he replied, "That's like wishing your child had blond hair instead of black.") Kathrin Tiedemann has already mentioned Castellucci in relation to iconoclasm, but since everyone reading this might not already know, I'll try to say just a little bit more.

Castellucci is an Italian theatre director who is currently one of the most, if not the most, famous on the European festival circuit. Gordana was proud to have presented him at Eurokaz back when he was starting out, back when most other festivals were still ignoring his work, found it too intellectual and visually challenging. His work often features strong, memorable, emotionally dark stage images bleeding into one another in gradual succession. A car falling from the ceiling and crashing onto the stage. Years ago, I saw a Castellucci show that opened with a woman masturbating a horse onto an overhead projector and then killing the sperm with iodine. I have not seen that many Castellucci shows, so I'm definitely not an expert, but to be honest I find his work fascist, pushing the audience to all feel the same disturbing things at the exact same time. At any rate, what I have seen leads me to believe that it is basically the opposite of everything I'm trying to do. He makes dramatic, memorable, surreal, controversial stage images based on what I'm told is an extensive and impressive theoretical research into various classical texts. I am trying to be myself in a performance situation, and speak about things that are important to me, in a direct, and hopefully very human, vulnerable, and intimate manner. So Gordana telling me my work should be more like Castellucci, in that moment, felt more than absurd.

It was around this time I became interested in Gianni Vattimo's concept Weak Thought. (I only just noticed that both Vattimo and Castellucci are Italian.) I'm not sure I fully understood it, then or now, but we might say that Weak Thought, which emerges from hermeneutics, is a way of approaching philosophy that believes not only that philosophy will always be incomplete, but that such incompleteness is central to its value, leading toward a plurality of positions that weaken one another, and in which no one position is ever taken for a final truth. Weak Thought is a positive concept often placed against and in relation to the strong thought of previous philosophical system building, where the philosopher might have believed, or wish the reader to believe, that their system in itself can be equated with the truth. It might have been a cheap analogy, but that night I was definitely feeling that my work was connected to Weak Thought in a way that might someday push effectively against Castellucci's apparent artistic strengths.

Gordana also told me about another show that had always stayed with her by the Japanese company Gekidan Kaitaisha. (Through which Hiromi first learned the term *post-mainstream* when they performed at Eurokaz.) The show began with a half-naked woman on her knees being hit across her back by a man standing above her. The woman was hit again and again until the audience couldn't take it anymore and an audience member would eventually run onstage to intervene. They would just keep going, keep hitting, until someone intervened. Gordana was saying this was an example I could learn from, but to me it sounded utterly and totally awful, and I made a joke in response that I've always somewhat regretted. I said: "Yes, I'm willing to make something like that, if you'll volunteer to be the woman." Gordana brushed it off – she never particularly got my sense of humour – but I regret that joke because there was something sexist about it. I was only trying to say that you might enjoy watching violence (which I certainly don't), find it powerful onstage, but you might not enjoy it so much if it were directed toward you. But it was also a joke about violence against women, the kind of joke I hope never to make again. And I wonder if the way it unthinkingly came out of my mouth had anything to do with the fact that I didn't like being told what to do, in this case by a woman (though in general I don't like being told what to do by anyone), a woman who had a certain degree of power over my work since she had given us a co-production and might someday do so again (though at that point it didn't seem likely), and was throwing so many suggestions at me that all felt so wildly off the mark. Yet for Gordana it was what she believed in and she was fighting for it. I wish I had been more able to respect, and therefore respectfully disagree with, her position at the time.

Years later, in her book *20 Years of Eurokaz*, Gordana wrote:

> With now already a third generation, *noble dilettantism* has become a widespread and solid market commodity. Many artists today think they have grasped an ideal care-free recipe for making theatre: you do not have to know anything; it suffices to be present onstage and there will always be someone who will inscribe the meaning into it. Rarely will there be someone to warn us that on the construction site

> of language, the most painful aspect is the silence and the most lasting is the anxiety. Iconoclastic theatre fell into its own trap and it seems there is no willingness to reinvent itself. For those of us who saw in it maybe too much, it is a somewhat sad statement, but we move on.

She certainly wasn't referring only to PME, but when I read this there was little question that, in her mind, these words very much applied to us. At the same time, I am able to find this phrase moving: "the most painful aspect is the silence and the most lasting is the anxiety." Silence and anxiety are realities I've always wanted to feel in performance, aspects of life and thought that, for me, far too much performance works too hard to avoid.

+ + + +

During this period I was also touring *Recent Experiences*, a show I co-wrote and co-directed with Nadia Ross and her company STO Union. It was something we had started back when I was still in Toronto, and we worked on it on and off for about six years until its premiere at the Theatre Centre in 2000, an event loosely connected to celebrations of the millennium. In it, we counted off the years from 1900 to 2000, as four generations of a family recounted episodes from their not-quite-reality lives, mixed with announcements of concurrent world historical events. Half the cast was black and half white, and as the generations progressed white couples gave birth to black children and vice versa, with no explanation given. It was a script we performed sitting around a large table with the audience, so actors performing scenes would be sitting across or directly next to you.

The following year we took *Recent Experiences* to the Festival de théâtre des Amériques in Montreal, where we got invitations. We went to Kunstenfestivaldesarts (Belgium), Wiener Festwoche (Austria), Theatre der Welt (Germany), Melbourne Arts Festival (obviously Australia), Hong Kong Arts Festival, etc. These were my first experiences with larger festivals, in a way the current version of the experimental mainstream circuit about which Knut Ove had written. And, perhaps naively, I was surprised to learn that while my own work was rapidly heading toward a place with no scripts and many different kinds of performers, all of these larger festivals were still committed to presenting challenging, contemporary theatre centred around good actors and good scripts. It made me anxious the extent to which my growing artistic desires were apparently so far outside of what was being celebrated on this circuit, and for this reason I found the positive festival reaction to *Recent Experiences* a bit overwhelming. It was a project we had been working on for seven years by the time we took it to Europe, and of course I loved it and believed in it, especially in the amazing cast (Andrew Moodie, Tracy Wright, Andrea Davis, Charles Officer, Ingrid Veninger, and Nadia Ross), but with my own work I was definitely searching for something else (since in my mind *Recent Experiences* was by STO Union, which meant that, even though it was a collaboration, it was primarily Nadia's initiative and part of her always amazing, ongoing body of work).

Because of the success of *Recent Experiences*, presenters who had loved it would then come to see *Unrehearsed Beauty-Le Génie des autres*. And, since *Unrehearsed Beauty-Le Génie des autres* was pretty much the opposite of *Recent Experiences,* they would often be confused or disappointed. They were expecting something more like the tightly scripted, beautifully acted table performance they remained enchanted by, not a destabilizing open question that required the audience's participation to complete it. (They should have come to the obvious conclusion that the genius of *Recent Experiences* belonged predominantly to Nadia, but I believe, because of unexamined European sexism, they often unfortunately did not.) Sylvie adamantly disagreed with me, but around this time I started to feel that PME would not be programmed at any of the big festivals, or at least not any time soon. Or maybe Sylvie didn't exactly disagree, but felt this difficulty was no reason not to try, no reason not to keep pushing.

Directly after Hamburg, we travelled to Berlin and performed *Unrehearsed Beauty-Le Génie des autres* at Prater. We had agreed to perform our show within the elaborate set of René Pollesch, which in hindsight was a mistake. Pollesch is a German writer and director who writes difficult, experimental, anti-capitalist texts that are then performed, often at a breakneck pace, by really good German actors who do so in a manner entirely specific to his work. (Once again, I thought, good scripts and good actors – everything I was against. And yes, I also know how insane this sounds.) His set was three entire walls of colourful, Berlin-glam-trash small stages, separated by thin frames, each featuring one or more gigantic manipulated images as a backdrop (for example, a close-up of the face of late-period Michael Jackson, like a modern-day tabloid freak show). It seemed clear our show was somewhat dwarfed by the scale and clashing patterns of this set, which was so tightly woven into the DNA of the René Pollesch aesthetic it was like performing our show in the middle of one of his. Opening night only a few went to the microphone, and after the show I got into a long discussion with Christine Peters, in which she did most of the talking, a conversation that felt like a continuation of the one I'd had with Gordana less than a week before. Christine had presented *Recent Experiences* at Mousonturm in Frankfurt. (Opening night in Frankfurt there was a critic sitting at the end of the table, furiously writing in her notebook, an absolutely miserable expression on her face. We were certain she hated it, but the next day her review was a rave with the headline: "A Masterpiece for the 20th Century." That was how I learned you can never tell what an audience member is thinking from their facial expression alone.)

I never felt that Christine loved *Recent Experiences*, but she definitely hated *Unrehearsed Beauty-Le Génie des autres*. She told me she had a really great story she could have told, but she didn't want to go to the microphone because she didn't want to help us. She told me that in this show it seemed we were only lost, only searching. She told me I should make work more like Forced Entertainment, because together they had decided what was important to them and they continue to insist on it. She told me that she preferred work that had, and clearly expressed, its convictions, and our work did not. (Sylvie says she thinks this is a good example of how people react when they see something new. They say they love to be shocked, but when they actually are shocked they might very well react against it.)

This discussion was yet another turning point for me. I had now been performing in Europe for almost five years but was just beginning to understand what I'd gotten myself into. I disagreed with many of the things Christine was telling me, but at the same time was trying to take all her complaints into full consideration. Because I did have a kind of conviction, but on a performative level perhaps it expressed itself as an anti-conviction, closer to everyday casual doubt. I had a conviction that one should not perform with skilled or impassioned conviction, that one should not hide the fact that one is vulnerable or feels lost, and to Christine this basically read as no conviction at all. She also said that I personally was trying too hard to charm the audience, smiling at them awkwardly, shuffling uncomfortably from side to side, which on that particular night – working to compete with Pollesch's set, to overcome the fact that so few were accepting our invitation to the microphone – I believe was far more true than I wanted to admit.

And yet, when I got home from Berlin, we got this email, like water in the desert, one of the many audience emails that have kept us going over the years:

> hello jacob,
>
> it was in december, the weather was bad and i was depressed. we were depressed, it was in berlin, in prater. a performance was going on, the audience was few, the people onstage were smart and beautiful, nothing really special, i mean: i was expecting it: everything fitting to berlin, december 2002, europe and so on.
>
> a microphone was put in the audience, somebody proposed: you can use this microphone – o.k. here we go – my public brain starts to work, slowly, our public brain(s), start(s) to work: an opportunity. can we use it? can i use it? economically? for my interest? for somebody else's interest? a mission? promising areas of 'yes and no' were opening and closing again, pros and cons and maybes

clouds:

->representative duties
-->skilled desires
----------------------------------> the coolnessfactor!!!!!!!!!!
->the uptightnesschique
->vague responsibilities
-> imperatives: shine -> hide
->oh YES: This is participation -----------> oh NO: This is participation
->this is history
->this is histery
->this is mud
->this is fog
->this is a mission
->this is history
->this is manipulation
------>this is propaganda
--------------------------------->attention: this is propaganda
--------------------------------->attention this is propaganda and i'm part of it.
->ATTENTION THIS IS PROPAGANDA, AND WE ARE ALL PART OF IT.

--->questions:
what is not propaganda? or: how not to propaganda?
DEMOCRACY – do we really like it? if not what else?
value? ----------------> what is the value of being invalid, when nobody is noticing? o.k.: value – now.... no, better: no value – now... so nobody will sell it.
shouldn't that all stop? stop – for example: now.

all this was a shock, an individualist shock. me and i and confronted with early death and all this shit. Publicly.

i looked around: the others – oh yes, they also suffered. same paradoxes: they were beautiful and alone and they and we were separated from each other, but anyways WE were a group gathering around this empty microphone.

nobody wanted. nobody wanted to use this microphone. it was beautiful. it was great. none of us did the steps. we refused collectively. passionately. it was an orgy of refusal. a party

this party was going on several times during that evening. (just in the end somebody said something half funny, which i forgot)

later we all laughed, cos we didn't clap and sing with this song, we laughed AT the performers cos they wanted us to clap, we laughed WITH the performers cos they didn't want us to clap at all... we laughed at us, cos we thought earlier that they really wanted us to clap.... we laughed at our smartness and that it doesn't help at all. (doesn't help: anyways we are all capitalists) anyways we laughed. we performed. the performance was called something like this: gods are laughing about the structural nothing or: i know, that you know, that i know (written by some ancient guy) i laughed. something like catharsis, didn't know that such a thing still exists.

yes, this was a community, but it didn't feel comfortable, i mean it was performing its skills [the delicate skill of inclusion (we ALL) and even more delicate: exclusion (WE all).] passionately to a really dead end...

and?

-------------------->

THANK YOU for putting up this microphone, if it wasn't you, please pass this text to the person who is responsible for it.

bianca

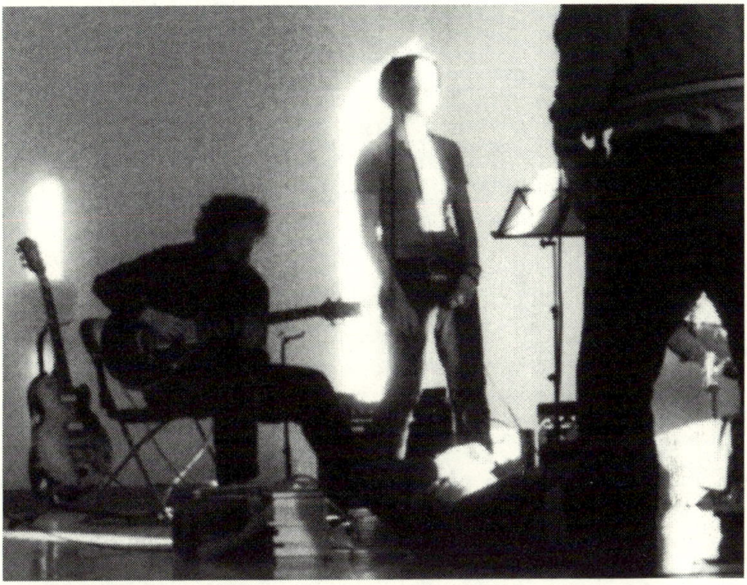

Jacob Wren and Julie Andrée T. in *Unrehearsed Beauty-Le Génie des autres*. Photo: Alexandra Rockingham Gill

Before *Unrehearsed Beauty-Le Génie des autres* was invited to Japan, there was apparently a great deal of discussion on their side as to whether or not to invite it. Unbeknownst to us, since we still hadn't met her, Hiromi Maruoka had come to see the show in Quebec City with some other Japanese artists and presenters, and they then debated what they'd seen for weeks, so much so that Hiromi came back to see it again in Montreal with a different group of interlocutors. Hiromi was definitely not sure it would work in Japan. She didn't exactly know how to deal with the difficult but necessary challenge of translating the often improvised text, as well as the contributions from the audience, into Japanese. When I heard we were being invited to the Tokyo Post-Mainstream Performing Arts Festival I could not believe the name. How had Knut Ove's term migrated from Norway to Japan (only later would I learn that the answer was of course: though Croatia). At that time Hiromi spoke little English, and communication was difficult. But during our first meeting it was clear to me that she felt she was taking a genuine risk by bringing us over, a situation that made me both nervous and grateful. It seemed to me she had started the Tokyo Post-Mainstream Performing Arts Festival with a clear intention to make an intervention, shift certain aspects of the Japanese performing arts scene, to open it up to work that took more artistic risks, was more international and contemporary, and her motives reminded me so much of the reasons Sylvie and Richard had founded Les 20 jours du théâtre à risque in 1988.

Our venue in Tokyo was SuperDeluxe, an artist-run white cube basement that normally hosted concerts and parties. Walking into SuperDeluxe for the first time was like stumbling into some sort of relaxed, effortless, next-level cool that could probably only exist in Japan. We spent many days working with our translators, Ayako Kuwabara and Adam Broinowski, integrating them into the show, trying to make the Japanese translation feel like a natural, transparent part of what we were doing. Each time one of us spoke, Ayako would translate it into Japanese, and each time an audience member went to the microphone, Adam would translate it into English. *Unrehearsed Beauty-Le Génie des autres* in Japan is unquestionably one of the most potent and unusual experiences of my performing life. (It was also my first time in Japan.) I wonder how I can convey the atmosphere in that room those three nights. Much like all of the performances I'm writing about in this book, you simply had to be there, which is the aspect of performance that most actively drew me toward it all those years ago. But since there is little chance you were at SuperDeluxe on the evenings of March 13, 14, or 15, 2003, I will do my best to describe some of it here.

I remember a Japanese woman getting up to the microphone. She said she was a translator and didn't know what to say because every time she had spoken in public she had only ever translated someone else's words, she had never spoken any of her own. Then a second Japanese woman got up, stood beside the first, and said she was also a translator, and she very much related to the first woman's predicament, so she would volunteer to translate her, and perhaps by translating each other they could help each other work their way out of this particular difficulty. Which is what they then proceeded to do.

I remember the U.S. had just invaded Iraq for a second time. How horrified and disgusted I was they had branded their first bombardment Shock and Awe. And people getting up to the microphone denouncing the U.S. invasion, but also expressing a fear, that was currently in the air, that North Korea might soon bomb Japan. One night an Australian company came and said they couldn't stand our show, because what we had created was a "peace church" where people took turns getting up and proclaiming their dedication to peace, and if someone had stood up to say they supported the U.S. invasion everyone present would have angrily pounced on them in the name of peace. SuperDeluxe was in the Western Roppongi district of Tokyo, and several times I saw U.S. soldiers walking down the street in small packs just outside the building.

I remember being told, after the first night, that several artists had stayed at SuperDeluxe to talk about the show, and had ended up getting into such a heated debate that they were still there talking about it the next morning. And then returning to Tokyo two years later and being told that artists were still debating the merits and demerits of our show. That they were still talking about it even then.

I remember giving a talk at the university. When I got to the classroom there was a black South African theatre director who was originally scheduled to give a talk, but had been asked, and agreed, to share his time with me. He gave a detailed and inspiring presentation about how they had used theatre to fight against apartheid, about how he and so many of his colleagues had been jailed, their theatre repeatedly shut down, but they never gave up and eventually prevailed. Then it was my turn to speak. I sheepishly got up and began by saying that I started making shows in Toronto when I was eighteen and since that time have always been working on how to be yourself in a performance situation. It felt almost comically anticlimactic after the victorious anti-apartheid struggle we had just heard recounted. However, when I got to Vattimo and Weak Thought, I definitely felt a certain spark of interest from the class.

I remember an eighties Toronto pop star who, by this point, was considerably bigger in Japan, getting up to the microphone and explaining how saddened and disappointed she was by everything she had witnessed. She spoke slowly, in carefully composed phrases, like she was a spoken-word artist reciting a poem, complaining that the topics the audience brought to the microphone felt so empty and soulless, that here we all had an opportunity to speak about important things, to speak from the heart, and instead we were wasting it on whatever popped into our heads. It felt a bit like my previous life from Toronto had followed me all the way to Japan to bash me one more time. But the room was having none of it, and directly after her a young man went to the microphone to say how much he loved eating meatball subs.

When we first arrived in Japan, we were told that people there were too shy to get up to the microphone and speak in front of a room full of strangers, that it went too much against the cultural norms, and we should be prepared for shows in which very few participated. But the exact opposite was true. So many got up and spoke, and so often you could feel that they were taking a risk, that they were pushing just a little bit past what might be a normal thing for them to do in public. This energy of so many moving past their previous comfort zone was something I don't think I'll ever experience again. (Also, I viewed it all through Western eyes, so I don't know if my impressions were even accurate.) *Unrehearsed Beauty-Le Génie des autres* normally lasted two hours, but each night in Tokyo it lasted well over four. Part of this was because of the translation, but it was also clearly because so many joined in. On the last night, as we played the final song, I could see Hiromi dancing at the back of the room, and I could feel her enormous relief that this show she was so nervous about, so unsure if it would work here in Japan, had worked far better than any of us had previously imagined.

+ + + +

The first night at SuperDeluxe, Toshiki Okada, from the company chelfitsch, was in attendance. Later he wrote a play partly about seeing our show called *Five Days in March*. The first half of his play takes place as two young men are watching *Unrehearsed Beauty-Le Génie des autres*, describing what they see and commenting on the action. This part is all fairly accurate. Then one of the men meets a woman and they go to a hotel room together for five days and five nights, talk and make love, while on the streets below there are massive protests against the just-starting Iraq war. The protests were happening, but the nights in the hotel were apparently pure fiction. *Five Days in March* won the Kishida Drama Award in 2004 and, I believe, launched Toshiki Okada's international theatre career. I don't think anyone who saw it ever realized that the show being described in the first act was PME's *Unrehearsed Beauty-Le Génie des autres*. Yet another moment in which we've infiltrated theatre in a manner that was practically invisible.

\+ + + +

Other things I remember from *Unrehearsed Beauty-Le Génie des autres*: Martin getting on all fours and performing "the last mammoth" before the species' extinction, lumbering up the side of the room in a choreographed, existential march of environmental collapse.

In Trondheim, Martin being lifted up by a class of Norwegian dance students and carried out of the building, the expression on his face as he looked back at us, as if to say: what the hell is happening.

Getting up on the small stage in Quebec City and reciting the sentence "loneliness must be recruited in the fight against capitalism" as a poem in which I added one word with every repetition:

Loneliness
Loneliness must
Loneliness must be
Loneliness must be recruited
Loneliness must be recruited in
Loneliness must be recruited in the
Loneliness must be recruited in the fight
Loneliness must be recruited in the fight against
Loneliness must be recruited in the fight against capitalism.

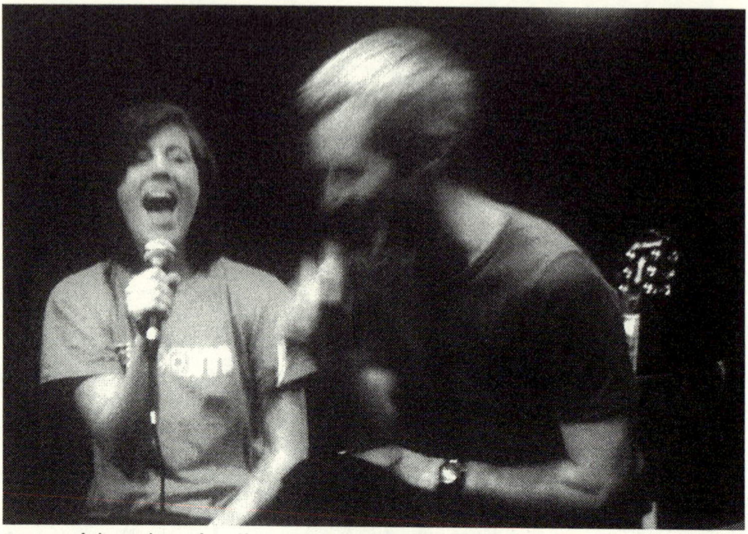

Tracy Wright and Martin Bélanger in *Unrehearsed Beauty-Le Génie des autres* at Le Carrefour international de théâtre in Quebec City. Photo: François Bergeron

When I think about being an artist, I always think the point is to have artistic breakthroughs, if it is even still possible to speak in such romantic terms. For me, *Unrehearsed Beauty-Le Génie des autres* was the most distinct experience I've had of an artistic breakthrough, of taking a leap into the void and fully experiencing what lay on the other side. So many unrehearsed moments that only happened that one time and will never happen again. So many nights when what we brought and what the audience brought gradually came together over the course of two hours to make something so much more than the sum of its part (and also many nights when it didn't). I also feel it was a show that half killed my career. Many loved it, were provoked or intrigued, but others, especially on the European festival circuit, took it as a clear sign that I was no longer an artist to watch. When we performed in Montreal, Danièle de Fontenay, who runs Usine C, the venue we've most often performed at in our hometown, came up to me after the show. This was back when we'd just started collaborating. We were talking and I said that sometimes it was important to go all the way, to follow the artistic questions all the way to the end and find out where they lead. "That's great," she replied, "just don't do it too often." A huge smile on her face as she said so.

As I've said, I fear I sometimes rely too much on parallels between art and politics, but all of this reminds me of a quote I've often thought about from an interview with the artist Paul Chan:

> At the time, the mid-'90s, the AFL-CIO [the American Federation of Labour and Congress of Industrial Organizations] was doing college recruitment, and big labour unions were going to colleges and universities talking about how they should organize. It was thrilling. It all culminated with the UPS strike in 1997 in Chicago with Ron Carey, the Teamster president. Here's a guy who came up from the rank and file of the Teamsters, who was forced into confronting a company that refused to negotiate with the workers on a new contract. 185,000 workers walked off the job, and UPS blinked. They broke the company and got a new contract. I lived close to a UPS processing center on the South Side of Chicago, and we'd bring them donuts. It was a great moment. Then of course Carey was booted; after the strike the Teamster hierarchy voted in the son of Jimmy Hoffa as president, even though Carey had just led this insane victory, and even though everyone knew Hoffa Jr. was shady. One of the lessons you learn is that changing things often means losing your job or getting jailed, or worse.

The parallel is not exact, perhaps not even obvious. The results of our (from my point of view) artistic breakthrough weren't so bad, certainly not losing my "job or getting jailed, or worse." But it was my first premonition of something that has haunted and confused me during my many years of making things: that the work I feel goes furthest, is the strangest and most strangely compelling, most likely won't be my most successful. And I still don't know what to do with this particular information.

Four:

# Families Are Formed Through Copulation

(2005–2006)

Created/Performed by:
Gaétan Nadeau, Laure Ottmann, and Tracy Wright

Written/Directed by:
Jacob Wren

We performed it in:
Montreal, Usine C • Brussels, Kaaitheater • Düsseldorf, Forum Freies Theater • Bergen, BIT Teatergarasjen • Tokyo, Post Mainstream Performing Arts Festival • Maubeuge, Le Manège/Via Festival • Dresden, Projekttheater • Créteil, Maison des Arts/Exit Festival • Prague, Divadlo Archa • Cardiff, Chapter Arts Centre

When you're no longer searching for beauty or love
just some sort of life with the edges taken off
– Pulp, "The Fear"

I remember having the first impulse for *Families Are Formed Through Copulation* on a train in Europe. I was thinking about melodrama, more specifically about a film: Thomas Vinterberg's *Festen* (and later also Lars von Trier's *The Idiots*). I was thinking about how they do so many things in those films that I would never let myself do onstage. Was it possible to have some form of melodrama folded into the act of being yourself onstage? I thought that what hit me so hard about *Festen* had to do with family, that the emotions we have in connection to our families are some of the most powerful emotions we're capable of experiencing. I had a fairly stable, loving, middle-class childhood (except the other children were mean to me and I still haven't gotten over it), but when I think about my family long and hard I feel a kind of pain that is completely out of proportion with anything that happened to me. These are negative emotions, I'm much better at the negative end of the emotional spectrum, but for someone else the same might be true for positive ones, they might feel a joy that is completely out of proportion. I was wondering if there was a way to keep doing what we were doing but to bring more emotional fiction into it, more storytelling.

Even the fact that I was considering such questions signalled a period of retreat. Sylvie once said to me: sometimes the best attack is a tactical retreat. I was learning that the European festival circuit most often preferred good scripts and good actors, and saw no reason I couldn't do that as well. (I now think of this time as a period of compromise that I basically regret. My regret is also most likely out of proportion.) How dedicated was I really to this project of no scripts, collaborative process, and different kinds of performers, and was my dedication little more than tilting at windmills? I could certainly see the absurdity of my position: practically everyone in the world thought theatre was one thing and, by pure force of will, I wanted it to be something else. I was single-minded, and incredibly stubborn, but I also, at times, believed in compromise. At the beginning of *Unrehearsed Beauty* I had already quoted Krzysztof Kieslowski on the topic:

> There's another aspect to all this. I, personally, believe that these compromises which you have to make and this agreement to relinquish your own convictions in certain matters – some better, some worse, of course – are healthy. Because absolute freedom only leads to great works if you're a genius. If you're not, it very often leads to pretentiousness, inferiority and something even worse, which is spending money and making films exclusively for yourself and your nearest friends. Restrictions, necessary restrictions and necessary compromises give rise to a certain ingenuity, inventiveness and inspire energies which enable you to find original solutions and ideas within the script.

This wasn't exactly the kind of compromise I was thinking of now. It wasn't exactly a compromise within art I was considering. It was more of a compromise with the world. To meet the festival circuit halfway and see if anything happens (it didn't).

\+ + + +

I wasn't only thinking of melodrama. I was also thinking about polemic. In *Unrehearsed Beauty* I had written:

> So often we say: art should only ask questions. Art should never provide answers. Art should be a field simply of exploration. And yet in our personal lives, in private conversation, we are so often a fountain of opinions. We have answers for everything. We know exactly what we think and exactly how we think it. We seem so sure of ourselves. And yet, as if out of some sort of near religious conviction, the art remains ambiguous. Is this not, I must now ask, somehow dishonest? And if so, then what is honesty? And what is art?

I was starting to feel that too much ambiguity in art let both the artist and the viewer off the hook. That if the artist is willing to make a strong statement within a work, take a stand, it gives the viewer something to push back against, allows them to agree or disagree, and in doing so further develop their own understanding and reflections. While with ambiguity it would often just wash over me like a warm bath, giving aesthetic pleasure but not changing me in any way. But perhaps this wasn't the real reason for my growing interest in combining polemic and art. When I was younger I distinctly remember being told that didactic art was bad art, and over the years the idea ate at me, I started to want to rebel against it. In some ways my interest in polemic was more like a teenage rebellion against something I had previously been told was not allowed. Of course, it was also part of an ongoing struggle to figure out how my work might become more political, what might be effective, what did I really think about art and politics after so many years of trying to understand.

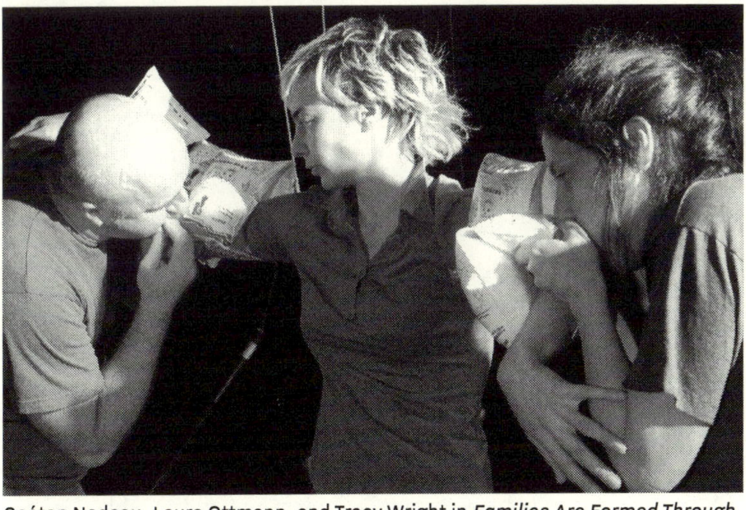

Gaétan Nadeau, Laure Ottmann, and Tracy Wright in *Families Are Formed Through Copulation* at Usine C in Montreal. Photo: Mathieu Chartrand

But before the decision was made, there was a much too long period, I think it must have dragged on for almost a year, that was probably the most intensive internal debate of my life, an impasse that drove Sylvie and Richard completely crazy, and that Sylvie sometimes still complains about to this day. Because I actually had two projects – *Extra-fin* and *Families Are Formed Through Copulation*

– and I found myself unable to choose between them, unable to decide which one we should do. When I fall deep enough into the indecision rabbit hole it is like I will never be able to decide anything again. One day I would come into the office convinced that *Extra-fin* should be our next show, then the next day it would be *Families Are Formed Through Copulation*, and the day after that it would once again be *Extra-fin*. Both were scripts I had written, but *Extra-fin* would be me alone onstage, a prospect that utterly terrified me, while at the same time telling myself that perhaps facing the challenge of this terror was something I had to do, something that would make me stronger in the long run.

After two difficult collaborative processes I didn't think I could face the reality of working with other people again, or at least not so soon. In fact, this must have been part of the impasse: could I face the terror of being alone onstage, which I had never done, or could I face the pain of once again attempting to enter into a collaborative (or pseudo-collective) process with others. It is only in retrospect that I wonder how much of this impasse had to do with feeling conflicted about returning to scripts after having so recently rejected them. Both projects were everything I'd said I never wanted to do again, and yet all I was doing was endlessly trying to choose between them, back and forth like a mental pendulum that doesn't completely understand what the problem is and therefore is never able to rest. I would probably still be debating the various merits and demerits of the two projects, still unable to decide between them, if it wasn't for Kathrin Tiedemann.

We first met Kathrin when we performed in Dresden in 1999. She came to see us with a small delegation – organized by Sylvie and Menno Plukker with the financial support of the Quebec Office – that also included Aenne Quinones, Johan Reyniers, and Frie Leysen. Soon after Kathrin was working at Kampnagel with Gordana, and was there for our unrehearsed discussions on the Bambule. In 2003 she invited me to the festival Reich & Berühmt at Podewil in Berlin. By the time I had reached my impasse, Kathrin had just become artistic director of the Forum Freies Theater in Düsseldorf. She had now been following our work for almost five years, and kindly offered to co-produce whatever we were planning to make next. We still had no idea which one we would do, I sent her both scripts, and she said for her there was no question: *Families Are Formed Through Copulation* was more interesting. So that is what we did. Forum Freies Theater has now done four co-productions with PME/PME-ART, and I have often felt, during our most difficult periods, that Kathrin's support was unquestionably one of the key factors keeping us alive.

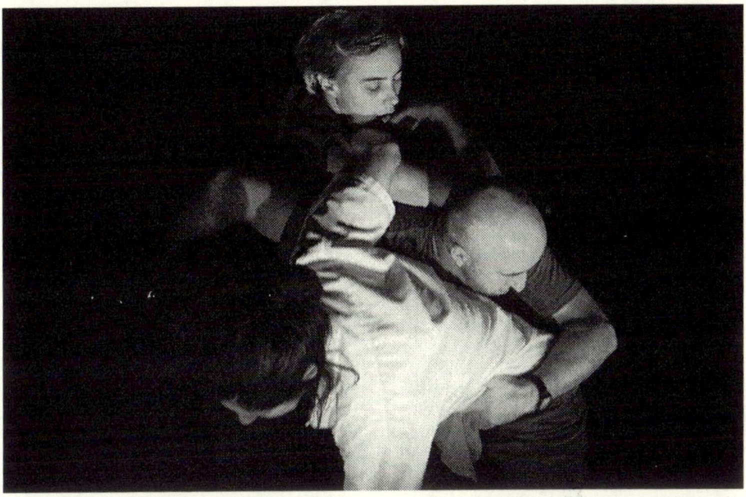

Laure Ottmann, Gaétan Nadeau, and Tracy Wright in *Families Are Formed Through Copulation* at Usine C in Montreal. Photo: Mathieu Chartrand

*Families Are Formed Through Copulation* was Gaétan Nadeau, Laure Ottmann, and Tracy Wright. It was the only PME show (so far) I haven't performed in, and of course the only one that began with a script. They were each, as usual, performing as themselves, but simultaneously they were also the father (Gaétan), mother (Tracy), and daughter (Laure) in a nuclear family. The oscillation between being yourself and being a (stock) character was something I was interested in, but perhaps also something we never quite achieved. Fragmented sections of text and dialogue alternated with performance activities, some of which echoed the text literally, others considerably less so. Tracy and Laure pulling at each other's arms in a kind of choreographed tug-of-war. Laure putting on a record as the others followed behind her, ending in a flowing tangle of bodies that might have been sexual, might have been violent, or might have only been playful. A pyramid of plastic wineglasses with a glowing liquid poured over them, like some toxic, nuclear champagne. Rows of tape measures spread across the stage, snapping back into their holsters in a sonic shattering that followed a text on 9/11. Playing one note each on their respective guitars as they slowly, one step at a time, walk toward the front of the stage, a snail-paced race in which music and movement merge through unclear rules. Sections were divided by Jean-Pierre Gauthier's installation: three brooms on one side of the stage and three folding chairs (or garbage bags) on the other, that when switched on flew and creaked in floating, ever-shifting patterns.

+ + + +

The most polemic part of the text is a section entitled "People, Stop Having Children":

> People, stop having children. You are not doing yourselves or the world any good. Take the energies you would have spent on child rearing and use them instead to fight American imperialism. The world is not as it used to be. Before you know it your children will be taken from you and indoctrinated in the ways of bad cartoons, overpriced toys, short attention spans, violent video games, stupid television, and the endless misinformation of the Internet. Stop for a moment and think. There are too many people in the world already. There is too much of everything. Your children will learn nothing from you. Is what you know really so valuable or important? People, stop having children. You think you are being generous but really you are only being selfish. You are doing it only to add surplus, disingenuous meaning to your already basically meaningless lives or as an unwitting slave of primitive biology. Your children will not look after you when you are old. They will be too busy trying to fend for themselves within the unyieldingly harsh economic realities you have created for them. Don't worry, the species will continue. Even if every single person who reads these words were to convince one hundred of their closest friends to stop having children, still the species will

continue. So people, stop having children. We must all stop and think. What are we actually doing? We are following a script. But is the script well written, does it serve the best interests of humanity? We have been following this script for thousands of years and look where we are today. Things are not going well. Well, I say let's change the script and stop having children. I am not simply trying to justify my own pathetic little life. This is a real question and each and every one of us must ask ourselves. Will the children I rear add anything to the world or will they only take up space? I'm not saying babies aren't cute, aren't adorable, aren't desirable commodities, perhaps the most desirable commodity any young couple could possibly hope for. But we all must look at the bigger picture. The planet is not infinite. In fact nothing is infinite. *Infinity* is a term we use to denote an impossible space. Infinity cannot be filled and yet we procreate as if it could be. People, stop having children. Let me tell you a story. There is a first world and a third world. In the third world they have lots of children and in the first world we have few. So that's all right, you might think quietly to yourself. The few babies we do have do not contribute significantly to the problem. And yet every baby we create contributes directly to the already considerable misery of children and adults alike halfway around the world. Everything we buy, every choice we make. Let me tell you another story. There was a young couple and they got married and had children. The couple were extremely liberal in both their thoughts and actions and thought that by raising their two children within the enlightenment tradition of their liberal ideas, they could, in their own small and humane fashion, make the world a better place. But their children were rebellious and, perhaps only out of misguided spite, grew up to espouse the most pernicious of conservative, pseudo-right-wing doctrines. The parents were heartbroken but their heartbreak was merely the result of naïveté. Your children might also rebel, might also grow up to represent the antithesis of everything you stand for and believe in, and what are you going to do about it. People, stop having children. The world we have created will not tolerate their still unformed humanity. The world we have created will destroy them and you will be at least partly responsible, or you will feel responsible, or you won't feel responsible but you should. Fascists believe in having children. Nazis believe in having children. Peasants believe in having children and it is time for us to get beyond all of that. And I want to be perfectly clear on this next point: the problem is not children. The problem is adults. But without children there would be no adults. And without adults there would be no children. And the cycle must be broken. As often as possible. Let me now outline what I hope we can all agree is a common enough scenario. A woman of child-bearing age attends her younger sister's wedding, during the course of which she is cornered by a distant relative she neither knows very well nor particularly likes. "So when's your turn," asks the relative, who is also perhaps more than a little bit drunk by this point in the late afternoon, meaning of course, when will it be your turn to get married. The woman of child-bearing age attempts to be polite, dodging the question, claiming she doesn't really know, when the right man comes along, etc. But the drunk relative is insistent: "Of course you're planning to have children," she continues, "you must be planning to have children." The woman of childbearing age has no immediate plans for children but doesn't want to cause a scene. "Yeah, maybe someday," she shrugs. Trying to be polite, trying to be evasive, wanting to leave this wedding and go back to a life in which human interaction is more familiar and ironic and benign. "No, not someday. You have to have them now, when you're still young, while you still have the energy. If you wait, if you wait..." The drunken relative trails off. Perhaps she has no children of her own. Or perhaps her children are all grown up and not treating her with the love and respect she knows in her heart she deserves. "You have to have children," the relative says, "you just have to." But she's wrong.

This text was written by a child who was never born. And you might think that because I was never born I'd be bitter or unhappy but you to would be wrong. Not having been born was the most perfect, wonderful, humane, enlightened thing to have ever happened to me. I am little more than a thought, a bit of whimsy, a pre-copulatory, never conceived twinkle in the eye of no one in particular and here is what I have learned. Nothing exists in isolation. Everything exists in relation to something else. If something is good, it is only good in relation to something else which is less good. If we can all agree with this premise we can see that there exists a sort of sliding scale of human endeavours in which the best thing is never to have been born, the next best thing is to be born but live your life without doing any harm, and the next best thing is to be born, do some harm, but never to reproduce. To be honest, it gets a little fuzzy after that. Life can be so difficult. But never having been born is a piece of cake.

In the show, this text is spoken by a computer, with white-on-black surtitles to make everything extra-clear. No explanation is given as to why the text is spoken by a computer, and it is the only thing like that in the show, or in any of my work, for that matter. Is the computer a voice from the future, warning us of the dangers of overpopulation, or simply an expression of all the computers we are constantly surrounded by, how they see us, what advice they might give if they had a chance.

I suppose it's a kind of polemic but, at the same time, it's a polemic drenched in paradox. Because it's a polemic written knowing that I would basically convince no one. Pieter De Buysser, who I co-created *An Anthology of Optimism* with, told me they had their first child pretty much nine months after he read the *Families Are Formed Through Copulation* book. "Jacob's not going to tell me what to do," he thought to himself at the time. When I read "People, Stop Having Children" at the Scream in High Park in Toronto, people at the back were holding up their babies and waving them back and forth. When we performed at the Kaaitheater in Brussels, two very pregnant women were sitting in the front row. They left immediately after and, curious, Sylvie chased them halfway down the hall. When she reached them she asked what they thought of the show. “We liked it,” they said, “but it’s too late for us,” both gesturing toward their bellies in unison. But then there was another story, a young woman I didn’t know trying to decide whether or not to have an abortion, and her friend read “People, Stop Having Children” to her over the phone, and she said it helped her make up her mind. Every rule has an exception.

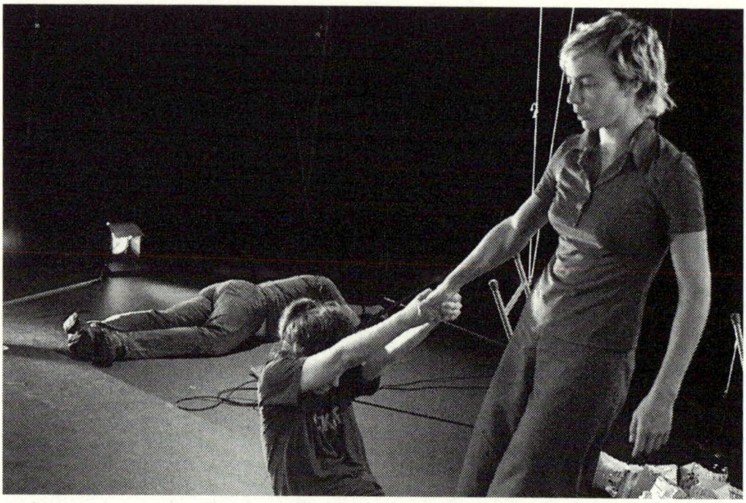

Gaétan Nadeau, Tracy Wright and Laure Ottmann in *Families Are Formed Through Copulation* at Usine C in Montreal. Photo: Mathieu Chartrand

In Montreal and France, *Families Are Formed Through Copulation* was the first show we performed entirely in French (in a beautiful translation by Eva Labarias). Especially in Montreal, I felt what an enormous difference it would make to the reception of my work in Quebec if I were a francophone. I have always felt out of place, in everything I’ve done and in every aspect of my life, and moving to Montreal, living and working here, always partly in a language I’ve been unable to learn, has been a way of making myself even more out of place, of making my feeling of being out of place correspond to my immediate surroundings and reality. *Families Are Formed Through Copulation* at Usine C in Montreal (where it was called *La famille se crée en copulant*) made me feel almost like a Québécois playwright whose work was being met with enthusiasm by a hometown crowd. This was such an uncanny sensation since, of course, nothing could be further from the truth.

+ + + +

Sometimes I say that my work across languages is based on productive misunderstandings. But there was a misunderstanding in the PME office that was more like a pure misunderstanding, neither productive nor unproductive. I had of course written *Families Are Formed Through Copulation* in English, and it had been translated into French. When we went on tour, what I assumed would happen was we would perform in French with (German, Japanese, Czech, etc.) surtitles. We had spent the entire process working with only the French text, therefore this, to me, seemed like the only logical option. However, what Sylvie assumed was that Gaétan, Laure, and Tracy would learn the text in the original English, and that's the version we'd perform on tour (with surtitles in German, Japanese, Czech, etc.). The text was written in English and, for Sylvie, there was no question it was best to perform it in the original language. We must have worked on the project for almost a year, each of us certain our assumption was correct, neither suspecting that the other had a completely different idea, before running into a series of confusions I found impossible to explain. I have spent most of my life reading literature in translation and, for me, there is nothing especially precious about work in its original language. However, since my unilingual mind doesn't have access to any of the originals, it is impossible for me to compare, and perhaps that is why, in the end, Sylvie's assumption won the day.

+ + + +

When we performed in Tokyo, Hiromi said I was doing something she had often been told you were never supposed to do in art: didactically tell the audience what to do, clearly state that one thing is right and another wrong. So the prohibition on didacticism in art that I was rebelling against, it seems, was also a truism in Japan. It was only much later that I thought ending my polemic with the admission that it was written by "a child who was never born" undercut the overall sentiment, made it even more absurd. And yet who could possibly be more of an expert on the topic than this unborn child. Hiromi always puts a great deal of thought and care into the venues where she presents us, and for *Families Are Formed Through Copulation* we were placed in a beautiful old movie theatre.

In general, the jet lag I have on tour is a constant, almost insurmountable, problem in my life, but the jet lag I experience in Japan is worse. I spend the entire time I'm there in a half-awake haze and fall asleep at the most inappropriate times. I know I watched the first two shows (but missed the third because I fell asleep in the hotel room and the alarm wouldn't wake me), but I remember so little, just staring at the Japanese surtitles, amazed they said what I had written. I believe this was also the trip in which Hiromi told me: "There is no such thing as a human being. The individual is little more than a Western invention."

In general, I have far fewer memories of *Families Are Formed Through Copulation*, I suspect because I wasn't performing, the experience of doing something being so much more visceral and memorable than the experience of simply watching. Or maybe because we had stumbled into the confusing middle, no longer in the thrall of the exciting, yet unsure, beginning. Laure said to me, at some point during one of the tours, that when she listened to us speak she had the feeling that Sylvie, Richard, and I all preferred *Unrehearsed Beauty-Le Génie des autres*, so why weren't we making more shows like that, instead of this one which in so many ways was constrained by its script. Of course, I knew exactly what she meant. (Sylvie reminds me that when we first decided to work with a script she was nervous that it might not be possible to work collaboratively or experimentally enough with a script as our starting point. But, after our first two shows, after two exhausting, back-to-back artistic breakthroughs, we perhaps felt like doing something with more of a net underneath us. Also, it was not an entirely traditional script, but rather a script with the history and memory of our process already woven into it.)

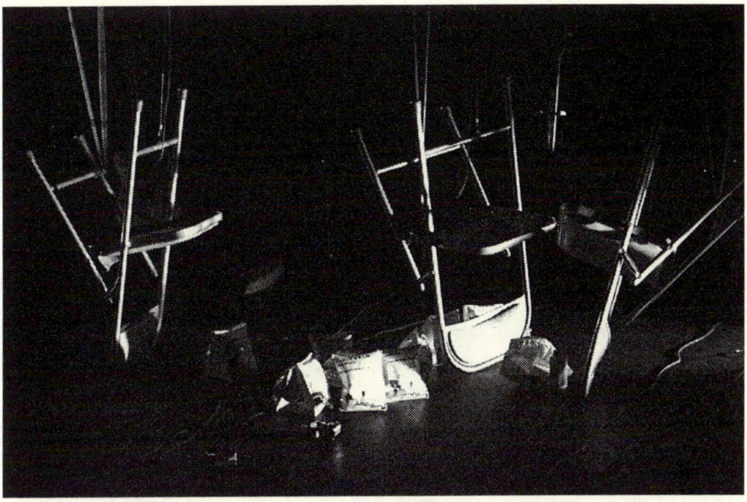

Jean-Pierre Gauthier's installation from *Families Are Formed Through Copulation* at Usine C in Montreal. Photo: Mathieu Chartrand

When we performed at the EXIT Festival in Créteil, during the final section, entitled "Reconciliation" (a title that gives you an idea how my attack on the nuclear family comes to an end), Laure was interrupted near the end of her text:

> And then I got older and I had children myself and I loved my children and my parents died and my children got older and they had children and I loved my grandchildren and then I died and on and on it went until the end of time, which was nice. Despite everything else we have said it was nice and I am dead and warm and happy and it was nice. But we're getting a bit ahead of ourselves. Today I woke up, made coffee, made toast, drank the coffee, ate the toast, went to school, flirted with a boy I sort of liked, failed a chemistry exam, ate lunch, got asked out by a different boy I didn't like nearly as much, said yes anyway hoping to make the first boy jealous, had irrational feelings, didn't pay attention in class (in fact I can't even remember what class it was), came home, ate dinner, pretended to do my homework, talked on the phone, checked my email, talked on the phone some more, and went to bed. In other words it was a perfectly normal day. On the one hand we have a perfectly normal

day like today and on the other hand we have my children and their children and their children's children on and on forever and ever until the sun burns out and how do these two seemingly opposite things relate to one another. Today, which I have to admit was just a little bit banal, and eternity, which will probably be a little bit banal as well, come to think about it. So today and eternity are both banal. Every day I wake up and think: today something will happen. And things do happen. Every day all sorts of things happen. And some things are less disappointing and other things are more disappointing and a few things are even kind of satisfying in their own everyday sort of way but nothing is THE THING that puts it all into perspective, makes all the other things more meaningful than they would otherwise ever be. Nothing is the epiphany. Still, once you grow up a little bit and realize that life is not a twenty-four-hour-a-day orgasm, it does begin to seem like time to cherish the little things, the little everyday things, and I'd just like us all to take a moment of silent prayer, pray to whatever god you can manage that we don't just fuck everything up, and that THE LITTLE THINGS will somehow manage to continue, perhaps even for all eternity. I'm still young so I'm still idealistic and I'd just like us all to take a moment and pray that we don't completely fuck everything up. Can we do that?

When she said, "I'd just like us all to take a moment of silent prayer, pray to whatever god you can manage that we don't just fuck everything up," someone from the audience yelled something, I'm not sure exactly what, something about not believing in any god, about being an atheist, about not wanting to listen to any of this religious or pious bullshit. There was then some other shouting in the audience, back and forth between a few different people, arguing about what was just said, about religion (Sylvie says some of them were shouting that, finally, something in the show made sense), and then others arguing to let us get back to it and finish the show.

As she walked offstage, the first thing Tracy said to me was: "I guess you haven't lost your edge." It was the first real heckling we'd had since five years ago in Croatia (but I guess, in *Unrehearsed Beauty-Le Génie des autres,* it was practically impossible to heckle since we literally put a microphone in the audience and invited them to speak). Tracy's comment also echoed a question we'd asked the audience in the early days of *Unrehearsed Beauty-Le Génie des autres*: "Have the Rolling Stones lost their edge?"

That was also the night that, after the show, we had to move all of our props out under a live horse that was blocking the loading dock. The horse was there for the performance by Sébastien Tellier and Xavier Veilhan that directly followed ours, in which Sébastien played music and Xavier created a series of stage visuals. I remember almost nothing of this show except that, near the end, when the music reached its final crescendo, a bag of water was released to make it seem as if the horse was urinating. Or maybe the horse really did urinate, I'm not sure. Is it possible to train a horse to urinate on cue? Passing each item from our show underneath the horse into the loading dock also felt like a moment that couldn't be real. I was laughing the entire time.

"I'm still young so I'm still idealistic" quickly became a running joke for us, the phrase from the show that was repeated most often. Sylvie would often say it. And we were still idealistic, though not as young as we used to be, trying to figure out how best to navigate between what we most wanted to do and the opportunities to do not-quite-it but something next to it that might or might not work for us. The packed house in Créteil had apparently not come to see us but to see Sébastien Tellier and Xavier Veilhan (and the urinating horse). For the same ticket you could see both. I had the feeling that the slight atheist kerfuffle in the audience made the experience better for everyone, that something had happened, some tension or pushback. The reason we go to a live performance, instead of a movie, is because there is always the possibility something might happen that wasn't planned.

\+ + + +

During this period I was also touring *Revolutions in Therapy*, another show I had made with Nadia Ross and STO Union. In *Revolutions in Therapy*, Nadia and Tracy take turns interviewing each other, partly inspired by Sandor Ferenczi's vision of a therapy in which both the patient and therapist take turns performing therapy on each other. (Ferenczi also suggested that therapy could take place with the therapist and the patient on the couch together hugging, something we didn't explore.) Halfway through the show, Nadia gets upset and storms offstage, and I return to replace her (once again replacing someone), answering to the name Nadia for the rest of the show. Among other things, the work explores Nadia's move to the country, in this sense putting her real life onstage.

Back when I was touring both *Unrehearsed Beauty-Le Génie des autres* and *Recent Experiences*, I had the feeling they were opposites, as far apart from one another as two projects I was involved in could possibly be. But by the time I got to *Families Are Formed Through Copulation* and *Revolutions in Therapy*, it was as if this dynamic had shifted, as if the two worlds had gradually contaminated each other over time, STO Union becoming more like PME and PME becoming more like STO Union. For me, *Revolutions in Therapy* had a loose, improvised feel I'd previously associated more with PME, a relaxed pacing with plenty of empty space. And, it's so obvious I can't believe I didn't previously see it, but I just realized both *Recent Experiences* and *Families Are Formed Through Copulation* are about family, another rather literal influence and reversal. It's amazing to me how, at times, I can be completely oblivious to the most straightforward and literal influences, perhaps out of a desire to protect certain illusions around being an artist and originality. (Of course, neither STO Union nor PME invented "family" as a possible theme for making theatre.)

This is probably a natural part of one's evolution as an artist, all the separate strands and aspects of one's work and influences gradually coming together over time, but it is an evolution I have such a strong desire to resist. On the one hand, I'm against purity in art, think the most exciting things happen only when approaches that normally don't go together crash and mix, creating unexpectedly hybrid forms, but on the other hand I want to keep all the aspects of my work separate from each other. It makes no sense. Or maybe, in another way, it does, if before things can properly mix they need to be kept separate for a while, each having enough time to develop its own trajectory. If everything mixes too soon there's no tension, no chance for significant differences to develop over time. The different strands would come together naturally, which is perhaps why I focus on the more difficult task of keeping them apart. When I started writing novels I wanted the books to be separate from my performance practice, to be literature, released in a literary context, a kind of fiction that was a near total escape from my endless and intractable struggles with theatre, anti-theatre, and performing, and for a while it genuinely felt like I'd broken free. And yet here and now I find myself writing a book about PME-ART, the separate strands once again intertwining. I wonder if in this book I'm giving away all my secrets. Then I think that's okay, if I live long enough I'll get new ones.

+ + + +

Gaétan Nadeau has a peanut allergy of the life-threatening variety. When we performed *Families Are Formed Through Copulation* in Prague, he carried around a scrap of paper that explained his condition in Czech, to show waiters in restaurants as he ordered. About two hours before our second show, Gaétan sat down next to me in the lobby of the Divadlo Archa. He was having difficulty breathing and turning a bright shade of red. He had eaten some Thai food (apparently with peanuts) a few hours ago and the reaction was kicking in hard. He had the injection in his pocket and self-administered it, inserting the needle through his jeans into his leg, while we waited for the ambulance. As we waited, we debated whether there was any way he could be back in time for the show at 8 p.m., whether we should cancel, or what our other options might be. It was decided that I'd fill in for Gaétan, holding the script in my hand, doing my best to follow along with the staging and choreography. (An echo of replacing Mads back in Bergen during my first trip to Europe.)

Performing in *Families Are Formed Through Copulation* for the first time that night, as a last-minute replacement, I had new insights into what was bothering me about the show. It was like a machine in which you had to follow the text, lighting, and movement, like a conveyer belt carrying me along from section to section without respite. I didn't feel anywhere near the same freedom I sometimes felt performing the previous two shows, freedom to improvise at times, adjust the pacing as we went, say something unexpected, or break the structure and then effortlessly return to it. Some of this was because I was only filling in, and didn't know the show well enough to fully play within it. Also, I was literally holding the script in my hand, following along with it page by page. But I don't think it was only that. The script, the narrative aspects of the script, the storytelling aspects, and the way we had organized them to alternate with performance actions, made the structure much harder to pull away from. It was tight rather than loose, a quality greatly admired in most theatre, but apparently not by me.

It was also one of the worst audiences we have ever performed for, consisting primarily of a school group of international students who texted, sniggered, made unpleasant noises, talked (only to be hushed by one of their teachers), and generally misbehaved from the first minute to the last. They were especially amused during moments when I seemed confused, when I wasn't sure what happened next, when I paused, unsure where to go or how long I should take to get there, and either Tracy or Laure had to give me the necessary hints in order to keep the show rolling. Mathieu Chartrand, our technical director, said listening to me speak the text changed his understanding of it. My delivery was considerably more ironic than Gaétan's. Mathieu said I had a way of speaking the text in which it sometimes meant almost the exact opposite of what it literally said.

The next day Sylvie went to pick up Gaétan at the hospital. She was talking with the nurse when the doctor arrived and, since the doctor spoke English well, Sylvie thought it would be all right to leave Gaétan there while she organized the insurance payment for his stay. But then the nurse looked more closely at Gaétan's chart, followed by an examination of the plate from the lunch he had just eaten. It was clear something was wrong; she was rapidly speaking to the doctor in Czech and gesturing at the chart and then to the plate. Gaétan had gone to the hospital with a peanut allergy and, the next day, they had served him peanuts for lunch. (There's a reason Kafka comes from Prague.) Because he was still on the anti-allergen drugs, he hadn't felt any negative reaction from what he had just eaten. But if he had left the hospital without realizing what had happened, the drugs would have worn off around 8 p.m. (the exact time he was meant to be onstage performing) and, with the peanuts still in his system, there is a possibility he might have died. It was only because the nurse and doctor noticed in time, before he left the hospital, that this calamity was avoided and Gaétan was back in time to perform our third and final show in Prague.

+ + + +

Later *Families Are Formed Through Copulation* became a book published by Pedlar Press. The book included the texts we had performed plus another ninety pages, turning it all into some sort of fragmented novel. It must have been around this time, or maybe a little bit later, that I decided I wanted to reinvent myself as a novelist. (As I've been writing it, I've also been thinking of this book as a novel about PME-ART.) I honestly didn't think it would work. I had been so disappointed with the non-reception of the *Unrehearsed Beauty* book that I hadn't put out another one for nine years (between 1998 and 2007). These were also the first nine years of my nomadic, travelling-way-too-much touring life, so perhaps the energy of being on the road simply took precedence.

I do remember having such a strong feeling around the time the *Families Are Formed Through Copulation* book came out. A feeling that what had first attracted me to performance was how ephemeral it was, that you had to be there, it was this unrepeatable moment of communal experience that came and went like a wind, or like everything in life. Yet I was now starting to experience this very aspect almost as a form of despair. I had been making shows for just under twenty years and felt I had practically nothing to show for it, no real evidence that I had spent that time doing anything of value, anything that still existed or that anyone remembered. Suddenly, the fact that you could hold a book in your hands meant something to me. I'm not exactly sure what. The fact that it might still be on someone's bookshelf ten years from now.

(I suspect all of this also has something to do with getting older, with mortality. With wanting to leave something behind after I die. What could be more futile.) Of course, I have always loved books. At times, reading them feels a little bit like the only space I am truly alive.

Two years later the *Families Are Formed Through Copulation* book was translated into French and published by Le Quartanier. This has led to a handful of stage productions. Long ago, I had decided I no longer wanted to be a playwright, but it seems I had accidentally stumbled back into being a playwright once again, only this time in French. There was a student production directed by Christian Lapointe at Cégep Garneau. A full production directed by Frédéric Dubois at Le Periscope. Another student production directed by Stéphane Olivier at INSAS in Brussels. I don't know if I should admit here that I didn't go see any of them. But maybe this is an aspect of being a playwright that I didn't previously appreciate. That one's words can be out there, spoken by someone in some other place, on a stage in front of an audience I'll never know anything about, and in some abstract way what I don't know can't hurt me.

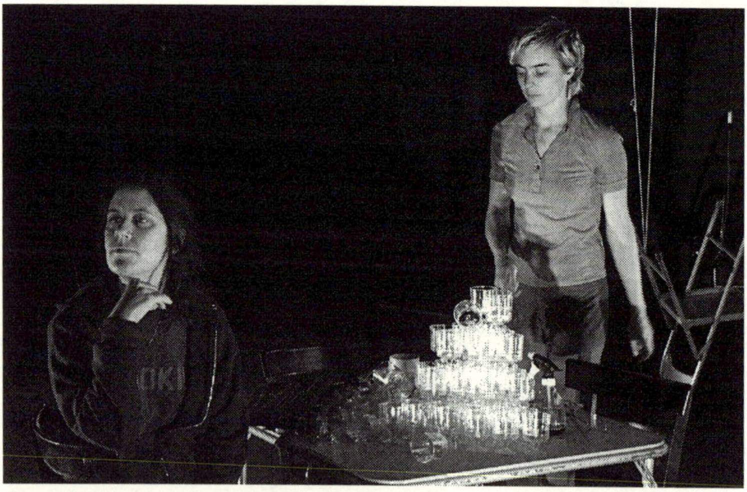

Tracy Wright and Laure Ottmann in *Families Are Formed Through Copulation* at Usine C in Montreal. Photo: Mathieu Chartrand

Projects emerge in reaction to other projects. I worry I've been too hard on *Families Are Formed Through Copulation*, sold it down the river (just a little bit down). For a lot of people, *Families Are Formed Through Copulation* remains their favourite PME show. Thinking about all this, I feel I should take a long, hard look in the mirror and ask myself: what the fuck is my problem? Or, more precisely: what the fuck is my problem with theatre? Richard once said to me that everyone has problems, but I was the only person he had ever met whose problem in life was that I hated theatre. (And do I really hate theatre, or do I only constantly compare it to some other form of theatre that doesn't yet exist but that, nonetheless, it seems I love too much.)

Sometimes the best attack is a tactical retreat, but in this case I'm not sure. Because the problem is that the problem is entirely in my head. It doesn't actually exist out in the world. Theatre isn't hurting anyone (which isn't to say it couldn't be more open, more artistically adventurous, and, in so many other ways, exponentially better). The fact that I see a kind of artistic potential for theatre that theatre doesn't want to embrace, or doesn't necessarily see for itself, or that artists making different kinds of theatre are routinely pushed out of the milieu, may be a metaphor for society-at-large, but this particular metaphor isn't theatre's only reality, though it does most often seem that way to me. Which is a kind of insanity on my part. Or a kind of self-sabotage. Or, if I want to put a positive spin on it, a kind of artistic vision.

Then again, something I'm noticing about my work is that, from project to project, it operates a bit like a pendulum, swinging back and forth between more theatre and less, more explicitly political and less so, and, since *Families Are Formed Through Copulation*, more polemic and more relaxed. There has been so much self-sabotage in my life. It often feels like I can't help it. (There have also been periods when I explicitly tell myself: no self-sabotage. And, surprisingly, that sometimes seems to work.) When I feel I've compromised too much, or in the wrong way, or against my better judgment, or for the wrong reasons, I get so depressed I can barely function. Self-sabotage seems to be the only way to break the depression. I now wonder if *Families Are Formed Through Cop-*

*ulation* would have toured more if I had been able to more fully get behind it, and if this would have been a good or a bad thing in my life, or in the trajectory of PME. One of the aspects I found so dispiriting about *Families Are Formed Through Copulation* was the way the text, the content of the text, dominated the audience's experience. When I went to Norway that first time, Lisbeth J. Bodd introduced me to the concept of "equivalent dramaturgy," in which sound, light, text, movement, objects, performance, etc., were all given equal weight. She said that when they discovered equivalent dramaturgy, so much of what they'd been trying to do all along suddenly made sense to them, they had a language with which to describe the ideals they were striving for. (Sylvie says equivalent dramaturgy was developed by Knut Ove Arntzen, and that Lisbeth was one of his students.)

When we were starting rehearsals for *Families Are Formed Through Copulation*, I remember saying to Sylvie that I wanted to make my version of a "good theatre show," if only to see what it would be like. I thought this was something one should be able to do as an artist, to not try to make a complete breakthrough with each and every project, but from time to time simply make something straightforward and strong. In my case, this also meant going back toward many of the things I had earlier rejected and having another look, thinking about why I had rejected them, and if there was anything I could now do from this new perspective of having left and come back. But it's possible I underestimated just how fierce and stubborn my original rejection was.

Interlude:

# For Tracy

When I'm onstage, I sometimes think about the degree to which my way of being onstage has been influenced by Tracy Wright. I have never told anyone this. The stillness, the care, the precision and anger and irony. Tracy died on June 22, 2010, just six and a half months after being diagnosed with pancreatic cancer. When I first heard the news I was on tour with *An Anthology of Optimism* in Italy. We were just about to perform in a former sports stadium in Polverigi. The next day we were invited to lunch at someone's house. From the large balcony I looked out at one of the most beautiful landscapes I had ever seen in my life, endless green rolling hills, and thought there was no possible way to reconcile such an idyllic setting with such completely fucked-up news. (Strangely, she died the day before my birthday.) I wouldn't make it back in time for the funeral, and later also missed her memorial service.

I worked with Tracy for fifteen years. We made at least nine shows together. We were on tour for many, many years. I've never worked with a better performer or a better artist. She is also one of the few artists PME worked with who is absolutely and unquestionably as stubborn as we are. This is the first time I've written about her since she died.

+ + + +

One of my clearest memories. We were walking down the street in Montreal, in the middle of rehearsals, making yet another show together, I don't remember which one, when she asked me why we were doing this, or why I was doing all this, what was the point of making all these shows, since it was often so difficult. Why were we doing it?

Without missing a beat, I said: "Just killing time before my eventual and inevitable suicide." It was a joke but, at the same time, one of the more honest things I've ever said. Now, when I think back on the exchange, I regret being so flippant. It is such a clear memory because it is a moment, an utterance, I so clearly regret. I wish I had said something more inspiring. Over the years I have tried my best not to take my depression out on other people, but that was a moment I remember when I used it as a club.

"Oh, is that all," she replied. Each word precisely withering in that way only Tracy could be.

I don't think it's any secret that much of my life is taken up in a struggle with depression. And yet, more and more, I'm not even sure *depression* is the right word. Melancholy, despair, sadness, self-sabotage, mourning for myself and for the world. It might have been during that same conversation, or it might have been a different one. But I remember Tracy saying to me that she had so many more reasons than me to be depressed, her life was more fucked up, she dealt with so much sexism in her work life, while I got away with murder in that way straight white male artists so effortlessly seem to do without even noticing it. Nonetheless, she had to admit, though she had so many more reasons to be, I was clearly the more depressed one. I think I just silently agreed. At any rate, I don't remember what I said in response.

+ + + +

For, I'm not sure, let's say the last seven or eight years I knew her, Tracy frequently complained about having no work. There were a number of lead film roles she was up for, some of which I believe had been written specifically for her, only to have her involvement vetoed by producers or distributors who were so intently focused on what the cast looked like that they unthinkingly blew straight past Tracy's obvious genius, both onstage and in front of the camera. As is well-documented, the film industry has little interest in women over forty. After she died, there was a wave of appreciation, people reminiscing about having met her, beautiful things she had done and said. Everyone agreeing how great she was in every role. But listening to all of this, reading every celebratory article, which of course I agreed with, there was always a part of me that couldn't help screaming: why didn't you hire her more when she was alive? Why praise her now? Where were you with the praise back when she had no work in 2006? Now, in writing this far too late, I can also direct some of these criticisms back toward myself.

+ + + +

The last show Tracy made with PME was *Families Are Formed Through Copulation*. After that she said she no longer wanted to work with me. I know her time with PME wasn't an entirely positive experience, though I also know there were many good times and beautifully bright spots. Perhaps, in the long run, she brought much more energy and brilliance to the shows than making the shows brought to the rest of her life. Often she took my negativity toward theatre personally, since she thought of herself as an actor, and starting to work with PME was also, for me, a process of moving away from working with actors. But if all theatre was as good as Tracy was onstage, I would be in the front row every night. I completely understood that she wanted to stop working with PME for a while. But I never considered that it was actually the end. I thought we would take a break for a few years and then find a way back into our collaboration over time. I also had the idea that it would be good for her to make some work on her own, to receive validation for performing her own writing in a context in which she had all the control, but maybe this was only my own idea for her, not something she was especially driven toward. She was a great writer, merciless and funny. Words that were so performative they demanded to be spoken aloud. But, in the end, I don't think she wrote very much. I wonder if she would have if she had been more encouraged to do so. If we had used more of her writing in PME.

Shortly after Tracy died, I had a conversation in Berlin that greatly disturbed me. I've used real names throughout this book but I've decided to refer to the person I had this conversation with only as X, though the identity I should be trying to protect is probably more my own. X didn't know Tracy especially well, was just starting to get to know her near the end. Some of their earlier interactions had been shaky, and I remember a conversation when X was trashing Tracy to my face, which also made me dislike X for many years. If you wanted to be friends with me you had to, at the very least, be a fan of Tracy Wright. But then later, unbeknownst to me, they started to get along better. And X told me about going to visit Tracy in the hospital. How Tracy told her that after we stopped working together she cried about it for weeks, but had the feeling it meant nothing to me, that she felt I wasn't upset about it at all. I hate so much to admit that she was right. I wanted to keep working with Tracy but understood that it was no longer working so well and respected her decision to leave. It had been a long time coming. But it is also one of the many instances when I was far too oblivious to things that were happening just an inch away.

And yet listening to X tell me this story, sitting outside in Berlin next to a skate park, a warm summer evening in which all seemed lost, all I could think is: why are you telling me this? Do you want to hurt me with this story? Do you want to make me feel bad? (If so, it worked.) To show me that, in the end, when it mattered most, you were a better friend to Tracy than I was? To show me how far your relationship had come from the early days when you didn't get along? Also, why are you telling me this story now, instead of Tracy telling it to me back when she was still alive? In the years after we stopped working together, we met from time to time, tried to clear the air, but I suppose we never really got it clean. And what if she had told me, what could I have said? All I could have done was apologize. Just as all I can do now is apologize, even though it is far too late.

+ + + +

I just remembered another time when I asked Tracy why she thought I was so depressed and she replied: "Because it's working for you." Meaning that I could be depressed and still be successful, so there was no real need for me to change. She never let me get away with any bullshit. There is simply no one in my life or work now who performs anything close to a similar role. And yet, by the end of our time working together, I was also starting to feel that she would let me get away with so little bullshit it was almost as if I couldn't do anything at all. I started to wonder if anything I would say or do would be real enough to pass the Tracy bullshit-meter. Looking back, I don't know if this had anything to do with Tracy, or was only the result of my own mounting insecurities. A feeling that even the best art ever made was really only a few steps away from bullshit, had no source of validation other than its own fragile desires and whatever praise it could scrape together in the marketplace of ideas. I've always been the kind of artist who believes the best thing an artist can do is stop, but continues because for some reason they can't help it.

One last depression-conversation memory. I swear depression wasn't the only thing we ever talked about, though I am thinking a lot about it now. I remember asking Tracy what she thought I should do about my depression. It was during one of my worst periods. She said she thought I should try to spend more time helping, thinking, and caring about other people. That depression came from thinking too much about oneself.

+ + + +

What made Tracy such a good performer. I'm afraid I have no great insights. I talk about being yourself onstage, but in whatever role she chose or was given, Tracy was always also herself. She had so much self, such a clear, unmistakable personality, that it quietly yet confidently filled every inch of every role. A lot of people probably think good acting means transforming yourself into the character, but I guess I think it means the opposite: to transform the character into yourself. Tracy took risks but got there step by careful step, maintaining control in some way in which any sense of, or desire for, control remained invisible. I must have seen her perform literally hundreds of times and I never saw her do a bad show. Also, I knew there was so much frustration and rage there, and yet it was all kept almost hidden, or came out mainly through humour, and at the same time it was always there, felt and present, like a melancholic or vicious bass line, low in the mix, that grounded every song.

+ + + +

I'm not sure exactly when – sometime between *Unrehearsed Beauty-Le Génie des autres* and *Families Are Formed Through Copulation* – that, in response to an invitation from STO Union, I proposed to Tracy we make a show together, just me and her. The title was based on something she once said to me: *It's A Sexist World, LaLa LaLa La La*. This is the proposal I wrote for it:

Tracy Wright and Jacob Wren have been working together on a regular basis for almost fifteen years in what has essentially been a collaborative actor/director relationship (with Tracy fulfilling the role of the actor and Jacob that of director).

With their new project *It's A Sexist World, LaLa LaLa La La* they would like to begin by altering the rules of this long-standing collaboration by working together as artistic equals. The reasons for this can be found in the show's deeply ironic title as well as in the following question: why, after such a long period of artistic collaboration, does Jacob remain the director and Tracy the actor, what are the underlying cultural assumptions behind this implicit hierarchy?

Starting with their own cultural experience, Tracy and Jacob will then work outward to deal with larger questions about society as a whole. While we generally live and work in a cultural milieu in which sexism is roundly condemned and men and women are at all times considered to be equals, the factual reality which surrounds us each and every day frequently does not comply with such assumptions. Again and again we bear witness to practical examples of every stripe in which men shoot ahead at the expense of women, or in which men make use of societal privileges which women of equal social standing simply do not have access to.

These are of course simplifications. The main goal of *It's A Sexist World, LaLa LaLa La La* will be to delve into these issues in all their subtlety and complexity, not shying away from the fact that women can sometimes be unintentionally complicit and men unintentionally oblivious to the sexist inequalities of everyday life.

Over the course of a two-week workshop, Tracy and Jacob will develop strategies for putting these inequalities onstage. Since they will be starting from their own unequal working relationship, the questions will never become too abstract. They will always remain personal and heartfelt, often quite emotionally wrenching, and in their accurate condemnation of widespread petty social hypocrisies, genuinely scathing.

Some of the strategies we will be starting with are lists, word association games, and songs, using the apparent lightness of these modes of expression to reveal a much darker subject matter to which everyone can relate.

I now don't remember exactly why it didn't happen. I got pulled away to other things, as usual. I was also probably afraid of it. In PME, I suspect a lot of the low-level conflict between Tracy and me was subsumed into the multiple, crossing and tangled conflicts that made up so much of those early years. I didn't know if I wanted to face it head-on, if I was up for the challenge. That was all a long time ago, and I like to think that maybe I would be now. But I'll never find out.

I also wonder if it would have changed anything if we'd actually done *It's A Sexist World, LaLa LaLa La La*, if something would have broken or shifted, if I would have understood something more about the dynamic or been able to work with it in some other way. I look at the proposal and am startled to see this language I no longer use: actor and director. It's been ten years since I've called myself a director, even though I still do many of the same things I did before. What I do know is that whatever difficulties we may or may not have experienced, it wouldn't have in any way harmed the work. This thing I sometimes tell myself, both the problem and the victory: no matter how depressed I get, I can still always work. There was something similar in our artistic dynamic, difficulties never got in the way of the work. Or maybe this is something I only tell myself. Maybe sometimes they did and I simply remained oblivious.

(Nadia says that *It's A Sexist World, LaLa LaLa La La* was STO Union's first attempt at producing other artists besides herself. She wanted to see what that would be like, to just raise funds to support projects she thought would be great. And it breaks her heart to think back upon the three projects STO Union proposed to develop together, which got turned down for funding. That refusal was a strong one. STO Union had been having success in Europe, and now were pushing for a kind of access into Canada, access for Charles Officer, a black man with a stunning talent, and for Tracy, a woman with a stunning talent, to give them more access. One can only imagine how different things would have been in all of our lives had we been told "yes.")

+ + + +

There are many aspects of Tracy's life that I won't write about here. Things that I don't know enough about, or that involve too many other people, most of whom I've lost touch with. Because there was a specific moment when I first thought to write this, or something like it. I was visiting Toronto, it was summertime, and I was sitting on the patio of Ideal Coffee in Kensington Market, reading, and drinking an Americano. As I was leaving I ran into Tracy's friend Laura Cowell, and we talked about a few things before she mentioned that I didn't come to Tracy's memorial service. That my absence was noted and my presence missed. I apologized, said we had rehearsals and I couldn't make it. "I guess there are more important things," Laura said, channelling that particular brand of scathing I've always associated with Tracy. And I started to think about it, why I didn't go, and am continuing to think about it now.

We had rehearsals scheduled for those days, and it was decided that Sylvie and Richard would go to the memorial and I would stay in Montreal to rehearse. At the time, I don't think I gave it a second thought. But later I wondered how much the decision had to do with Tracy, because of course she wouldn't be there to note my absence. Who would be there were all the people I used to know and be part of a community with in Toronto. (I should probably write more about this time but I don't think I have the strength.) People who, when I now run into them from time to time, I have no idea what to say. And then I think, in this book, I've also been too hard on Toronto. That my working life in Toronto had at least two stages: an early period when I was the world's youngest playwright and actually received an enormous amount of support, and a later period, just before I left, when Mike Harris's Common Sense Revolution was setting the agenda and I felt all professional possibilities were in rapid retreat. Being who I am, I mainly focus on the second stage. Also in a positive way, because it forced me to leave and see the rest of the world. From Toronto, nothing like that seemed imminent or possible. But, despite (or maybe even because of) the early support I received, I suppose my grudge against Toronto was also about something else: I felt it was a place that would never encourage taking greater and greater artistic risks over time. Having now worked in many more places, I now see this is, to some degree, a fact of culture everywhere.

Tracy was my last link to my previous life in Toronto (also Nadia, but by that point she had been living in Wakefield for a while, and I associated her more with that). I still know lots of people in Toronto, but Tracy was the last, or most active, link to the work I had made there when I was young, and to the specific place and time, the specific community, I had made it in. That community doesn't exist anymore, has scattered in every direction, and though I am now partly able to romanticize it, when I think back to that time, mainly what I feel is something awful. It must be that awful feeling that, once again oblivious, I didn't want to return to, didn't want to face at the memorial service. I think it's a feeling that has to do with starting out much too young, not knowing what I was doing, with nothing but my youthful ambition to guide me. But it is also a feeling of broken idealism, of thinking something was possible, that this community could create a different kind of theatre and, over time, this different kind of theatre would become the mainstream, and then realizing I was deluded, that nothing could be further from where things were actually headed. But there's no arguing with youthful naïveté and idealism.

For me at least, in whatever kind of show she was in, Tracy remained resonant with this other possibility for theatre, stubbornly taking the stage in the only way she knew how. I also think she would probably call bullshit on what I'm saying now. She was focused only on the task at hand. She would have also said to me:

you should have come to my fucking memorial service. And, as usual, she'd be right. (Sylvie reminds me that Tracy wasn't focused only on the task at hand. That I once told her Tracy always had such a strong overview of the dramaturgy and overall concerns of the work. Which is also true.)

+ + + +

Just after Tracy died, when there was a wave of moving appreciations, I had the feeling that people were speaking of her as if she was a saint, and the portrayals were so far away from the complex, intractable Tracy I knew and worked with for so long. And that if I were to someday write about her I would try to bring some of that complexity back, to show some of the overlapping and often profound difficulties that made her not worse but simply more human, the struggles that were always there and most likely made much of her brilliance and sharpness possible. (Sylvie says this also has to do with the strong opinions Tracy so often held. With the originality of her position.) But, to be honest, I can't really bring myself to do it. Despite thinking myself different, I am also bound under the injunction not to speak ill of the dead. I also seem to find myself writing about Saint Tracy. And maybe that's how it should be. Because she definitely had a kind of greatness and, in the end, that's what I find myself remembering most.

I don't actually think life is so great, so I never feel that sad when someone dies. But for Tracy I'll make an exception. As an author, I've often been taught that the worst kind of literature is a story with a trite moral. But, in a sense, this is a story that does: deal with things now because there might not be another chance in the future. Things were okay between us but I was still hoping they would continue to improve.

But this is a book about PME, also my life within it, and for me Tracy basically defined PME for our first three shows. She was there at the centre of it all, showing us how it's done. Just how fierce and stubborn and quiet and still and precise and human and vulnerable and honest you actually have to be just to be yourself onstage. I would be a very different performer if I hadn't spent all those years watching her. I would be a considerably less honest one. I should have told her all this more often, then remember times when I did, then remember how hard it was to give Tracy a compliment, how often she would throw the compliment right back in your face in the form of a self-deprecating joke. It was some kind of defensiveness. As if, if she admitted how good she was, it would go to her head, or make work rejections more painful, or undermine her ability to keep working honestly. I often felt Sylvie had a way of complimenting her that really seemed to connect. (Reading this, Sylvie says she also felt it was hard to compliment Tracy because she was so hard to fool, or not hard but impossible. But then she says she was at least able, at times, to connect a little.)

For better or worse, I think this is also something I've learned from Tracy, something I often find myself doing. Or perhaps something we had in common from the start. Being unable to honestly take a compliment might be the downside, the pain of not being able to genuinely take in heartfelt praise. But I also feel there's something valuable in it: to not think so much about praise, or its absence, or whether or not people will like it, whatever I happen to be working on at the time. Simply focus on the immediate task at hand.

How fierce, stubborn, quiet, still, precise, human, vulnerable, and honest you actually have to be just to be yourself. I wonder if Tracy would agree with any of this. It's a shame I can't ask her. It's a shame it's all now relegated, at least partly, to the past, to a series of complex memories. It's a shame Tracy's not performing somewhere right now. That I can't get on a train to Toronto and go see her onstage tonight, effortlessly making someone's work better than it has any right to be.

Part Two:

# 10 Years of PME-ART

(2008–2018)

Six:

# Prehistory

(2003–2007)

I spent most of 2007 making a show at Sophiensæle in Berlin. *Der Tod in Rom* (*Death in Rome*) was a stage adaptation of Wolfgang Koeppen's 1954 novel of the same name. The project had begun at least five years earlier, when Gordana first got the job running Kampnagel. She invited me to do a project, specifying that she wanted me to work outside my previous comfort zone. From the nature of the invitation, I understood, or perhaps misunderstood, that she wanted me to do something more spectacular. I also had a feeling she wanted it to be more theatre. (Sylvie reminds me that Gordana's very first invitation in 2000 was actually to work on one of the classics: a Greek text from antiquity. I think I instantaneously rejected this possibility and then immediately erased the suggestion from my memory. My idea of the canon has always been works from the twentieth century onward.)

Having now worked in Norwegian and French, I was curious if I could also begin to work in other languages, also curious what I could do with a book I loved. Someone had told me something about Wolfgang Koeppen that I was fascinated by. Koeppen had stayed in Germany during World War II, and when asked how he survived the war without moral compromise, he apparently replied that in his job at UFA, the national German film company, he survived the war by writing screenplays that were good enough not to get him fired, but not good enough to ever be made. (And then, much later, I learned Wolfgang Koeppen was born on the same date as me. Perhaps also a partial explanation for why I was so enamoured with his work.)

In 2003 I had a residency at Kampnagel during which I adapted (basically edited) the English translation of the novel *Der Tod in Rom* into a script, which was then recreated in German using the original German book. Kampnagel applied for money to produce the project but was refused, at which point it seemed like the project was no longer going to happen. Around this time, I had also met Marie Zimmermann, when we had performed *Recent Experiences* at Theatre der Welt. She seemed interested in *Der Tod in Rom*, and for a while there was a possibility Theatre der Welt might co-produce it, reviving the project in the process. I met with Marie in 2005, when we performed *Revolutions in Therapy* at Theatre der Welt, and hoped she would commit to a co-production, but she remained only interested. I left feeling that, after working on the project steadily for three years, *Der Tod in Rom* was now dead in the water. However, as I was leaving the meeting, I ran into Tomas Frank, who told me he had just gotten the job co-running Sophiensæle. When he asked me what I was working on, I was actually holding the German script for *Der Tod in Rom* in my hands, and I gave it to him. It was another two years before the project happened in Berlin, and by that time Tomas had already left Sophiensæle to run BRUT in Vienna. (This is what we sometimes call the "musical chairs" of European presenters. Often the presenters you meet who are running one venue or festival are already working somewhere completely different by the next time you see them.)

+ + + +

As a heartbreaking aside, I feel I have to mention that Marie Zimmermann killed herself in 2007, the year *Der Tod in Rom* premiered. I have such a vivid memory of her wandering across the festival grounds at Theatre der Welt. Something had gone wrong, didn't happen in the way it was supposed to, and Marie was doing her best to take it all in stride, explaining to us that "the festival is a living thing." The way she said it made me feel that something was terribly wrong, she was putting a brave face on an enormous degree of stress, trying to hold everything together in some way that was perhaps unnecessary, at the same time claiming to do the opposite, that the festival was "a living thing" and she was just letting it live. But I must also be reading far too much into this, the memory charged by the fact it was the last, or at least one of the last, times I ever saw her.

I also thought about Marie Zimmermann a great deal again when Niels Ewerbeck killed himself in 2012. I barely knew Niels. He ran Forum Freies Theater for many years before Kathrin Tiedemann took over from him. I worked with him once at Gessnerallee in Zurich and then had dinner with him in 2011 in Munich. But remembering Marie and Niels, I find myself thinking about the enormous pressure the presenters we work with must sometimes feel they're under. In my interactions with them, there is often such an unspoken blurring between work and socializing. We are talking like we're friends but I also want them to invite our show to their venue. The power dynamic distorts everything, and for the most part it would never occur to me to feel concerned about their mental health.

+ + + +

A large part of my depression consists of constant, obsessive thoughts of suicide, and therefore I must in some way be fascinated by it. If we leave aside what I'm writing here and now, for the most part I keep these thoughts to myself, though at times they do slip out, when I let down my guard or momentarily think it's an acceptable topic for humour. Or when the depression simply, in some way, overflows. Since so much of my performance work is about authenticity, it does occasionally strike me as ironic that there is such a large gap between my inner life and outer persona – people who don't know me very well often find me upbeat and happy – and yet all the times I've behaved in an outwardly more depressed manner have led me to believe that my current solution, imperfect as it is, is probably for the best (at least at the level of smoothly operating social interactions with acquaintances and strangers).

Once again, there is a paradox at the heart of all this. I was drawn toward performance in search of more authentic forms of art, the desire for an artistic space that felt more connected, and yet spend most of my waking hours performing a less suicidal version of myself that often feels ridiculously false. When I drift too far down this rabbit hole I begin to no longer know what is true and what is false. I have spent most of my life obsessively thinking about suicide but I'm still alive, another way I'm not particularly consequent. There is this quote from E. M. Cioran:

> The obsession with suicide is characteristic of the man who can neither live nor die, and whose attention never swerves from this double impossibility.

And this one from Andrew Solomon:

> Suicide is a crime of loneliness, and adulated people can be frighteningly alone. Intelligence does not help in these circumstances; brilliance is almost always profoundly isolating.

It feels almost self-comforting to present these thoughts not as my own, but as citations from others. As if they were about me, but also about the world.

\+ + + +

I'm not able to think of *Der Tod in Rom* without also thinking about Marie Zimmermann. I met with her, was irritated she didn't commit to the project, and the next thing I heard she was gone. At that last meeting she told me she thought an artist should follow their artistic desire, as long as it was a desire they felt strongly. I wasn't sure if I agreed with her at the time, and still don't know. In one sense, all she was saying was that if I had the impulse to stage *Der Tod in Rom* then I should go for it. But what she didn't know was that this impulse was tangled up in the original invitation from Gordana, in the complex dynamic between us, as well as with trying to figure out what kind of artist I might be if I worked more in Europe. Also, a bit too obviously, with my opportunism. How I thought about all these questions when I was first invited in 2000 was also considerably different from how I thought about them by the time the project eventually happened in 2007. I still had a great deal to learn about how to usefully interrogate my own artistic desires, connected to something I have always wondered so much about: how to make a good decision.

\+ + + +

*Der Tod in Rom* was even more of a return to theatre than *Families Are Formed Through Copulation*, but in every other way it was ideal. The German cast (Matthias Breitenbach, Simon Brusis, Miriam Fiordeponti, Christoph Grothaus, Swantje Henke, and Lajos Talamonti) were present and extraordinarily willing to collaborate, Sophiensæle provided complete support for our process, and our assistant, Katharina Stephan, understood what we were doing in a way that made everything feel possible. Tomas Frank said the cast came out of rehearsals with such big smiles on their faces he was worried I had brainwashed them and was starting a cult. But when the project was over I felt destroyed. I could find no way to reconcile how beautifully everything had gone – including reviews and audience reaction – with how far away it all felt from what I was actually searching for in art.

These feelings echoed many of the themes of the novel itself. For example, the scene in which Siegfried, a young German serial-music composer in Italy just after World War II, is on his way to attend the orchestral premiere of his first composition:

> I didn't have a white tie, but I could have bought myself a white tie, or I should have hired a white tie, there must be people in Rome who make a living by hiring out white ties, but I didn't want to buy a white tie nor did I want to hire one; I didn't see why one had to have a white tie in order to be able to listen to music.

When he gets to the concert hall:

> Kurenberg was waiting for me in the conductor's room. He saw that I had turned up without a white tie and that must have annoyed him. He stood above convention, and he told me that, by scorning the white tie and not subjecting myself to custom, I had given dress and convention a significance they didn't deserve.

I both knew and didn't know exactly what had bothered me so much about my experience in Berlin. It felt like whatever you did onstage, the conventions of the experience dominated: that the actors were trained as actors (albeit in a theoretical and Brechtian German tradition), that there was a script, that the audience had bought tickets and had certain expectations, that they applauded just before it was time to go home. I wondered if I was giving all of these conventions a "significance they didn't deserve," or if I should continue with my mad plan to try to escape them once and for all.

But I fear I'm repeating myself too much. It was a lesson I had already learned, but it seemed I had to learn it at least one more time.

\+ + + +

In my book *Polyamorous Love Song* I write about feeling lost in Berlin:

> I left the shop and made my way down Torstr. I had no plans for the rest of the day. The haircut was it, and had been a relative disaster. As I walked I could catch an occasional glimpse of myself in the shop windows. My hair looked terrible but when did I start worrying about such things. No, I didn't give a shit about the haircut, it was only a stand-in for the fact that I was here wandering aimlessly through the streets of Berlin along with thousands of other Canadians, Danes, Swedes, Americans, Mexicans, Norwegians, artists from every country you could possibly name, and we all wanted something from this place. Berlin was a kind of signifier, evidence we were searching for the next (or more accurately last) exciting moment, some sort of zeitgeist or locus, in our otherwise grievously dull and tepid times. Somehow, in that moment, my haircut seemed like the deflating, other-side-of-the-coin hangover to this earlier, first adventurous impulse to search.

I find myself thinking about all this again now, but from the other side: am I currently challenging myself enough? Would I have more challenging discussions if I lived in Berlin? Everything went so well there, and I met so many people from all over, often artists and thinkers with striking perspectives that have continued to inform my understanding of the world. During my entire time in Berlin I was constantly wondering if I should move there, felt that for so many reasons I probably should, but couldn't do it. An artist moving to Berlin was a cliché I couldn't bring myself to become. Also, I was drinking more in Berlin than I ever had in my life, and I definitely don't have the physical constitution for that quantity of alcohol.

+ + + +

During this time in Berlin, the performance group I heard about most frequently was Rimini Protokoll, who made shows with "real people": firefighters, race-car drivers, chefs, children attending upper-class boarding schools, economists, etc. Rimini Protokoll referred to the people they worked with as performers as "experts," because each was an expert on the topic they were being put onstage to speak about, for example: a firefighter was an expert in being a firefighter, and could present this expertise in the form of a Rimini Protokoll show. Reading the book *Experts of the Everyday: The Theatre of Rimini Protokoll*, I wondered how to position this notion of experts in relation to my own quixotic project of being yourself in a performance situation. Should I also be working with "real people," would that somehow be more authentic than the dancers and visual artists I currently found myself performing alongside in PME? I realized I had almost no interest in this particular understanding of the question. I wasn't looking for especially real people who were to be found somewhere out there in the world, just as I wasn't searching for some special forms of authenticity or vulnerability that were to be found during particularly intense moments of one's life. I was more interested in the casual, everyday being yourself that happens to all of us all of the time but seems difficult to put onstage. In the fact that we, in fact anyone, were "real people" as well.

However, there was also a sense in which Rimini Protokoll were working in territory similar to my own but, from a certain perspective that seemed generally held, had found a way to take it much further, using their "real people" as Duchampian readymades, foregrounding the reality of and within the situation. They had also found a way to effectively brand their work, something I had been unable, and also most likely had made little attempt, to do. Everyone on the circuit knew exactly what Rimini Protokoll stood for and what they were working on – there was such an immediate clarity to it: real people onstage – while there seemed to be a certain degree of confusion as to what exactly PME were working on and why. I had always thought that art was deeply intertwined with such confusion, but in Berlin it became clearer to me that current avant-garde success was often connected to a single, clear, manifesto-like endeavour: conceptual dance, real people onstage, relational aesthetics, art as political activism, Tino Sehgal's dance as museum-ready sculpture, even Christoph Schlingensief's theatre of political controversy. (In comparison, the manifesto I wrote around that time was called "Manifesto for Confusion, Struggle, and Conflicted Feelings.")

Rimini Protokoll were making work that, on the surface, seemed remarkably close to what I was searching for, but that I felt (yet was not certain) had very little to do with it at all. And I still don't precisely know what this distinction I'm making actually is or is about. I wasn't interested in finding someone out in the world and using them as a readymade. I was interested in the fact that I, and everyone I met and knew, was already a readymade, and yet the ways we were already made were so rarely seen in performance.

(Caroline agrees, and says there was a real difference between her experience of working with us and with other companies using the idea of the readymade. In the work of the other companies, the content of the work is generated from the life of the person involved via the creative process. From this process, a text and a structure is created by the artistic team and then used by the subject in the performance. Their performances are directed and controlled. With PME-ART, there is no construction of the readymade, no dramatization of the self, no censor, not a single person telling you what to do or what to say when. You really don't have to be charming if you don't feel like it. Caroline doesn't think we ever gave each other notes or feedback on our performance qualities. A real freedom. As a performer, you are completely in charge of yourself. We gave each other feedback on ideas and content, but never on how to perform. And this difference took her a while to understand, ten years of working with us.)

Compared to the work I was seeing in Berlin, my artistic desires felt almost self-effacingly anti-spectacular. And yet, despite or because of my ongoing struggle to place my work in relation to it, everything I saw in Europe and in Berlin continued to influence me. I just wasn't sure how. I often felt I was more influenced by work I couldn't stand: by wondering what it was about it that I hated, how I might approach a similar idea yet do it completely differently. Was there a kernel in the hated work I might be able to use, if only as a thought experiment, discarding all the rest?

+ + + +

Both *Families Are Formed Through Copulation* and *Der Tod in Rom* were like a long, hard, considered look back at where I had come from and, much like the biblical story, I felt they had turned me into a pillar of salt. But I say all this now like I knew what was happening. At the time I basically understood nothing, was only confused, didn't know what kind of artist I wanted to be or where such an artist might live or work. It seemed to me that the kinds of work I most wanted to make couldn't exist in the theatre, but it didn't particularly seem like they could exist anywhere else either. In Berlin, I remember meeting Aenne Quinones for a drink. She had previously presented *Unrehearsed Beauty-Le Génie des autres* in Berlin at Prater. I remember telling her that I was thinking so much about all these questions, that I wasn't sure there was any right place to present the kind of work we were making with PME. She replied quickly and with great certainty: "That's because there's not. There's no place work like that will ever fit." (I now mostly think of this "not fitting" as an artistic and philosophical virtue. But at that moment I was on a different line, mentally drowning in the real-life practical difficulties such a position entailed.)

When I got back from Berlin I had an overwhelming feeling that it was time to shut down PME. I simply felt it was all too hard. Funding difficulties were also at the forefront of my mind. Sylvie doesn't remember this, but I have such a clear memory of telling her that I thought it was time for us to stop, and her telling me that she thought exactly the opposite, that now was the time for us to keep going, that she genuinely felt we were on the verge of getting somewhere. Sylvie is perhaps the only person I consistently listen to, though she might also not see things in precisely this way. But there was no question that Sylvie and Richard's will to keep going was considerably stronger than my will to quit. I also had nothing resembling another plan.

Seven:

# HOSPITALITY 3: Individualism Was A Mistake

[2008–2012]

Created/Performed by:
Caroline Dubois, Claudia Fancello, and Jacob Wren

We performed it in:
Toronto, Harbourfront Centre World Stage • Montreal, Usine C • Stockholm, Perfect Performance Festival • Malmö, Inkonst • Vienna, Brut • Düsseldorf, Forum Freies Theater • Montreal, Studio 303/SPARK • Mannheim, Zeitraumexit/Wunder der Prärie Festival • Oslo, Black Box/Ultima Music Festival • Trondheim, Teaterhuset Avant Garden • Nottingham, Dance4/Nottingham Contemporary • Cardiff, Chapter Arts Centre • Tallin, Nu Performance Festival • Saint-Jean-Port-Joli, La Biennale de sculpture

> There is no "human individual." There is a psyche that is socialized and, in this socialization, in the final result, there is almost nothing individual in the true sense of the term.
> – Cornelius Castoriadis

> In the 1960s many people came to realize that in a truly revolutionary collective experience what comes into being is not a faceless or anonymous crowd or "mass" but, rather, a new level of being... in which individuality is not effaced but completed by collectivity. It is an experience that has now slowly been forgotten, its traces systematically effaced by the return of desperate individualisms of all kinds.
> – Fredric Jameson

Before there was *HOSPITALITY 3: Individualism Was A Mistake*, there was another project, or at least a proposal, also entitled *Individualism Was A Mistake*. The thing I most remember about it is that it was designed for a large theatre in which the audience would be seated only in every other row. I imagined how uncanny it might feel to take your assigned seat and only moments later realize the entire audience has been arranged in this simple, unusual pattern. We would then walk through the empty rows and interview audience members with video cameras, their faces projected on a giant screen at the front of the room. We applied for funding and were turned down by everyone (these rejections only added to my feeling that it was time to end PME). We had already asked several people to be part of the project, and when I met with Caroline Dubois and Claudia Fancello to tell them the project was cancelled (at least for now), they suggested the three of us simply start working together anyway. (The moment I write this I suddenly wonder: was it actually their suggestion or was it mine. Caroline says she also can't remember.) Sylvie and Richard have always believed so deeply in paying the artists we work with properly, or at least to the best of our ability, so the idea that we would start working for free felt not quite right. Nonetheless, it was a generous offer from Caroline and Claudia and that's what we did.

That meeting between the three of us on the patio of Café Olimpico must have been the very first seed, the earliest moments of

*HOSPITALITY/HOSPITALITÉ*. And yet, starting after that first moment, I feel confused about the exact order it all occurred. We had a residency at Usine C. I wrote a project description in which I proposed not one but rather a series of projects in and around the theme of hospitality. We performed *HOSPITALITY 1: The Title Is Constantly Changing* at Studio 303 in Montreal. These things must have happened in roughly that order, or in some order, one after another, but when I think back it feels as if they all happened at the same time.

(Claudia says she remembers that first meeting at Olimpico very well. Mostly she remembers being curious about Caroline and me and what we could do together. She knows it was very unPME to not pay our invited artists, but she was coming from a long practice of self-producing dance and collective creations, so being paid still felt strangely like a bonus. When we were in the studio together, for some reason the void of money exchange gave a stronger sense of agency, of coming into the work with no expectation and no need to compromise. It felt like there was nothing to lose. Claudia really wasn't sure of what we were going to do or how we would function. And that unknowing was welcome. She has wondered a lot over the years if it would have changed the dynamics of our process if we had been paid at the beginning to work together. In our initial process all exchanges felt pertinent: our tangential conversations, checking out cafés, meals, gallery visits, record shop visits, seeing shows together, going out dancing together. It all mattered.)

Another part of all this was reinventing PME as an interdisciplinary group that would now be called PME-ART. It didn't happen all at once, but during these years there was more of a definitive break from theatre, more frequently presenting our work in a visual-arts context, as I constantly found myself questioning just how definitive the break actually was. As the *HOSPITALITY/HOSPITALITÉ* project progressed, it was clear that something had changed. We were no longer seen only as artists making theatre, or experimental theatre, or even anti-theatre. More and more, what we were doing was now seen as something else. In the transition toward this something else I feel there has also been a change in my personality, which could most accurately be characterized as relief.

+ + + +

The idea of working on the theme of hospitality might have first begun when I overheard two women at an art opening in Berlin talking about how *hospitality* was one of the key terms of late Derrida, and for them one of the most important qualities in contemporary art. (One of the things about my lack of French in Montreal is that it makes it much more difficult for me to eavesdrop, which in the long run I believe is for the best.) Or it might have started when I was thinking back to *En français comme en anglais, it's easy to criticize* and *Unrehearsed Beauty-Le Génie des autres*, how certain audience members took the avant-garde position of the work as some kind of aggression coming out toward them. I wondered if it was possible to make work with similar aims that would not be experienced as aggressive, if there were forms of hospitality we could develop that would create a more open dynamic between us and those watching and/or participating. I was also, as always, thinking about politics.

As with many Canadians, there is a part of me that – like a bystander watching a car crash (and perhaps catching a few shards of shrapnel along the way) – couldn't help but be fascinated by American electoral politics. The divide between left and right seemed so ridiculous and overwhelming. I was asking myself if there were forms of hospitality that might begin to open up a conversation where previously no communication seemed possible. Was there some form of hospitality that might allow me to open a dialogue with someone I had nothing in common with, or with someone I disagreed with completely? Was there some form of hospitality that would allow me to begin some form of useful dialogue with a fascist?

When I used this example, Sylvie said she disagreed. She thought there was nothing to do with fascists, only to fight against them. She absolutely doesn't remember telling me this, but I remember that she told me a story about an author who attended a public memorial commemorating Pinochet's death. He went up to one of the mourners and said he understood how they felt, since he had felt the same with when Salvador Allende died. But the Pinochet supporter basically just spit in his face. I don't know if someone else told me this story or if I simply made it up.

(What Caroline remembers is that I used the example: could I have a conversation with George W. Bush, who was in power back then. That my position was that it wouldn't actually be possible for me to do so. She remembers her feelings about my stated incapacity, because she could project herself having a conversation with him. Not only that but she had the willingness to try, the hope to open a dialogue with someone she disagrees with, and it was difficult for her to understand why I could not.)

But, of course, I didn't actually want to open a dialogue with any fascists, it was only a provocative example. What I did want was to open up a different kind of dynamic between us and the audience, a dynamic where you might be seeing or experiencing something you've never seen before but nonetheless feel welcomed toward it. And also feel that your own reaction – however positive or negative it might be – was a welcome part of whatever we happened to be presenting.

+ + + +

I proposed that we start by playing music together. Previous PME work had started with talking, and talking seemed to lead too quickly toward certain misunderstandings and limitations. I was wondering if there was some other way to begin (other than searching for a quote in the wrong book and therefore never being able to find it). We had no money so we began with things we already had: the musical instruments from *Unrehearsed Beauty-Le Génie des autres*, the record player from *Families Are Formed Through Copulation*, some blue metal sawhorses that were also used in that show, other objects I no longer remember.

Slowly the rules for *HOSPITALITY 1: The Title Is Constantly Changing* began to form: 1) place the musical instrument in a physically awkward or unexpected relation to your own body or to the body of one or both of the other performers; 2) stay connected to the other two performers and to the audience at all times; 3) try to make it sound like pop music, which was difficult because we were really not musicians. (Caroline suggests it was because of these rules that we never improved musically. And that in fact we never tried to improve either.) What resulted from these rules was a kind of ever-shifting, awkward, music-playing dance, an attempt to make something together in real time, to show the reality of us making things together as it was actually happening. Key words later became *cooperation* and *discord*, moments when we were making music together and moments when one of us would break the pattern, send everything spiralling off in some other direction.

As it progressed, new tendencies emerged: to keep things moving, not get fixed in any one position or rhythm for too long, but also the opposite, at times to go deeper and more fully into certain actions or patterns. To keep the instruments and objects moving through the space. To form constellations in which we were all really close or really far away. When Richard first saw an early run he said he thought we were approaching something a bit like shamanism, a structured yet structureless performance that felt as if it was making itself up, magically inventing and reinventing itself, as it went along. Something not based on words, nor music, nor dance – but simply based on energy.

I remember the first showing of *HOSPITALITY 1: The Title Is Constantly Changing* at Studio 303 as something terrifying. I had never walked out in front of an audience with less of an idea of exactly what we would be doing or how it would be received. What we did that night felt so slow, tentative, and uncanny. It was on a mixed program, and there were other pieces that I remember as virtuosic dancing, precisely rehearsed sounds and movement, while what we did was almost the opposite. I had the feeling we were more like children, trying both to figure out and invent the game as it was already in play. To me it also felt like a moment of starting over, as if it was at least somewhat possible, so many years into a career and artistic practice, to find a tabula rasa, to start again with a blank slate.

One month later we found ourselves doing the same thing at the Rhubarb! Festival in Toronto as a late-night presentation. (Rhubarb! was the festival where I had started out, where I had made my first performances twenty years before.) We were supposed to go on at 10 p.m. but the other shows ran long so we didn't end up starting until just before midnight. I was sick that night with a flu, sitting in the basement, drinking ginger tea, waiting to go on as the hour got later and later. By the time we hit the stage, much of the audience had left, and I felt myself pushing to keep the attention of those who remained. I think that was the first time I did the almost-splits while playing guitar, and I could also feel Caroline and Claudia pushing themselves as well. If Studio 303 had been spacious and strange, here in Toronto I felt we were almost rocking out (the emphasis should definitely be on the "almost").

After the show I immediately went to sleep off my flu, but Sylvie stayed and talked with Tracy, who had come to see us. Tracy felt that I was a better musician than I let on during *HOSPITALITY 1: The Title Is Constantly Changing*, that I was slumming, faking being less musically proficient for the sake of some sort of presentational artistic naïveté. Sylvie told me she had listened to Tracy and thought: yes, but he's doing some other things at the same time, (for example, on that particular night, the almost-splits). But later I realized, as usual, Tracy was probably right. Caroline and Claudia were both non-musicians, while I had spent my teenage years playing in bands (though even now, when I play with good musicians, I definitely feel like a non-musician in comparison), and I was most likely on some level, conscious or subconscious, attempting to equalize the musical situation, playing at a level that fit more with the group. In this sense there was definitely something fake about it. It is only now I realize that night in Toronto was the first time Tracy had seen a PME show she wasn't in. That must have been strange.

+ + + +

The very first record we got was a reissue of *Colossal Youth*, the seminal 1981 post-punk recording by the Young Marble Giants. (Caroline reminds me that when we started, it was actually the CD;

we got the record only later.) At some of those early rehearsals we would put it on and play along, hitting the guitar with a drumstick in time with the recorded drum machine. Later, we would read the first paragraph from the liner notes, written by Simon Reynolds, before playing *Colossal Youth* in the show:

> Postpunk and "perfection" rarely went together. This was an era of experimental over-reach, of bands catalyzed by the punk do-it-yourself principle attempting to expand the music by embracing genres (funk, reggae, jazz) that in their original context relied on virtuosity and slickness. Artistic ambition and anyone-can-do-it amateurism make for uneasy bedfellows, and many of the key groups of the period made records that were closer to sketches toward an ideal of a new music than the fully-realised deal. Even some of the accredited classics that defined the era [...] have the odd moment or several that are substandard, botched, or simply misconceived. And really, that's okay, because perfection wasn't the point of postpunk. What was? Throwing out ideas, setting challenges for band and audience alike, keeping the collective conversation moving.

This felt like a manifesto for so many of the things we were working on. So much of the performance work in dance and theatre that surrounded us seemed to be aiming for an over-rehearsed perfection that felt, to me, mediocre and lifeless. That last sentence: "Throwing out ideas, setting challenges for band and audience alike, keeping the collective conversation moving." What else was there in life and in art?

\+ + + +

The title *Individualism Was A Mistake* was a constant source of debate between the three of us. I was pushing hard for an idea that had begun for me near the end of *En français comme en anglais, it's easy to criticize*. The idea had something to do with one of the premises for that show: that the left was only able to criticize capitalism, had difficulty altering it in any effective or ongoing manner. One of the reasons for this, I thought at the time, is that it's impossible to change anything by yourself – fighting for real change involves solidarity, involves working together with others in a committed and continuous manner, and our culture's overemphasis on individualism makes such working together difficult. I think it's fair to say that Caroline and Claudia never completely agreed with all aspects of this premise. (Claudia says this is true, and she also remembers me articulating early on that we didn't have to agree with each other's individual choices. This was a new way of working for her, as she was previously used to working with a lot of consensus decision-making and compromise. This agreement of non-agreement feels to her very distinctive to the process we had.)

In a way, for me, this central disagreement was a flashback to the process for *En français comme en anglais, it's easy to criticize*, in which none of the group particularly agreed with any of the things I had hoped to say with the show, and what's more, for the most part, didn't even pretend to be interested in them. It's only now as I'm writing this that I think: maybe this is what PME-ART actually is. I bring a theme and thesis to the group, the group doesn't agree with my thesis, and this situation becomes a starting point from which we can begin to work. (Caroline says this is true, and that it is probably one of the things she likes most about PME-ART.) But if in that one small way it was a flashback, in every other way it was different. If *En français comme en anglais, it's easy to criticize* was a dysfunctional family, *HOSPITALITY/HOSPITALITÉ* was one of the most artistically functional ongoing collaborations I have ever been a part of. In that sense, the fact that we were working together, the ways we were working together, disproved the arguments underlying my title. Our culture might overemphasize individualism, but it must still be possible for people to work together effectively because we were doing so. And why should everyone in a collaboration always agree? Our differences were part of the work and (as Claudia has already said) we tried not to hide them, but let them be present and visible in the things we were making, to use our differences to the work's advantage.

The way I think about these questions now has changed a great deal. I still believe there are no individual solutions to collective problems. But I now feel that my original premise confused different levels of reality. Since it must also be true that you need some consequent sense of yourself as an individual in order to work effectively with others. (This is an idea that came from Caroline.)

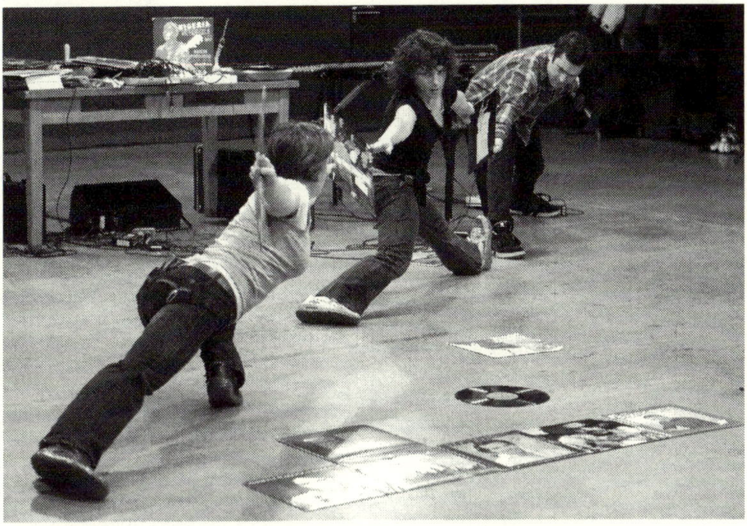

Caroline Dubois, Claudia Fancello, and Jacob Wren in *HOSPITALITY 3: Individualism Was A Mistake* at Usine C in Montreal. Photo: David Jacques

The other aspect of my original idea was that artists had a lot to answer for in terms of our culture's overemphasis on the individual. The idea of the solitary artist, pushing alone against the stagnant conventions of society, against the status quo, was in so many ways at the root of the problem. When I write this I am mainly criticizing myself. Even though I have dedicated the bulk of my artistic life toward collaboration, as I get older it becomes increasingly clear to me just how internally divided I am across the chasm of these questions and difficulties. This is probably the deepest, most pernicious contradiction in my ongoing work with PME-ART: that I want to be a famous (or at least semi-famous) individual artist and, at the same time, I also want to work collaboratively in a manner that often teeters on the brink of pure collectivity. This contradiction is very much present in the writing of this book. (And, Caroline says, also very present in her experience of working in collaboration with me.)

Western narratives are so often about one lone hero rather than about a group or collective. The improbable eighties Hollywood action hero, one man endlessly fighting off armies of opponents and in the end prevailing, is a pure cartoon of everything that is wrong with our thinking around how things change and how injustice might actually be defeated over the course of a long struggle. And artists are also so often at the centre of their own ridiculous cartoon, with (in the case of more successful artists) a lot of praise and encouragement to prop up this personal mythology.

(Caroline says that I am quite well known in contemporary theatre in Europe, Canada, and the U.S. and so is PME-ART and, for her, working with me was a way of getting out of Montreal. The fact that I'm known and respected gave her great opportunities and also difficulties, simply because the work was largely perceived as being by me and not so much as being what it actually was: a collaboration between the three of us. She remembers how sometimes our co-authorship of the work was hard for people from festivals, theatres, and events to understand. How we needed to fight and ask for corrections in their programs. She also remembers being in a festival in Germany and her and Claudia both having to wear a lanyard with "Jacob Wren" written on it.)

There are no individual solutions to collective problems. Nonetheless, it is individuals who must come together and figure out what to do. In all of this, there is the unaddressed question of leadership. The anarchist in me genuinely believes rotating leadership is a solution: people take turns taking the lead in the areas of their greatest competence, interest, or desire. Another similar collaborative idea might be: best idea wins. But art is so subjective, and for five different people five different ideas might each seem best. It has always been my thinking that if someone in the group feels strongly that we should do something, then we should do it, their strong desire shouldn't be watered or sanded down by the democratic entropy of the group. I want the projects to be open enough to welcome the strongest impulses of each of the participants. This is my ideal, and like all ideals it is something I often fall short of achieving. Perhaps this ideal is not even best for every collaborative situation. In a sense, it is just another way of saying that I want to work in ways that are deeply collaborative while at the same time keeping our most intense individual artistic differences more alive than alive.

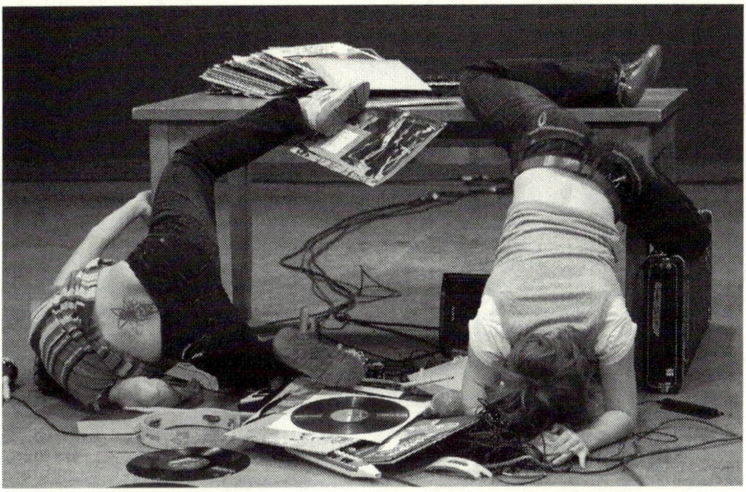

Claudia Fancello and Caroline Dubois in *HOSPITALITY 3: Individualism Was A Mistake* at Usine C in Montreal. Photo: David Jacques

We spent weeks and weeks talking about all these questions. What did it mean to offer someone hospitality? What did it mean to offer it to the audience? What is the relationship between the individual and the group? Our conversations were loose and free-ranging. What, if anything, do I remember from those many weeks of talking? The conversations took no particular path, anything and everything could enter into them. It was as if there was no plan, and at times I felt as if I had significantly renounced my previous tendency to lead. A conversation between three people can be so lively and focused, so much more focused than discussions in a larger group. Suddenly it seemed not so difficult for everyone to have a more or less equal chance to speak. We talked about our daily lives just as frequently as we spoke of artistic or thematic questions and, in this, the work drifted toward questions of how the personal is political, how our friendships and romances mirrored and informed so many of the thematic questions we were struggling with. Years later I saw a talk by Paige Sarlin in which she presented her research on the feminist origins of the phrase "the personal is political," explaining that at its origin the phrase had a second part that was equally important: "the personal is political, no I without a we."

Many of our conversations also circled around the question of questions. What was a good question? Could we enact some sense of hospitality by asking the audience questions, by being interested in what they thought? How interested was it actually possible for us to be within the artifice of the performance situation? If we were to ask questions, what might we honestly want to know?

+ + + +

The show *HOSPITALITY 3: Individualism Was A Mistake* was divided into four sections. For the first section, each of us brought the audience into the space in small groups of six or eight and, once inside, each group sat around one of three separate tables. On the tables were Post-it notes and pens. We then asked our group four questions, one question at a time, instructing them to write each of their answers on a separate Post-it. (Claudia reminds me that we also allowed people to write their answers in the language of their choice and, when we read back the answers at the end of the show, we would, if necessary, ask other audience members to translate.) The questions were:

- How do you decide when to fight and when to compromise?
- What do you learn from your enemies?
- How do you get power?
- When is the best time to lie?

After each question, we collected the Post-its and placed them on the back wall. There was of course something unfair about this exercise: a question that pulled in so many different directions and yet you had to fit your entire answer on a single Post-it.

The second section began with a brief explanation of how the wall of Post-it notes reflected the individual and the collective. We explained that if you read the notes down the column, you had a single individual's answer to all four questions. While if you read across the row, you had everyone in the room's answer to a single question. I gestured down the column to suggest the individual and across the row to indicate the collective.

We then each picked up a musical instrument. There was a tense, sometimes comical, moment as we glanced at one another, unclear how we could or should begin. Each of us as individuals, and the three of us as some abstract mini-collective, searching for an opening that would lead toward the music we were about to attempt to play. Once again we followed the rules: put your body in awkward relation to the instrument, stay in contact with the other performers and the audience, try to make it sound like music.

Playing music on a random assortment of musical instruments led into the next section: putting on records, playing music on vinyl. It's now hard for me to remember that at the beginning we started with only twenty records. We would each tell a story about the record before playing it. Many of these stories were about the individual versus the collective – for example, how some musicians were solo artists who presented themselves as individuals while others chose to present themselves more collectively as bands.

Finally we would get to work balancing all the objects onstage in various precarious assemblages. While we did this, a final song played on the record player, most often "Just Take Your Time" by Al Green. We each took turns turning down the music and speaking about the title of the show, what it meant to us, in what ways we each agreed and disagreed with the sentiment. We had come together to work around this title I had provided, and after many months of working in and around it our disagreements on the topic had perhaps only deepened. And this was also something about the individual and the collective, that we hadn't managed to convince each other but still found ways to work together, within and against our differences, to hold our collaboration in fragile, precarious balance.

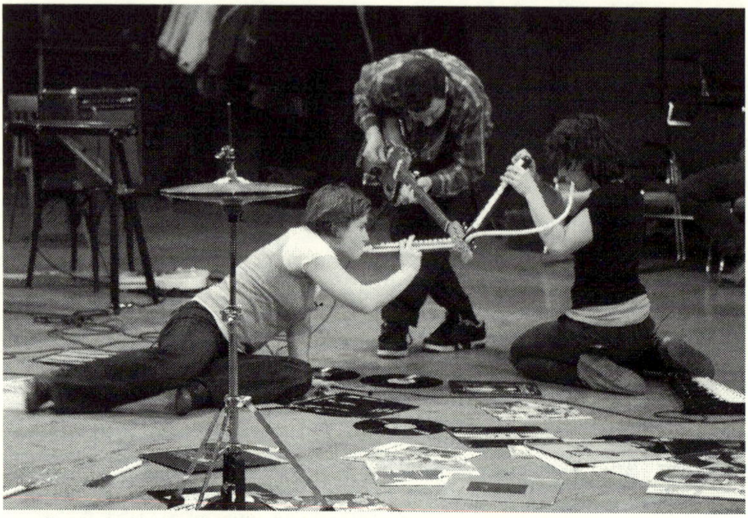

Caroline Dubois, Jacob Wren, and Claudia Fancello in *HOSPITALITY 3: Individualism Was A Mistake* at Usine C in Montreal. Photo: David Jacques

The *HOSPITALITY 3: Individualism Was A Mistake* premiere at Harbourfront Centre World Stage in Toronto was one of the most stressful of my life. The show I just described is in fact what the show evolved into over the course of the following year. But in the days leading up to the premiere we weren't quite there. I felt so strongly that it still wasn't working and at the same time had lost perspective, couldn't see what we had or what might still need to change. In Toronto I would lie awake in bed trying to think my way toward a solution but my thinking did little more than spin in repetitive circles. After the premiere a man stormed onstage and started kicking over all of our precarious assemblages. He was obviously infuriated. When someone tried to intervene, asking him what he was doing and why, he responded that this was a moment he had "decided to fight."

I was so nervous that first night that I told one of the record stories completely wrong. We had a record called *Flesh* by the London band Worldbackwards, one of the records from my teenage collection. When we began researching the records I was surprised to find there was absolutely no information about Worldbackwards online. We have the feeling we can find absolutely anything on the Internet and yet here was a clear example to the contrary. On the inner sleeve of the record there are photographs of the four members of the band (Nigel Lackey, David Henderson, Dinah Mulholland, Paul Hood) and I would stare at it and wonder what had happened to them: were they alive or dead, were they still making music, what were they now doing with their lives. They had made this record that I'd listened to over and over again, that was once so much a part of my life, and now all four of them had vanished without a trace. However, during the premiere I was nervous and held up the wrong record. So instead of saying there was nothing on the Internet about Worldbackwards, I said there was nothing on the Internet about the Red Guitars. If you check you will find there is lots and lots of information about the Red Guitars, as many people wrote me in the following days, to set me straight, irritated that I had said something so verifiably false during the course of our performance.

Tracy was also there. I can't remember if she came the first or second night. However, I do remember her coming onstage after the show as we were cleaning up. She said the show was great, but then pointed to Claudia and Caroline and said: "Except for one thing. Who are these girls?" Tracy had been in every PME show and now she was making a joke about the fact that this was no longer the case. I don't think I laughed. But I remember her exact tone of voice as she said it, that absolutely particular comedic tone. (Caroline also remembers this very well.) It was perhaps the moment when I had the first premonition of just how much had changed. That we weren't quite making theatre anymore. Back in Toronto yet returning to where I started as if from another world.

\+ + + +

Two weeks later we were doing nine shows at Usine C in Montreal. I remember this as the time in which we really started to figure it out. But what I remember even more is how difficult it was to work there. I decided before I started writing this book that I wasn't going to use it to settle old scores, and this will be one of only two unfortunate exceptions. (This book is being written for PME-ART's twentieth anniversary, and it's bad sportsmanship to use a birthday present for purposes of revenge.) But my feeling was that after the success we'd previously with *Families Are Formed Through Copulation*, Usine C resented how our work had now taken an unexpected swerve in a much more experimental direction. (In a later conversation, I remember being told: "Jacob, you're just too radical for me." I didn't know what to say in response.) Their resentment was summarized in the fact that they told the restaurant that not many people would be coming and therefore they didn't need to serve meals or keep the bar open after the show. It was a feeling I'd definitely had before: we were in the process of an artistic breakthrough, making work I'd previously not even thought possible, and our breakthrough was being met by a noticeable lack of support.

At the same time, if we didn't feel enough support from the venue, I clearly felt a strange kind of support from the audience. The curiosity of the Montreal audiences, their openness to witnessing something we were all in the process of discovering together, was palpable during each of our shows at Usine C. I felt I was once again learning in public and that there was still a certain degree of room for this kind of risk-taking in Montreal. Each night we would try something different with the ending, no ending feeling satisfying, but we were determined to keep searching for one that did, not to give up.

\+ + + +

There was no time to process what had happened at Usine C because a few days later I travelled to Belgium to continue work on *An Anthology of Optimism*. A series of pre-premieres in Linz, Krakow, Vienna, and Copenhagen, leading up to its official opening at the Kunstenfestivaldesarts in Brussels that spring.

*An Anthology of Optimism* had begun many years earlier with just a title. Geert Opsomer at the Nieuwpoorttheater in Ghent had invited me to propose a project and the title *An Anthology of Optimism* was basically all I had. I think I was considering it mainly as a critique of my own ongoing pessimism, a kind of wondering aloud what kind of optimism it might be possible for me to compile or embody in the world today. Geert applied for money to begin something but didn't get it. However, in the meantime he told Pieter de Buyser about the title and Pieter contacted me, explaining that it felt to him like a project we should be working on together. (This made sense to me because, at the time, I thought of Pieter as one of the most optimistic people I had ever met.)

I had met Pieter many years earlier, when PME performed *En français comme en anglais, it's easy to criticize* at the ICA in London in 2000. Pieter had been one of our few audience members in London, but he had subsequently written to me many times about how much the work had meant to him. He invited me to Brussels to work with him for a week or two and figure out how we might begin to conceive of a project entitled *An Anthology of Optimism*, what it might become. Together we came up with the concept of "critical optimism." For me critical optimism has to do with seeing all the unbearable, heartbreaking things in the world with open eyes but still finding a way to have hope, simply because one knows that without a certain degree of lived hope it is impossible to fight for any kind of change. I believe Pieter's definition of critical optimism might be considerably different. During these first meetings we also decided to write a letter to many artists, thinkers, and public figures, asking them to respond to our idea of critical optimism. We would send out the letter, a kind of message in a bottle, and then structure our performance around whatever responses we eventually received.

*An Anthology of Optimism* is probably the show I've been a part of that has toured not only the most but also to the most large festivals. (This is partly because it was produced by CAMPO, a Ghent-based organization that is exceptionally good at touring things.) And once again I was in the middle of some strange divide: on the one hand touring a show by PME-ART that was very close to my heart but often considered to be difficult work, and on the other touring *An Anthology of Optimism*, a show that was much more successful and that for many years kept me afloat financially. The work I most wanted to do always seemed to have some more successful shadow, reminding me that if I were to make different artistic decisions my life might be considerably easier.

*An Anthology of Optimism* was a kind of lecture/performance in which Pieter and I showed the responses we had gotten from our letter on an overhead projector and used them as a framework for our own reflections on the questions our letter raised. In these reflections, Pieter most often took the more optimistic stance while I was generally the voice of pessimism. As I said in the show: "The fact that air and water are still sometimes free is a deep pain in the hearts of capitalists everywhere."

The obvious observation, likely no less true due to its obviousness, is that *An Anthology of Optimism* was more successful on the circuit because it was simply more optimistic. The ending especially gave the audience an up feeling. Unfortunately, touring it so extensively did little to make me feel more optimistic about the world. Or perhaps it did. Many have told me they think the project changed something about me, that since that time I'm apparently more comfortable expressing certain optimistic ideas. Why do I resist the possibility that it changed me? Even as I'm writing it here I want to delete it. It's still not something I'm ready to own.

\+ + + +

For some reason, with *HOSPITALITY/HOSPITALITÉ* we did the numbers out of order. I believe it was my idea, but I have absolutely no idea why I wanted it like that, or what exactly I was thinking. Counting to five, but in some slightly off-kilter manner: 1,3,2,5. (We still haven't made a HOSPITALITY 4, so that might be the reunion tour.)

*HOSPITALITY 2: Gradually This Overview* took place at the artist-run centre Articule in Montreal. When someone came into the gallery we sat them at a table with Post-it notes and asked the following six questions:

- How do you enjoy being difficult?
- How do you know when you are part of a community?
- What is one rule you love to break?
- Where is the vulnerability in power?

- How do you alter the system?
- What song most shaped your personality?

Once again we put each Post-it on the wall as soon as it had received an answer, and slowly the entire gallery filled up with Post-its, gradually forming the overview of the title. For three weeks people came into the gallery and answered our questions, their answers forming an unsummarizable survey of a community that was partly the artists in the neighbourhood and partly a community brought into being by our proposal and presence in the gallery.

My original idea was that once all six answers were up, we would immediately take the participant to the wall and rearrange their answers in front of them, placing their answers, along with the answers of others, into a series of unexpected categories, then immediately rearranging them again into yet other categories. Creating new possibilities for what their individual answers might mean and how they might also be placed in relation to all the other answers that surrounded them and had accumulated over the past weeks. Unfortunately, the three of us could never quite agree on exactly how to do this and therefore it didn't happen. This is one of my greatest small artistic regrets. I was hoping there was a way to destabilize each viewer's experience of the game, to slightly unravel their understanding of themselves as a unique individual as represented by their six short answers. I thought that doing this the moment they finished answering the questions had a certain potential, to get in there while their engagement with the questions was still recent and fresh. I was hoping to destabilize them but I didn't have the nerve or conviction to really push it through. It was an idea that was so important to me but I didn't know how exactly I wanted to do it. I was also nervous that it crossed a line, that it was overly unfair to the viewer. At the same time, I had the feeling that the hospitality we were offering up was too smooth, needed a little bit more discomfort and grit to bring it more fully to life. A collaborative process can at times feel like little more than an impasse and this was one particular impasse we remained unable to break. At the time, I remember feeling a collaborative frustration so intense it kept me awake night after night. I felt the project could go so much further and we remained utterly stalled. The more I left theatre, the more these other questions would arise, questions I realized I was only beginning to grapple with. Now, with the clarity of hindsight, I only wish I had pushed harder. That I had been able to take my uncertainty regarding an addition that was clearly important to me as a positive sign. A positive sign that the only way out was through.

I don't know how many artists openly admit to past artistic shortcomings and failures. When you write about your work, I believe, you are encouraged to do so as if everything has always worked out for the best. An artist today is somehow supposed to be their own most enthusiastic cheerleader. But this is basically the opposite of how I experience my own struggles to make work and make collaborative work. There have been so many shortcomings along the way, some of which we've overcome, while others got the best of us. Periods where our disagreements coalesced into something unexpectedly great and other moments where we stalled within them and ran out of time before making the necessary breakthrough. *HOSPITALITY 2: Gradually This Overview* is one of the few projects we did only once. It is also possible that if we'd had further opportunities to present it, if we had continued to work on it, it very well could have begun to move again.

+ + + +

As *HOSPITALITY 3: Individualism Was A Mistake* continued to tour I could feel it gradually becoming something else. At many junctures we continued to simplify the work. There were so many moments where actions we had been doing from the beginning fell away, we realized we didn't need them anymore, and what remained became so much more precise and uncompromising. (For example, an action we had at the beginning where we slowly slid a portable record player down our back while it was playing.) In the end, I believe *HOSPITALITY 3: Individualism Was A Mistake* was the most collaborative and uncompromising project I have ever been a part of. (Caroline says she feels the same.) Each of the four sections had its own separate, clear logic and, at the same time, so strangely resonated with the others in ways one could never quite pin down.

It was a show you could think endlessly about and whose awkward grace and gracelessness produced so many shades of productive discomfort that pulled one away from such thoughts. Caroline, Claudia, and I didn't let each other compromise, didn't let each other off the hook, even though we weren't necessarily aware what was happening at the time. For a while there was an off-kilter balance in which each of us managed to keep the other two honest, a process that took on a life of its own. I'm not sure the way I'm describing it here can give any real sense of what I mean. It was a breakthrough and I'm still hoping its full consequences continue to filter into our future work.

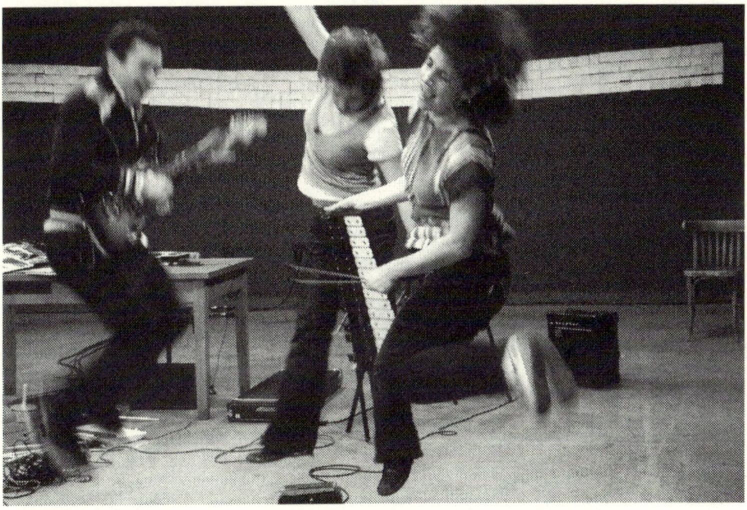

Jacob Wren, Caroline Dubois, and Claudia Fancello in ***HOSPITALITY 3: Individualism Was A Mistake*** at Usine C in Montreal. Photo: Mathieu Chartrand

The connection between hospitality and performance is both obvious and perhaps not obvious to everyone who makes performances. In the dynamic between performer and spectator there is always the potential for at least a certain degree of hospitality on both sides. How open-minded am I going to be when I begin to watch a performance? How open to the spectator is any performance I might make? Sometimes being too open, taking the spectator too much by the hand, might come off as condescending, and keeping this in mind it is possible to convey a greater hospitality by making work that is in fact more challenging.

Everyone just wants to be treated with respect. You can disagree with someone and still treat them with respect. You can hate someone and still treat them with respect. You can even kill someone and still treat them with respect. This approach also merges with my feelings around the theme of hospitality. Hospitality, it seems to me, is fundamentally about respect. You welcome a stranger, you don't yet know anything about them, but already you have decided they deserve to be treated with respect. Later they might do something to prove you wrong, but the starting point remains the same. You can convey respect by honestly telling about yourself, or by asking about them. Or by respecting their privacy, if that's what seems to be required. At the same time, too much respect might turn back on itself, might backfire. Sometimes the necessary respect might involve giving a push or asking hard questions. Hospitality might mean having a feel for these different necessities, how certain moments might call for different, or even opposite, ways of being respectful.

Many who saw *HOSPITALITY 3: Individualism Was A Mistake* commented that the element of hospitality was what most differentiated it from previous PME work. Previous work might have been characterized as being at war with theatre. Now such battles were drifting into the past, replaced by feelings of welcoming. Perhaps I was only mellowing with age. (Claudia says I might be mellowing with age, but the more significant factor in this shift is my collaboration with her and Caroline, who both take the act of hospitality very seriously. This is absolutely true. Thinking about it now, it is more than obvious that the genuine, thoughtful, and embodied hospitality in the *HOSPITALITY/HOSPITALITÉ* project comes predominantly from them.)

But also, for me, the battle might have simply moved to other places. Something I often felt around this time: some strange and misguided nostalgia for a recent past when my self-appointed mission was to change theatre, and no matter how much I failed, the mission remained clear. Without such a mission I was sometimes feeling confused (in a different way than before). What was I now doing and what was I now trying to do? Around this time I was at a party, having a conversation about different kinds of hybrid forms, how difficult they often seemed to be to describe or explain. A writer who was also an artist was asking everyone, "If I'm not exactly making poetry and I'm not exactly making performance, what am I making? How should I describe it to people?" They then turned to me: "How do you describe what you do?" Without missing a beat I replied: "I'm co-artistic director of an interdisciplinary performance group." Everyone laughed.

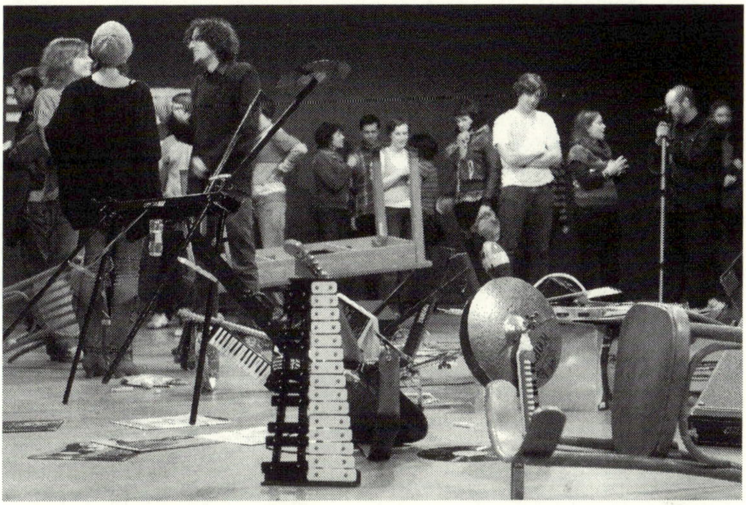

The audience at the end of *HOSPITALITY 3: Individualism Was A Mistake* at Usine C in Montreal. Photo: David Jacques

Eight:

# The DJ Who Gave Too Much Information [HOSPITALITY 5]

## (2011–)

Created/Performed by:
Caroline Dubois, Claudia Fancello, and Jacob Wren

Continued/Performed by:
Adam Kinner and Marie Claire Forté

We performed it in:
Montreal, Escales improbables/SPARK • Groningen, Noorderzon Festival • Mannheim, Zeitraumexit/Wunder der Prärie Festival • Oslo, Black Box/Ultima Music Festival • Malmö, Inkonst • Ghent, CAMPO • Montreal, Musée d'Art Contemporain/La Triennale québécoise • Tallin, Nu Performance Festival • Düsseldorf, Forum Freies Theater • Montreal, OFFTA/Phonopolis • Peterborough, Artspace • Toronto, Mercer Union/FADO • Kingston, Modern Fuel • Montreal, Maison de la culture tour: Borough of St-Léonard, Maison de la culture Villeray-Jarry Park, City of Westmount • Regina, Dunlop Gallery/Curtain Razors • Austin, Fusebox Festival • Marseille, Actoral Festival • Quebec City, Mois Multi Festival • Birmingham, Fierce Festival • Manchester, Contact Theatre/The Whitworth • Bordeaux, Festival Novart • Munich, Spielart Festival /Pathos • Cardiff, Experimentica Festival/Chapter Arts Centre • Fribourg, Festival Belluard Bollwerk International • Salzburg, Sommerszene/Szene Salzburg • Helsinki, URB Festival

When we performed *The DJ Who Gave Too Much Information (HOSPITALITY 5)* in Düsseldorf, I was asked to write a letter to the audience:

Dear curious spectator,

I am currently reading the book *Love Saves the Day: A History of American Dance Music Culture, 1970-1979* by Tim Lawrence. (It is essentially a history of disco.) In it, there was one particular anecdote that fascinated me. In 1965, when the New York club Shepheard's replaced its house band with a DJ, the American Federation of Musicians picketed in protest.

This story echoes many of my questions and artistic concerns. Is there something fundamentally different between the experience of going to see a live band and listening to a recording? Are there some essential attributes that make a performance situation "live," and if so how do they differ from attributes of recorded media? Is a live experience more intense? More real? More immediate? More unexpected? I don't have precise answers for any of these questions, but it's my hope that our work itself is a kind of an answer, or at the very least a way of making such questions more rich, more complicated, of making them resonate.

In the above anecdote the DJ is literally putting the musicians out of work. (In such matters I always side with the union, but can't fail to admit I love, and perhaps even prefer, listening to records.) It also suggests a certain dynamic between the individual and the community: the musicians cooperate with each other, they work, play (and in this case picket) together, while the DJ spins alone.

As we now know, the future was in many ways on the DJ's side. We live in a world in which we are constantly surrounded by mediated experiences: photographs, television, movies, music, Internet, advertising of every kind. I have always wondered if making a live performance might offer alternative ways of watching and of being together, ways that differ significantly from watching a movie or being on the Internet.

In our new show *The DJ Who Gave Too Much Information* we play records and tell stories about them. We tell every kind of story: about bands, things that happened to us, to our friends, and to complete strangers, theories about the world, about love, and about life. They are stories that suggest the songs we listen to also affect how we think, live, and understand our daily lives. The alternation between telling (live) stories and listening to (recorded) music also feels important to me. We have records by A Tribe Called Quest, Al Green, Broadcast, Burial, Caetano Veloso, Jacques Brel, Kronos Quartet, LCD Soundsystem, Omar Khorshid, Pavement, Prince, Public Enemy, Red Guitars, Robert Wyatt, Selda, Sister Nancy, the Ramones, Eddie Kendricks, Cate Le Bon, Hefner, Jane Weaver, Dirty Three, THEESatisfaction, the Jackson 5, Lloyd Miller, Nina Simone, and so many more. (I think we have almost a hundred and seventy.)

I don't think there's anything particular you have to do to prepare yourself. For me this work is simply a place to relax, listen, and enjoy. We don't anticipate dancing, but then again, why not.

Hope to see you there.

\+ + + +

*The DJ Who Gave Too Much Information* was a show we made without ever actually making it. Strangely, in making a show through not making it, I suspect we made a show that we can continue to do forever. It clearly developed directly out of the previous project. As we accumulated more and more records, and stories about them, we realized it was an activity that could be not only one short section in *HOSPITALITY 3: Individualism Was A Mistake* (where we did it for about twenty minutes) but could also develop into an entire show. What's more, it was an activity we could do for any length of time: one hour, three hours, eight hours, etc. Over the years we have continued to accumulate even more records and stories. Weaker stories have fallen away, to be replaced by apparently more compelling ones.

*The DJ Who Gave Too Much Information* is also the first project I've written about in these pages while still in the middle of it. The previous chapters each ended with some sort of muted closure, but these next few might each end in a manner considerably more open. This book that started in the past is now finally catching up to the present. A kind of perspective I feel I might have had about older projects now seems to be slipping away. Or maybe I simply haven't yet had time to mythologize more recent work. However, saying it's the middle might be overstating the case. We've now been performing it for about eight years, and I don't exactly know what it is that gives me the feeling it might continue for at least another ten, if not indefinitely. (After a recent Skype meeting with Sylvie, Claudia, and me, Caroline posted on her Facebook wall: "Tonight I agreed with PME-ART to keep performing *The DJ Who Gave Too Much Information* until I die. So did Claudia Fancello. I think it's a good deal.")

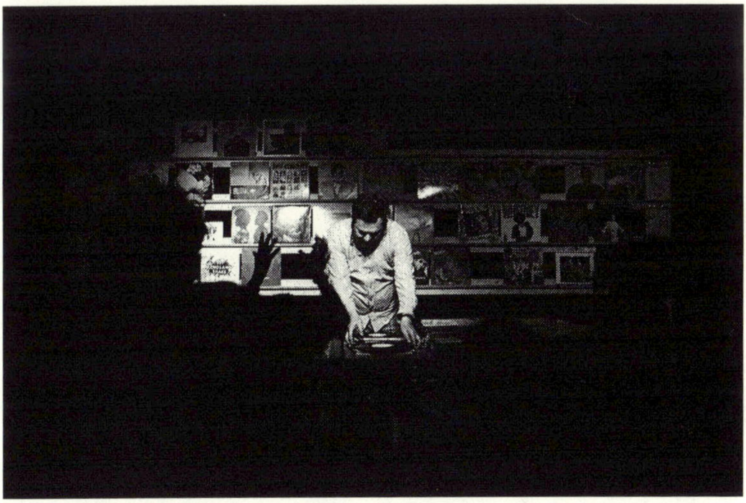

Jacob Wren in *The DJ Who Gave Too Much Information* at La Vitrola in Montreal. Photo: Sergio Conde

The premiere took place at the Noorderzon festival in Groningen. But unlike with previous projects, there was no specific creation process. We simply decided that this activity, which we had previously done for twenty minutes, would now be done for an hour and a half. In Groningen we had scheduled a dress rehearsal. (Strange to call it a dress rehearsal since we only ever wear our normal clothing. Residue from the fact that I began in theatre.) Mark Russell, who at the time was running P.S. 122 in New York, was in town, but would be leaving before our premiere. We invited him to the dress rehearsal, and he asked if he could bring a few friends. We were then extremely surprised when thirty U.S. presenters showed up. It was the first time we had ever done the show and we were doing it for more U.S. presenters than had ever previously seen our work. I suppose it went all right but I still wonder if it was a good idea. What I remember most is all of them spontaneously singing along to Lionel Richie's "All Night Long." It was the first moment I was truly struck by how different the relation to American pop culture was in Europe than it was in the U.S. In Europe they're intrigued and have a desire to analyze it. In the U.S. it's their culture, they somehow experience it as their own.

A few days later, at the premiere, we decided to perform for forty-five minutes, take a break, and then continue for another forty-five. (Something we in fact never tried again.) There was a bar in the space, and we were thinking it might be good to give the audience a chance to get a drink. The moment the intermission began, a man from the audience made a beeline for me as I was putting on a record. He was visibly irritated.

Him: What is this? What are you doing?

Me: The performance is called *The DJ Who Gave Too Much Information.* We're playing records and giving too much information about them.

Him: None of those stories are interesting to me. None of the information you're giving interests me in any way.

Me: I'm sorry. I can assure you that wasn't our intention.

He looks at me for a long moment, realizes he's not going to convince me that our proposition is uninteresting, and storms off. I now wish I had asked him more questions: What he found interesting in life and in art. What kind of performances he most liked to watch. I finished putting on the record, went to the bar, and told Claudia and Caroline what had just happened. I believe I was visibly shaken. And yet he had every right to confront me, to have his own opinion about the work we were doing, and engage me on the topic. These are discussions I want to have but so often they catch me off guard and therefore I'm unable to push them toward something productive.

+ + + +

Soon after, we decided to begin each show with statistics about the records we had on the table. Here are the statistics from our show in Fribourg, Switzerland:

> 140 records in total
>
> -----------------------
>
> 41 records by men
> 32 records by women
> 43 records by bands
> 6 compilations
> 6 records by duos
> 7 record by trios
> 2 soundtracks
>
> -----------------------
>
> 96 records by artists who are still alive
> 25 records by artists who are now dead
> 7 records by groups that contain a mix of living and dead artists
> 2 records by artists that we were unable to find out if they are dead or alive

-----------------------

89 records by artists with English as their first language
16 records by artists with French as their first language
3 records by artists with German as their first language
2 records by artists with Spanish as their first language
2 from Sweden / 3 from Egypt / 2 from Denmark / 1 from the former Yugoslavia / 2 from Norway / 1 from Greece / 1 from Brazil / 1 from Finland / 1 from Iceland / 1 from Syria / 1 from Estonia / 1 from Nunavut / 1 from Belgium

-----------------------

8 records by artists singing in English even though it's not their first language
1 record by an artist singing in French even though it's not their first language
1 record by an artist singing in Spanish even though it's not their first language
3 records by artists singing in both English and French even though neither is their first language

-----------------------

15 records that were part of Jacob's teenage record collection
1 record that was part of Claudia's teenage record collection
7 records that were given to us as gifts on tour
4 records that are on coloured vinyl

-----------------------

96 records that all three of us like
13 records that only two of us like
8 records that only one of us like
13 records that none of us like
20 records that not all of us have heard

Looking at these statistics, I find myself thinking about how eccentric our record collection is. We have the Jackson 5 but not the

Beatles, we have Al Green but not Dylan, we have Big Star but not the Rolling Stones, we have Destroyer but not Nirvana, etc. I believe, when we started the statistics, men outnumbered women by a far greater margin than they do now, but I would still prefer it if we could get to 50/50. (It also occurred to me just now that we don't have any records by transgender or non-binary artists, but that could also conceivably soon change.) But, then again, the biases and inequalities of the world find their way into the show and the statistics then lay them bare. At times we push against these biases but at other times they push, equally, against us.

+ + + +

*The DJ Who Gave Too Much Information* works as a kind of game between the three of us. Someone starts by choosing a record from the pile and telling the story about it. They then put on the record. While they are doing this, the other two need to think of another story in the pile that relates to the first one. These relations between stories can be thematic or tangential, but often we try to surprise each other, to find new connections between stories, stories that might have (previous to that moment) felt unrelated. We then listen to the record for a moment or two, or a few minutes, interrupting it with the next story. (This sense of interruption, of frustration, of rarely getting to hear an entire song, gives the show, for me at least, a kind of frantic uncanniness.) And on it goes, finding seemingly endless connections between the records and stories, in a sense a new dramaturgy, each and every time we perform. Sometimes we hit a vein and mine it for a while – for example, a series of stories about drugs (with musicians there are many) or a series of stories about love – until someone breaks the thread and sends the connections spiralling in some other direction. We often say, now that we've been performing it for about eight years, that each of us should take a moment to question our first impulse before going up, decide if we want to find the obvious connection or reach for something more unexpected. Playing the game involves mixing different kinds of connections between stories over the course of the show. Sometimes the most obvious connection might still be the right one.

After you've finished your story, and put on the record, you place the empty sleeve face forward on the shelves behind you. Gradually, over the course of the show, the shelves fill up with all the images from the music we've been listening to together. These images, the images the musicians or record labels chose to visually represent their sound, are also such an essential part of the work. A constant visual reminder of the story so far. Cassettes, CDs, and mp3s have all had their day, but no other format's packaging has yet to match the perfect dimensions of the album cover.

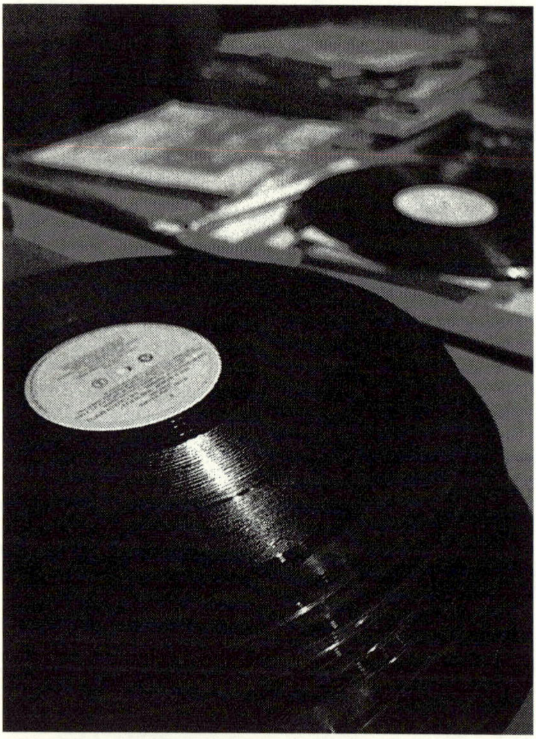

Some of the records from *The DJ Who Gave Too Much Information* at La Vitrola in Montreal. Photo: Sergio Conde

I often like the metaphor of art as a game with rules. A game where you can push the rules toward their breaking point, or make breakthroughs in the other direction by following the rules even more religiously than their intention. I often think there is a strange connection between freedom and rules. That freedom without rules is simply a freedom that refuses to acknowledge whatever unspoken rules might already be present. And that one can only increase one's artistic freedom by bringing the rules into sharper focus. Also, when necessary, by breaking them.

During the process for *HOSPITALITY 3: Individualism Was A Mistake*, Caroline once insisted that for her art is like a good meal: you want to enjoy eating it, you don't want to read the recipe as you are doing so. Knowing "the recipe" was an unnecessary distraction, wouldn't improve the artistic experience. I don't know if Caroline would still agree with this assertion. (Caroline says that, yes, she still thinks this. She in fact feels this way about art, food, and sport. For example, she enjoys watching tennis but doesn't know the rules very well and somehow wants to keep it this way. If she eats something someone else made, she doesn't want to know the recipe, it somehow kills her experience. And it's the same for art, she doesn't want to know the recipe, for her it takes something magical away. Although she does appreciate when things are in a way simple and conceptually concise, but appreciates this mainly when she can understand it through her own interpretation.)

I had previously written that I prefer to know the rules – that for me art should be more like watching sports (where those watching most often know the rules) and less like being served a meal – but reading Caroline's response I'm no longer certain. I was mainly thinking back to an experience during my residency at Alkantara in Lisbon. My host, Thomas Walgrave, took me to see a soccer match, I believe it was England versus Portugal, and, while we were watching, I asked him a series of questions. For example, I didn't understand how they knew when to start playing again after the whistle blew. There was a short break and then, as if by magic, it would all start up again in unison. At times I wasn't even sure where the ball was or why the referee blew the whistle in the first place. Without the frame of the television screen the field was too open for me to follow. "The questions you're asking are so basic," Thomas at one point told me, either amused or annoyed, I couldn't tell which.

However, what I remember most about that day was that before the game was over, but when it was already clear that Portugal could not win, the Portugal fans started leaving in droves, not waiting for the game to finish. There seemed to me something extremely strange, almost disloyal, about this: not wanting to be a fan to the bitter end, not wanting to stay a fan to the bitter end even if your team badly loses, not wanting to watch your team lose. The other thing I remember is that after the match ended there was an announcement over the loudspeakers, in English, telling the England fans, who were all seated together in their own section, that they must remain seated until everyone else had left. This message was repeated several times. Thomas explained to me that the point was to keep the England fans and the Portugal fans separate in order to avoid violence. So many rules I didn't know.

\+ + + +

Claudia noticed it much more than I did. In fact, I don't think I would have even known about it if she hadn't told me. What she noticed, when we performed at Zeitraumexit in Mannheim, was an older couple in the audience. Apparently, after every single story, the man would make like he was ready to leave, and the woman would say: "Just one more story." It went on like this for well over an hour, maybe almost two. Each time, "Just one more story." Like our show was a bowl of potato chips and you couldn't stop eating them. But with each chip you ate you told yourself: this is going to be the last one.

\+ + + +

When we performed at OFFTA in Montreal, we decided it would be a durational version. For the first time we would play every single record and tell every single story we had. We estimated this would take about eight hours. This was the summer of 2012, when it seemed like the entire city was alive with protest. When I think back to the most heartfelt, inspiring protests I have ever witnessed first-hand, the city-wide protests known as the Printemps érable (a play on words on the Printemps arabe happening then Tunisia, Egypt, Libya, Syria, Yemen, etc., and very much at the forefront of everyone's minds) will always be at the top of the list. Very quickly, for those readers not living in Montreal at the time: at first there was the widespread student strike against a proposed tuition hike, then the *loi spéciale 78* put in place to suppress the protests and force students back to school. The Canadian Association of University Teachers condemned the law for "violating fundamental freedoms of association, assembly, and expression," its president calling it "a terrible act of mass repression." In response to this "special law," the protests generalized in a way I had never seen before, everyone on the street to prove that the right to protest, the right to the streets, was still an non-negotiable part of democratic culture. Every night at 8 p.m. everyone would be on their balconies, and on the streets, banging pots and pans as part of the *casserole*, a strategy most associated with Argentinian protests against the banks shutting down in 2001, but that had also been used in many other Spanish-speaking countries.

So on that night, as we were performing for eight hours at OFFTA, at 8 p.m. we paused our show to go out onto the street to bang pots and pans with the rest of the city. Well, we didn't exactly pause the show. We announced that there were pots and pans and people could stand outside the theatre to join the ruckus while we would continue to perform. The entire audience left, and for a while we were nervous they might not return. We told very few stories to the empty room, letting each song play out in full, until eventually the audience came back. At 2 a.m. we were still performing when someone from the theatre came in and told us we had to stop. There were nine unplayed records left on the table, nine stories we hadn't told. Jasmine Catudal from OFFTA said we should just quickly tell the rest of the stories but the people from Théâtre d'Aujourd'hui insisted we had to stop. I believe the reason was it would cost more, overtime for the staff, etc. It was late and they wanted to go home.

I don't know if *ironic* is the right word, but I often think there's something a bit funny about the fact that if we hadn't paused and sent the audience outside to protest for about thirty minutes in the middle of our performance, we most likely would have made it to the end of the show. I sometimes feel this says something about the relationship between art and politics, though I'm never entirely sure what. Perhaps only that sometimes you need to pause your artmaking, or leave an artwork unfinished, in order to go out and join the protests that are happening now and only now, that might never happen again. Or, at least, never again in quite the same way.

+ + + +

(Claudia also remembers that OFFTA was the first time the audience spontaneously broke into song and dance during Mylène Farmer's "Désenchantée." It was one of the first times the audience took over – the first must have been in Groningen to the Lionel Ritchie song – completely unplanned and unexpected. There was something about having the time and space between stories that also gave room for the audience to respond in whatever ways they wanted. They would listen, leave, get bored, get rowdy, tell their own stories to their neighbours, groove out. Even though we did not plan, nor could we, on this kind of interaction, having that space with only music created a certain audience autonomy. So many unexpected actions have been the by-product of *The DJ Who Gave Too Much Information*, creating situations she could have never previously imagined.)

+ + + +

The first *Bring Your Own Record/Listening Party* took place the next day. I believe it was Jasmine's idea. There have been a few times over the years in which presenters have proposed additions to our performances, and these additions most often involve some more direct interaction with the public. There is such a strong desire on the part of these organizations to be open to the public, or at least to be seen as being more open. (Probably, more often than not, it's a genuine desire. I don't know why I'm so suspicious.) My first reaction to such suggestions is always to say no, to bristle at the idea that someone else, someone who has some kind of power over me, is interfering with our work so directly. But we generally ignore my first impulse and accept the proposal in some form or other. Perhaps, in the end, I also want to be seen as being as open as possible to our various publics (publics that somehow include the very presenters who are making the suggestions). Jasmine first suggested doing the *Bring Your Own Record/Listening Party* directly after the durational performance, but we thought after eight hours of playing records and telling stories we would not be especially receptive to the stories of the audience, so instead decided to do it the next day.

The *Bring Your Own Record/Listening Party* is an invitation for anyone to bring a song (in any format) and tell a story about it. After their story we all listen to the song together in its entirety. (This differentiates it substantially from *The DJ Who Gave Too Much Information*, where each song is most often interrupted by the next.) We have now heard so many incredible heartbreaking and heartwarming music-related stories in so many different places. I wish I had taken notes, jotted down a few of my favourites as we went along. But unfortunately I did not, so instead I will just quickly sketch out what I can from memory.

A story about a woman's brother who had cut off all ties with her and her family, but she could still listen to the songs he recorded with his old band. And we all listened to one as well. As we listened, I believe I cried.

A story about a woman's first day on the job as a chauffeur and she's assigned to drive Duran Duran around. During their concert she accidentally locks her keys in the limousine. The band comes out, they don't want to engage with the fans who are waiting outside for them, so the drummer rushes over to the chauffeur and asks her what's the problem, why aren't they leaving already, as she nervously explains the situation, that it's her first day, etc. The drummer is wearing a fistful of big metal rings and he swings his arm down, smashing the limo window and says, "Get in, let's go."

In Bordeaux I was surprised by how almost every single song they brought was a French New Wave song from the eighties, which they danced to with generational élan, as their many children danced around them.

A story about purchasing a box set of Wagner on vinyl but never, until now, having a record player to listen to it on.

A story about growing up in Australia and encountering rock 'n' roll for the first time in the late fifties, of being startled that there could be something that sexual and primal performed in front of a stadium of screaming fans. (Caroline reminds me he also had a strict religious upbringing and therefore expressing himself and being loud, for example screaming, was not something he was used to.)

I don't actually know if I have the right to retell any of these stories. I hope I haven't crossed any ethical lines. But stories want to be shared.

\+ + + +

There was one story at the *Bring Your Own Record/Listening Party* at the Belluard Bollwerk festival in Fribourg that seemed especially powerful, also especially about the relationship between art and politics, which has always been my theme. It was told in French, so I didn't follow it at the time, but after we were done it was translated for me several times. I'm sure I'll get it at least partly wrong, but stories want to be shared and in the process distorted and transformed.

The story was about hearing a song on the radio that the person telling the story loved, and finding out that the singer of the song came from Israel. The person telling the story was fiercely anti-Zionist and pro-Palestine, but she still loved the song and didn't know what to make of this dilemma. (Caroline says the person who told the story was from Lebanon and her political feelings were deeply rooted in this history.) Soon after, she found out that the singer was coming to play a concert in her hometown. She still loved the song, but at the same time didn't want to support the Israeli singer by buying a ticket to the concert, and wasn't sure if she should go to the concert at all. After much inner debate, she finally came up with a solution she could live with: she would go to the concert, but bring with her a pro-Palestinian protest sign, and hold it aloft for the entirety of the show. A few songs in, the singer noticed her holding the sign in the audience, and invited her up onto the stage to show her sign to everyone and discuss the question with him. My understanding was that this discussion was productive, and that they were not as far apart on the issue as she had first imagined. We then all listened to the song she had first heard on the radio and loved.

We didn't think to take down the names of any the people who were kind enough to show up and share their stories. These stories are somehow as ephemeral as performance itself, existing only in the memories of those who told and heard them. But if you're reading this now and at some point in the past (or future) you attended a *Bring Your Own Record/Listening Party* and shared a story, I would like to take this opportunity to thank you again.

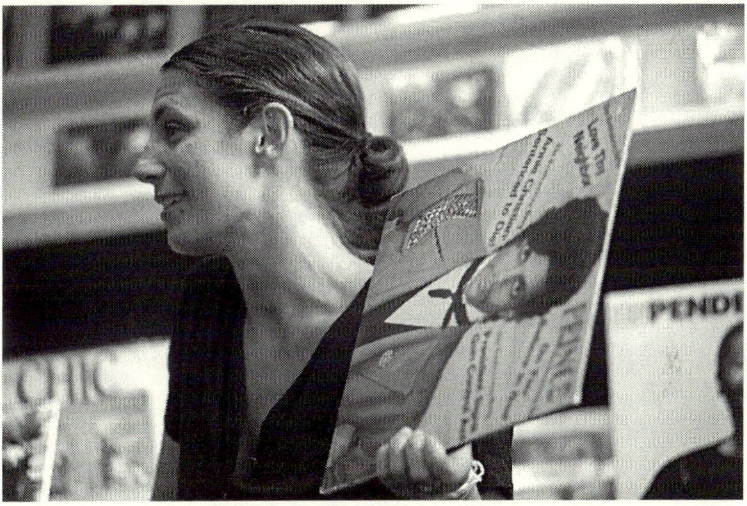

Claudia Fancello in *The DJ Who Gave Too Much Information* at a record store as part of the Noorderzon festival in Groningen. Photo: Pierre Borasci

There are a few stories we tell (and don't tell) in *The DJ Who Gave Too Much Information* that so clearly resonate with my own ongoing struggles with collaboration:

A story about the Fall. About how the Fall had over sixty members, and the reason there were so many is that Mark E. Smith kept firing them. It goes without saying that many former members were less than happy about this situation. Mark E. Smith didn't write any music and didn't play an instrument. He only wrote the (generally brilliant) lyrics and spoke/sang them, and also gave commands in the studio and onstage as to how precisely the songs should be played. (In general he wanted them played with greater simplicity and more ferocity.) So members who were no longer with the Fall had written all of their best-known riffs and melodies, and then were later replaced with others who did the same. But Mark E. Smith said they shouldn't complain, that if past members were all so great then why hadn't they done anything as great after they left. For Mark E. Smith, himself plus anyone was the Fall. Or as he once notoriously put it: "If it's me and yer granny on bongos, it's the Fall."

I believe, or at least hope, that I'm a much gentler soul than Mark E. Smith was. (Or at least more Canadian. And I'm certain that I drink exponentially less.) But the evidence on the table shows that there are many who have worked with PME-ART in the past who no longer work with us. I certainly didn't fire them, but perhaps there were some who wanted to continue further than they did. Or maybe, on the other hand, they really, really didn't. I don't actually know. Over the years there have not been many conversations along these lines. In one sense, this is simply our roots showing: we are structured like an (experimental) theatre company that works with creator/performers on a project-to-project basis. We invite people to work with us on a specific project and then see how it goes. But most of the work is so highly collaborative that this way of explaining the structure never feels completely right to me. I do gravitate toward the idea of "projects," artistic endeavours with a beginning, middle, and end (as one can see from the way this book is structured). And, at times, I have also felt that me and anyone (and yer granny on bongos) is PME-ART. But most of the time I realize just how untrue this actually is.

(Perhaps all of this also reflects a decision semi-made all those years ago, after sitting in on the Forced Entertainment rehearsals, when I asked them if we should stick with the same people or open up to new collaborators. But it also seems to be a decision I am continuously making and unmaking. I can't quite let it rest one way or the other.)

The story we tell in *The DJ Who Gave Too Much Information* about Pavement has to do with their final concert before they broke up (and also a few years before they once again reformed). The lead singer, Stephen Malkmus, walked onstage wearing handcuffs, holding his cuffed hands high above his head, and said: "If you want to know what it feels like to be in a band, this is what it feels like to be in a band."

But there are also two stories about Pavement that I've never told in the show. The first is about how, after Pavement broke up, I read an interview with Malkmus in which he said that Pavement was basically all him: he wrote all the songs, wrote all the guitar parts, and often had to teach the rest of the band the songs several times before they were able to properly play them. (In their early days Pavement recorded a number of songs that were a bit too obviously influenced by the Fall.) Malkmus has now released a number of solo albums (some with his new band, the Jicks) that, in my humble opinion, are nowhere near as good as anything he made with Pavement. So the other members of Pavement clearly must have been contributing a great deal. (Also, to give Malkmus the benefit of the doubt, that was just one interview, maybe he was having a bad day.)

The second untold Pavement story is more apocryphal. I believe my favourite Pavement record is *Wowee Zowee*, made while they were still high off their first somewhat mainstream success, *Crooked Rain, Crooked Rain*, and its single "Cut Your Hair." *Wowee Zowee* was their most experimental and adventurous album, pushing in different directions with every track while still holding it all together. It was also a relative flop. And I feel they were overly stung by its reception. After that they were less likely to take risks, more likely to play it safe. Somehow I've had analogous experiences with PME-ART. Some of our most adventurous works (*Unrehearsed Beauty-Le Génie des autres, HOSPITALITY 3: Individualism Was A Mistake*) have also been the hardest to tour. I always need to push myself back toward taking artistic risks again. To remember that *Wowee Zowee* is still the best Pavement record and the world just needs to catch up.

These stories about Pavement and the Fall are perhaps ways for me to reflect on my different position within the group, within any given PME-ART creation process. How I am both one of the gang and the boss, and I suppose it's not really possible to be both. And yet that is the struggle of the work. The ethical/artistic struggle that can never entirely be solved. Since, at the same time, I'm never only in charge. Within a PME-ART process it is always possible for me to be outvoted or to change course based on the desires of the group. It's happened often. How to be transparent about my role within the collaborative dynamic? I often hate the lived experience of collaboration but somehow still so fiercely believe in it, knowing it would be so much better if it was the opposite: if I loved collaboration then I wouldn't even particularly need to believe in it.

(Marie Claire writes that, yes, within PME-ART the leadership is pretty clear, even though it is subject to discussion. But also, it was only through her learning *The DJ Who Gave Too Much Information* that she came to understand just how much Claudia and Caroline hold and lead the work with me. For the *HOSPITALITY/HOSPITALITÉ* series, this has been absolutely true.)

The story about Parenthetical Girls is one we used to tell in the show but for some reason don't anymore. When I saw the Parenthetical Girls play in Berlin there was one moment that will always stick with me. During a split-second pause in a song (I no longer remember which one) they all smoothly and effortlessly switched instruments. The drummer stepped over his drum kit and slid into the guitar strap that was held open for him, as the guitarist stepped over to the keyboard, the keyboard player was handed the bass, and the bass player sat down behind the drums without missing a beat. Or at least that's how I remember it. This is also a story about collaboration, about those ecstatic moments when it really works, all the pieces sliding together without a hitch. I wonder how many times they had to rehearse it before it worked, or if it happened that smoothly every night. A moment of grace that can only be achieved through fully working together. (This actually isn't the kind of thing I usually like in performance. Too virtuosic for my tastes. But in this case it caught me off guard and lodged in my memory accordingly.)

Another story about Parenthetical Girls. In 2016 I had a residency in their hometown of Portland, Oregon. And, while there, I would tell everyone I met that I loved the band. And everyone responded that they knew frontman Zac Pennington, or one of the other members, but no one had ever seen them live or listened to any of their records. (Parenthetical Girls put on a phenomenal live show.) As someone said to me: "Of course I know Zac. He's really good at karaoke. Is his band any good?" As the French expression goes: you can never be a prophet in your own village.

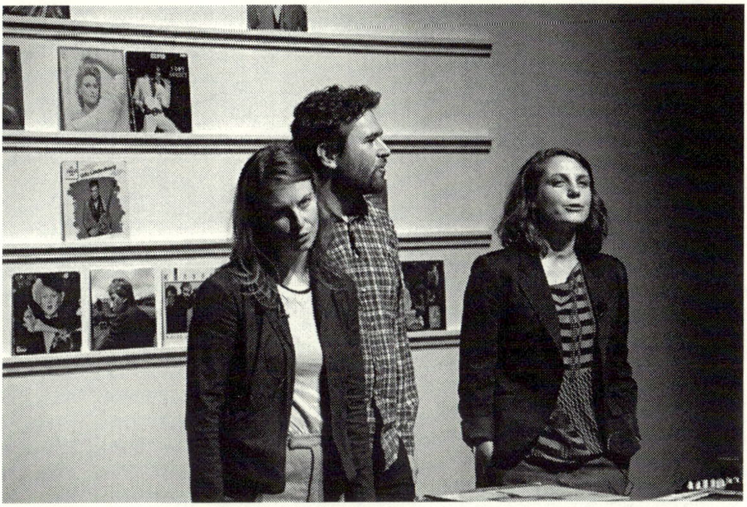

Caroline Dubois, Jacob Wren, and Claudia Fancello in *The DJ Who Gave Too Much Information* at La Triennale québécoise-Musée d'art contemporain de Montréal. Photo: Mathieu Chartrand

When we performed at Curtain Razors in Regina, Saskatchewan, after the show and the listening party, we had a day off. Michele Sereda, who had invited us, said she would take us to a round dance that night. (I'm embarrassed to admit I can no longer remember the name of the community.) I had never been to anything like that before and had almost no idea what to expect. I want to write about this experience but, to be honest, I don't know enough about what I witnessed to be sure I will write about it without being unintentionally offensive. It was in October 2013. We drove for about thirty or forty minutes to get there. Outside the low building was a bonfire with a few people smoking and a dog wandering around them (there might have been more than one dog). Inside was a large room that reminded me of a high-school gym, which it might have actually been. Michele instructed us to sit with her in the chairs against the far wall. Claudia was with us and one other person who I no longer quite remember. (Caroline was off with her brother, who had driven several hours to see our show for the first time.) In the car on the way up, Michele told us that she wouldn't be participating in the dance tonight because she was menstruating, but if we wanted we were allowed to join in. I don't think we did.

At the far end of the room, on a raised platform, were two callers with microphones who announced what would happen next. They were also surrounded by prizes for a raffle, which were given away occasionally throughout the night. In the centre were different performers, groups of singers with drums. They would lead one or two dances and then the next singers would replace them, the callers announcing the transitions. Everyone else in the room danced around the performers in a large circle, always with the same side-to-side step. People would join and leave the dance in the most casual way I have ever seen.

Shortly after we arrived, one of the callers announced: "We have some guests with us here tonight, can you go see who they are." We were the guests. I had no idea to what extent we were or were not invited, or what our role was there. As far as I could tell, we were the only non-indigenous people in the room. Someone came over and Michele explained to them who had invited us and who she was and, though I didn't hear everything she said, it all seemed to be all right. Michele had been doing a project with artists from this community but I now can't remember exactly what she told me about it.

Sitting there against the wall, in a folding chair in a long row of folding chairs, listening to the drums and listening to the singing, watching everyone move in and out of the dance, I had a feeling that also didn't seem quite right to me: that this was what I'd always been looking for in art. The way everyone could participate or not participate, how the dancing and singing and drumming was just going on in and around us, part of daily life, and at the same time we were all always part of it. (Well... I wasn't but everyone else seemed to be.) Since, of course, this wasn't only or even mainly art, it was culture in a larger sense. Much older yet very much in the here and now. I had a desire to take something from this experience and use it in my work and then immediately realized I couldn't, that it wasn't mine to take. There is such a long, disturbing history of modern/avant-garde Western artists experiencing various traditional forms and taking from them without permission. And yet I couldn't help but think: wasn't this related to what I've always been working on. A performative feeling of community where the performers were no different from the audience, where everyone knew the rules yet engaged with them in some way where the rules barely seemed to matter at all. I was of course watching all of this as an outsider and a settler. I had no idea what it was like for the others here who did this every week or every month. It seemed like a regular part of their lives.

A year and a half later Michele Sereda was in a car with Michael Green, Narcisse Blood, and Lacy Morin-Desjarlais. The car crashed into two other vehicles and they were all killed. They were driving to the Piapot First Nation community to discuss a project. I believe this was the same community where we went to see the round dance but I'm not sure, and the only person who can absolutely confirm it is now gone. An article about the tragedy in the *Globe & Mail* explains:

> Ms. Sereda had worked with the Piapot students for five years after establishing a drama program called *Spirit of the Story* with Nicole Crowe, a teacher and consultant based at the school. Ms. Morin-Desjarlais had recently joined the effort. Ms. Crowe had the gym set up for the presentation and became alarmed when she could not reach Ms. Sereda after 9:30 a.m. on Tuesday and heard about an accident on the highway.
>
> "Everything was set up and noon came around and I just waited in the front for their vehicle to pull in, just hoping that they were stuck in traffic and were on their way," said Ms. Crowe, who adds that the school did not open on

Wednesday because of the tragedy. "Our school is lost. She had a huge impact on our students."

I barely knew Michele Sereda, but the fact that she's now gone gives my memory of the round dance a different cast. It felt to me that she really wanted to take us there, wanted that experience to be part of our first visit to Saskatchewan. I feel she also wanted to encourage PME-ART to consider future collaborations with indigenous artists, which I hope someday will happen. I knew Michael Green more. He had presented *I Cut, You Bleed* at the High Performance Rodeo in Calgary in 1999 and I had seen him regularly ever since. So strange they were both in the same car. An old friend from 1999 and a new friend from 2013. So strange they're both now gone.

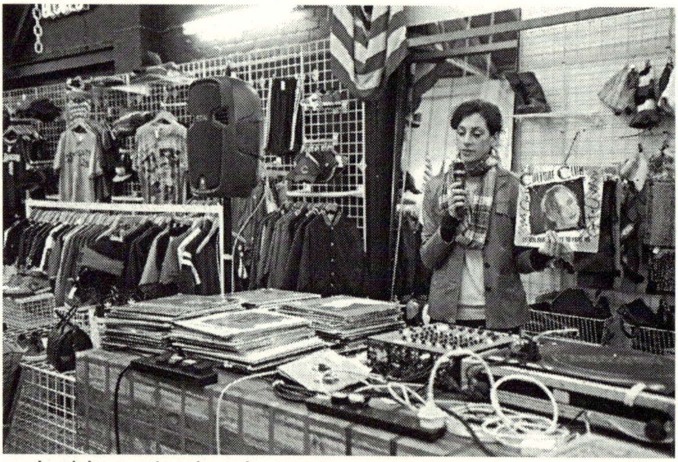

Marie Claire Forté at the *Bring Your Own Record/Listening Party* at the Fierce Festival in Birmingham. Photo: Meg Lavender

When we performed at the Fusebox Festival in Austin, Texas, the audience turned the last hour of *The DJ Who Gave Too Much Information* into a raging dance party. Thinking we were in their town and therefore should be doing it Austin-style, they rapidly cleared away the chairs, creating an impromptu dance floor. When each song finished they would all momentarily pause their dancing and attentively listen to the next story, and then when the next track kicked in they would resume dancing with renewed fervour.

We did our best to oblige by playing our most danceable records: Prince, the Jackson 5, Madonna, Donna Summer, I'm not sure what else, perhaps Erik B. & Rakim, Burial, or P. Diddy (whose "Let's Get Ill" featuring Kelis is an amazingly danceable house-flavoured rave-up). Afterwards we wondered if we had pandered to the crowd, if we had let them take over the show and use it for their own ends. But it's difficult to argue with a crowd that so enthusiastically wants to dance. I don't think we could have slowed them down even if we'd tried.

(Caroline reminds me that we were also invited by OFFTA to DJ at the Festival TransAmériques headquarters with our record collection. And that it was rather difficult to keep a dance floor going for a long time using only what we had. She remembers playing things twice and trying to explain to people making requests that all we had were our records from another project, a project that was about telling stories and not about keeping a dance floor alive, but surprisingly we managed to do it and it was okay.)

+ + + +

As I'm writing part two of this book, I sense such an intense shift from part one. And I think: this change is a change in my life. Everything now is allegedly more stable. Fewer things are being experienced for the first time. Touring is no longer an escape from the static claustrophobia of my early years but has become its own kind of stability (albeit a rather unstable one). These changes are my life today. When I left Berlin after *Der Tod in Rom*, when I left Brussels after *An Anthology of Optimism* – since I had spent more or less three years working in each city – I had such a strong feeling that I had made an entire life for myself and both times felt I was leaving those lives behind. Friends, institutions I was working within, places I went and could be found. And I suppose I was leaving them behind to return to PME-ART.

As I'm thinking all this through, I read a sentence in Carl Wilson's review of the Bruce Springsteen memoir: "Most celebrity memoirs fall apart in the second half, when the compelling origin and rise narrative is followed by the dull triumph and lists of charity works and award shows." Well... I'm not a celebrity and so far there are no charity works or award shows in my path. (Actually, this isn't even true: PME-ART was nominated for the 27th Conseil des arts de Montréal Grand Prix in the category of New Artistic Practices and I've also been nominated for a few literary prizes. But it's definitely not as exciting when you don't win. Or, since I've never won, I don't know. It's possible I would find it equally unexciting either way.)

It also feels completely insane to hear myself say that my life is now more stable, since all stability within the marginalized arts is built only on quicksand. But something has definitely shifted and if I try to articulate precisely what, it becomes increasingly clear: we can no longer in any way trade on some imagined future artistic potential. Whatever we are doing, good or bad, is what we are actually doing now. At times thinking this way also feels like a trap. A pressure to do what we already know and just do it better, rather than continue to venture into the semi-unknown, continue to surprise ourselves with unexpected risks. (*Wowee Zowee* is still the best Pavement record.) I am reminded of graffiti I once saw in the bathroom of the much-loved Montreal venue Sala Rosa: "Find your style before you sell out." And I just thought of some graffiti I might have written underneath: "Keep searching for your style long after you're washed up." Or to be more concise: "Keep searching."

+ + + +

Somewhere in the middle of *HOSPITALITY/HOSPITALITÉ*, Caroline moved to Manchester. For me, *HOSPITALITY/HOSPITALITÉ* was a project, a series of performances, made by Claudia, Caroline, and myself. Just before the project began, I had decided it was no longer a good idea to mix collaborators from Toronto and Montreal, as we had done with our first three projects, that logistically it made everything too difficult, and if we were going to continue we now had to focus on artists who lived in Montreal. I know there are other groups who work together from different cities, but I couldn't see how we could do it. (The fact that Caroline now had two young children in Manchester was definitely a factor in this not knowing. But I also realize it is not a good reason to do or not do anything.) So though we still continue to tour *The DJ Who Gave Too Much Information*, since Caroline moved away, the three of us haven't made anything new together.

In 2014, Claudia had a last-minute pizza party at her apartment to entertain a few visiting presenters and introduce them to Montreal artists. The following year we had a tour planned: Birmingham, Manchester, Bordeaux, Munich, and Cardiff. The tour was confirmed, and since Sylvie hadn't heard back from Claudia about the dates, we incorrectly assumed they were fine. (Sylvie reminds me that there was an earlier discussion about the dates for this tour in which the availability of Caroline was also uncertain.) At the pizza party, Claudia told us she was planning to open her own wine bar the following year and wouldn't be able to do the tour. The next day I panicked. (Sylvie feels I shouldn't take the blame alone as she was also part of this decision.) We had a tour that was mostly confirmed and grants we were already in the process of writing. I couldn't quite imagine the consequences if we were to cancel it all. Over the years, especially since Caroline moved, there had been off-and-on-again discussion about adding new people to *The DJ Who Gave Too Much Information*, and in principle everyone agreed the prospect was artistically intriguing. But because *HOSPITALITY/HOSPITALITÉ* had always been just the three of us, I seemed continuously hesitant to do so, to make the first steps in that direction. However, in my panic the day after the pizza party, all hesitation washed away. And that's how Adam Kinner and Marie Claire Forté were invited to join.

\+ + + +

To bring Adam and Marie Claire up to speed we came up with the idea of *The DJ Who Gave Too Much Information – Monthly Rework*. I suppose the first impulse must have been to do the show in a bar (La Vitrola) once a month for a year. After a year of learning and adding stories, we were sure that everyone would be on the same page. But before we could implement such a plan, Claudia announced that she wasn't leaving after all and suddenly the plan seemed considerably less pressing. Nonetheless, we still thought we should do something, so arbitrarily decided on four *Monthly*

*Reworks*, just to publicly welcome the new people in. After checking and rechecking everyone's schedule, it seemed only two were possible. So in the end the *Monthly Rework* happened twice.

The first was on a stormy Easter Monday. The weather outside was cold, wet, and awful – and it was a holiday Monday, a long weekend – so I was convinced no one would show up. I remember Sylvie and Richard were sick that day, so Mathieu and I did the load-in by ourselves. La Vitrola is on the third floor, and after an hour of carrying equipment up the three flights I felt so exhausted I could barely stand up. I was wet, drained, and seriously out of shape, and had a moment when I honestly questioned what I was doing with my life. Then I had a coffee, after which Claudia, Adam, and Marie Claire showed up and we went through the records one by one, holding them up like flash cards to refresh our memories. It would be the first time we had ever done the show without Caroline (we had already done it without Claudia in Birmingham, Manchester, and Bordeaux). At 7 p.m. there was only one person in the audience (the writer Mathieu Arsenault, slightly embarrassed he had shown up too early), and I was certain this *Monthly Rework* idea was turning out to be a disaster, but by eight it was starting to fill up and by nine we were bringing out more chairs for the relatively packed room.

I remember something so particular and special about that night. It was looser than usual, partly because Adam and Marie Claire were still learning as they went, but also because of the audience. We had performed in bars before, but never with such a warm, attentive, relaxed hometown crowd. People were drinking and talking during the songs but absolutely with us during the stories. And Adam and Marie Claire brought their own energies and insights to the work. They weren't doing anything so different from us and yet everything was different all at once. The magic of being yourself in a performance situation: with new people everything changes. I was also really drunk, having done my best to drink away the stress of the day, a fact I announced mid-show to laughter and applause. Because Adam and Marie Claire were still figuring it out, I also found myself (drunkenly) figuring it out anew, telling stories differently than I had told them before, surprising myself. Once again, like in the very beginning, at least for one night, I wasn't quite sure what I was doing.

\+ + + +

(Marie Claire says that one relevant difference between PME-ART and other ways of working might be, given the baseline engagement of the artists present, that there is no artistic right and wrong. Trying something new in performance and rehearsal always feels possible because even if a discussion ensues about this new thing, even if the new thing is deemed as not appropriate or right for the work, it is understood that it is appropriate and right for the work to try something new. And it is often the artists themselves who question their trials with the group, and the group supports the questioning. And we have changed our minds about things in both *The DJ Who Gave Too Much Information* and *Adventures can be found anywhere, même dans la mélancolie*.

Marie Claire goes on to say that perhaps she is not doing justice to how this value of holding questions, truly holding them without judgment, although still having strong aesthetic and ethical positions, is precious. She doesn't know if it is precious for art or just for her, and doesn't particularly care. She remembers after her first performance of *The DJ Who Gave Too Much Information* in Birmingham, at a party where an Austrian classical-theatre dude tried to make her feel bad for having been so visibly nervous and shaky, for nearly failing to put the paper sleeve back into the record cover because of her trembling. That he almost succeeded in making her feel bad, but not really, and especially not in retrospect, because she had been nervous, we were jetlagged, none of us had had coffee, there was a loud buffet in the same room, the conditions were horrible, and she really wanted to do a good job. Why not be visibly fucking nervous? She told a story and played a record. She cared. Why consider this a failure in any way?

She is still riddled with questions and self-doubt when working with PME-ART. But in a good way, because she holds these questions and self-doubt as valuable tools to consider what we are doing, not as a sign that we don't know what we are doing, or that I know but she doesn't.)

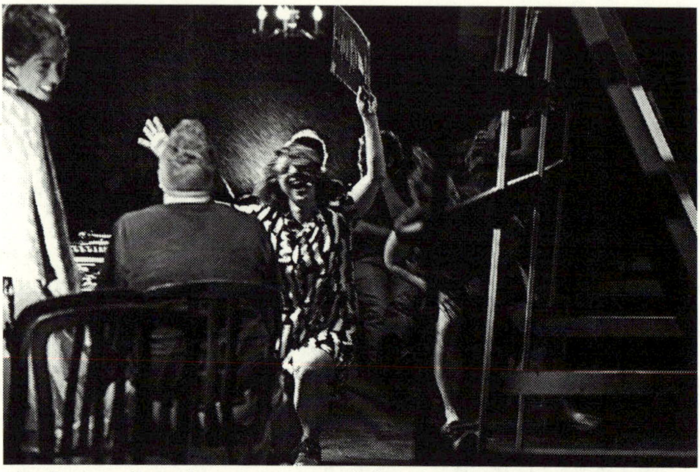

Claudia Fancello as the storm mounts during *The DJ Who Gave Too Much Information* at the Belluard Bollwerk festival in Fribourg. Photo: Tania El Khoury

In 2015 (the years are now getting closer to the present) we were invited to present *The DJ Who Gave Too Much Information* for a second time at OFFTA, as part of their Décalogue program celebrating the tenth anniversary of the festival. All of the Décalogue events took place outdoors at Place Émilie-Gamelin: a large concrete area, with long strips of greenery, taking up an entire city block. Around this time, many of us could not help but notice that the rapid transformation of Place Émilie-Gamelin into a space that featured performances, concerts, and art projects had the distinct feel of a top-down gentrification project. It seemed likely that the homeless people who had previously made use of the area, and considered it their own, also could not help but notice this fact.

It was an extremely windy day and, during the set-up, the shelves almost blew over. Then, while we were soundchecking, a record blew up from the turntable and hit me in the face. We had performed *The DJ Who Gave Too Much Information* outside twice before, but this time I wasn't entirely sure it was going to work. For the entire show record sleeves would blow off of the shelves and we would chase them out into the audience, like the wind was turning our show into some start-and-stop episode of *Keystone Kops*. There was something so stupidly comical about it all. Mathieu had anticipated the problem and had stapled thin strips of elastic across the front of each shelf to hold the records in place, but the elastic was not much of a match for the strong gusts of wind.

Several times colourful figures from the square would come in front of the stage and give their best dance routine, taking up as much attention as they could get. Watching them dance, I had such a strong sense that this was their place, and we were the gentrifying intruders. They were dancing wildly and eating up the imagined adoration of the crowd, and we were calmly telling stories and occasionally chasing record sleeves as they flew out of our hands. In the following weeks one audience member told me it was the best show they had ever seen us do, that the way we dealt with all the chaos that swirled around us was beautiful to behold. And another audience member told me they viewed it almost as a betrayal of the carefully balanced intimacy we had managed to create at La Vitrola. I've always thought of *The DJ Who Gave Too Much Information* as a show we could do anywhere, as a work that would respond to the specific challenges of each new situation. But chasing a record sleeve across Place Émilie-Gamelin – and with each time I thought I had it, it would once again fly just out of range – I had the suspicion this was a shade of "being myself in a performance situation" I wasn't entirely cut out for. (I can't run very fast.)

+ + + +

There was a storm announced for the night we were scheduled to perform at the Belluard Bollwerk festival in Fribourg. As I arrived at the venue, my first thought was that I hadn't previously realized the degree to which the roof was open. Once again we were performing (more or less) outside. The venue was a bit like a coliseum, round with an open circle of sky above. A large awning had been built to protect the stage from rain, and we were assured that many had performed there in difficult weather before. A moment before we started, I looked up and saw repeated flashes of ominous yet spectacular lightning, and then a few records into the show it began to rain. But the audience took out their umbrellas and stayed, and the stage remained dry, and I was just starting to feel like it was going to be a good show after all when it began to rain considerably harder. Asking the organizers what to do, we were told that if we wanted to we could keep going, so, after a brief consultation between the three of us, that's what we did. It continued to rain harder and harder, the rain turning gradually to hail, strong gusts of wind blowing rain and hail onto the stage. It was then suggested we could invite the audience onto the stage with us, and most of them climbed up, surrounding us, holding their umbrellas over the turntable to protect it, a beautiful act of community and participation.

It was also the day after the Brexit vote, the day after the U.K. had racistly voted to leave the European Union. Since Caroline had moved to Manchester, she would often tell a story about what it was like to live there and then play the song "England" by PJ Harvey. That night she talked about how upset she was by the results of the referendum and how she had witnessed increased acts of racism over the course of the Brexit campaign. And the moment the needle dropped onto the PJ Harvey track, the storm really started to build, almost perfectly in time to the mounting swell of the music, rain and hail slamming onto the stage, as if we were soundtracking the end of the world. The music and the storm and the recent Brexit vote all swirled up into some kind of tangled poetry. I couldn't quite believe it was happening or that it felt so much like part of our performance. Someone tapped me on the shoulder and pointed down. When I looked, the stage was quickly filling with water, the water rolling toward the electricity, toward the tangle of cables powering the sound. As PJ Harvey faded out we paused the show. Moments later the stage was full of technicians with mops and rags, clearing away the water as it fell. Half an hour later the storm had subsided. We finished the show for those brave and kind enough to stick around.

+ + + +

It is almost impossible for me to recognize it as such, but *The DJ Who Gave Too Much Information* somehow manages to achieve what

I've been aiming for, or toward, for the entire time I've been making performances. It's like meeting your doppelgänger in the street and being unable to recognize the resemblance. Is it really possible to achieve a goal that was never actually meant to be achieved? Probably not. But *The DJ Who Gave Too Much Information* does feel like some satisfying approximation that simultaneously, and unsurprisingly, raises more questions for me than it answers. What were these goals and how does *The DJ Who Gave Too Much Information* slide so freely in and around them? The balancing act between structure and spontaneity. A performance that is reinvented every single time we do it. A structure that makes room for everything, every kind of story and material. And such a wide range, such a varied spectrum, of ways to be yourself. It is a show that, in theory, could easily keep going forever. As we keep adding more records, more stories. (And, why not, also more people.)

My musical tastes have changed so much in recent years. I still like the Fall and Pavement, but think of them mainly as bands I listened to in my twenties. Tastes change over time. I don't know if I would have been as interested in *The DJ Who Gave Too Much Information* in my twenties as I am now. These days I listen mainly to hip hop, disco, soul, R&B, African reissues (I highly recommend the compilation *Brand New Wayo: Funk, Fast Times & Nigerian Boogie Badness 1979-1983*), the Japanese band Maher Shalal Hash Baz and the Colombian band Las Malas Amistades. Sometimes, when I now listen to the music that I listened to in my twenties, I simply find it too white. But I expect this will all change again, several times over, and at some point in the near or distant future it will all be mixed together, all the various periods of my musical listening life freely intertwining.

Come to think of it, in *The DJ Who Gave Too Much Information* all the various periods of my musical listening life *are* freely intertwined, placed on the shuffle setting of our collaborative game. Listening to music so often brings back memories, is related to youth, connects the present back to some earlier moment. I thought, in this chapter, of including more stories, stories about Frank Ocean, Lewis, Jean Leloup, Catherine Ribeiro + Alpes, the Fania All-Stars, Jeremy Jay, Bonnie "Prince" Billy, Annette Peacock, Paris, Talk Talk, Irma

Thomas, Mammane Sani et son Orgue, Fabulous Diamonds, etc. But, for me, writing these stories down doesn't nearly do them justice. Our performance has so much more to do with how the stories fall into relation with one another, with how they become different each and every time. Like most "being yourself in a performance situation," and like (I suppose) this book, it's all in the way you tell it. So much of its reality is contained in the intentional and unintentional intonations and suggestions of the voice. It's all in the telling. And in the music.

Nine:

# Every Song I've Ever Written

(2012–)

We performed it in:
Düsseldorf, Forum Freies Theater • Montreal, Usine C, Nuit Blanche, Phenomena Festival • Mannheim, Zeitraumexit/Wunder der Prärie Festival • Helsinki, Baltic Circle Festival • Malmö, Inkonst • Austin, Fusebox Festival • Toronto, Harbourfront Centre World Stage • Tokyo, Sound Live Tokyo • Montreal, La Chapelle Scènes Contemporaines/La Biennale de Montréal/Musée d'Art Contemporain/Actoral Festival • Stavanger, Rimi/Imir • Bergen, BIT Teatergarasjen/Meteor Festival

When I was young, at times, I felt certain about what I was going to do with my life: write songs and sing them for people. I was going to become Leonard Cohen. There was a time when this path felt so clear and then a later time when it felt less clear, until eventually, around the period I was starting to tour in Europe, I stopped writing songs altogether. When we're young we think our lives will be one way and then later they turn out differently.

Above my desk there is a hand-drawn diagram. Across the top of the page is the underlined title: "Diagram for a New Project." The diagram has four categories. Around each category is a circle and between each circle is a line with an arrow on each end. The project is clearly meant to move between all categories, equally in all directions. The categories are: The Internet, The Stage, The World, and Another Place. (This last category is rather vague, but I think in the end this "other place" turned out to be the songs I wrote when I was young.) This was an early note, a first impulse. How to move things from the Internet out into the world and back again?

By this point in my life, like many of us, I was spending all my time online. My addiction to social media was becoming a real problem. It is difficult for me to take this problem seriously but lately I've been trying. I got rid of my iPhone and am living with no Internet at home. (Also, after about ten years of being mainly nomadic, I signed a lease in 2013 and now have an apartment.) When I tell people I'm addicted to Facebook their first response is: so am I. But I feel my addiction is something else. I sit mesmerized by the screen so intensely I can't even get up to go to the bathroom. (I'm writing this now longhand in a notebook in a café in order to be as far away as possible from my computer.) I still don't know what to do about this situation, how to break the addiction or how much I actually have to, but at the time I made the diagram I definitely felt we needed to find ways to make the Internet more part of our work.

\+ + + +

*Every Song I've Ever Written* is a project with four parts:

1. A Website where you can listen to and download the fifty-eight songs I wrote between ages fourteen and twenty-nine. (Also record your own version, send it to us, and we'll put it on the site.)

2. A Solo Performance where I play all the songs in chronological order. (It takes over five hours, and I get more and more tired the older my songwriting self gets, a tiredness related to aging, which has also been my experience in life.)

3. A Karaoke Night where anyone can get up and sing the songs. (Even if they've never heard them before.)

4. A Band Night in which five local bands get up and perform one of my teenage songs each. (And I interview them about songwriting and the Internet after they do so.)

It seems to me that *Every Song I've Ever Written* is most interesting if you think of all four of its parts together. Which is strange, since few experience all four. But the more we've done it, the more I've come to understand that even experiencing one of the parts will be considerably more intriguing if you're aware of the existence of the other three. That they're out there somewhere and what you're watching is only one part of a larger whole.

\+ + + +

The very first Solo took place in Düsseldorf at the Salon des Amateurs, a long, narrow bar connected to the Kunsthalle. I remember feeling that I had no idea if I could make it to the end of all fifty-eight songs without losing my voice. (I made it.) Every time I do the Solo, so many memories flash through my mind, and as I become more exhausted the memories become more fluid and exhausted as well. So many things I haven't thought about for years. Between songs I often mention these flashes, describe them to the best of my ability. Writing songs about relationships before I'd ever been in a relationship, and imagining such never-experienced relationships only as horrible. Buying polyester shirts and not realizing why I was sweating so much, not knowing it was the synthetic qualities of the fabric that were to blame. Discovering Serge Gainsbourg and realizing that songs could actually be that dirty. Or discovering Brecht/Weill and realizing songs could be catchy and more political because of it.

About six months later I'm back in Düsseldorf for the first ever Band Night. A few weeks before, one of the performers had dropped out because his child went into the hospital. I remember reading the email and feeling so incredibly sad about the situation, about the wellbeing of the child, which made no sense because I had never met the musician and had certainly never met his child. I guess I had already begun to feel a connection simply through listening to his music non-stop. So the plan was to have five bands, but we were unable to find a last-minute replacement, so in the end we only had four: Fragil, Kreidler, Niobe and PDR. The day of the show I sat in the dressing room during sound check, occasionally poking my head into the theatre. I hadn't heard any of their versions yet and had absolutely no idea what to expect. But, one by one, one cover version at a time, I was reassured. They had each done something so different from each other, and so different from anything I might have expected. That had been my original hope for the project. I had no idea if it could possibly work and now it was happening. Afterwards, we all went out for drinks and I began to understand how difficult it had been for the bands, how some of them had struggled with the invitation, struggled to understand my most basic intentions. Why was I even asking them to do this? As the project progressed, we would need to make it clearer.

During the Solo at Zeitraumexit in Mannheim, a pattern emerged that would later recur. Word got around that I was playing all my songs, that it would take five hours, and that I was unsure whether or not I could make it to the end. So into my fourth hour the crowd started to increase, all coming to find out if I'd make it. I was surprised how different the second ever Band Night in Mannheim (with Ape Diem, the Alicka Problem, Betina, callahaan, and Hans Reffert) felt from the first one. I wondered if I had gotten better at the interviews, if I was starting to figure out how to do them, or if the bands were simply more honest and forthcoming this time around. Because the bands were so different in each place, I was starting to feel there would be no way to learn from, or prepare for, the differences. The structure was exactly the same, yet each Band Night felt like a different show. We had gotten away with it the first two times, but there was no guarantee it would continue to work.

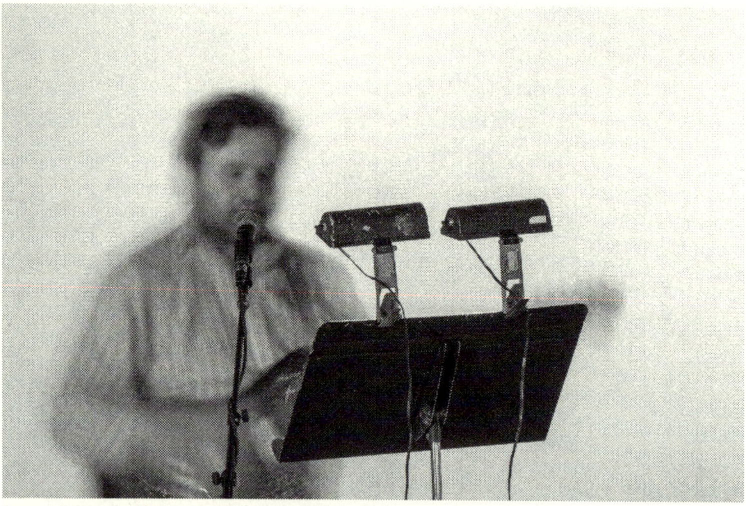

Jacob Wren in the *Every Song I've Ever Written Solo* at the Power Plant in Toronto. Photo: Brian Medina/Harbourfront Centre

Perhaps the best Band Night we've had so far was at the Baltic Circle festival in Helsinki (with Tiiu Helinä, Kanerva, Kap Kap, Samuli Putro, and Tundramatiks). I keep asking myself: what made it work so well? And I believe it had a great deal to do with our musical coordinator, Janne Masalin (whose band Tundramatiks was also part of the night). Something about the precise way the invitation was made to each of the bands, the care that was taken in doing so. As we progressed through more and more Band Nights, what became most important in this invitation was the idea of "extra-freedom." That each band should take extra-freedom with their cover of my teenage song. That, if they wanted, they could change the lyrics, change the melody, remake it in their own image or in any other way they saw fit. What did it mean to say that a song was a cover version of another song in the light of this extra-freedom, if neither the lyrics nor the melody were the same? Sometimes I would say: what would it mean to say "God Save the Queen" was a cover version of "I Want to Hold Your Hand"? Sometimes I would point out that there are different songs that have the same chords, in almost the same order, and yet we still think of them as completely different songs.

There was one particular moment during the set-up in Helsinki that really sent the night spinning in the right direction. My original idea was that Kap Kap would play last. They were the most people onstage, and rocked out hard, so it felt like the natural, high-energy way to finish. However, when we were all talking through the order, it turned out that one or two of their members had another gig that night and had to leave early, so they asked if they could play earlier. As a spontaneous, in-the-moment decision, I suggested that Samuli Putro would go last instead. Samuli really wasn't sure this was a good idea. What he had planned was to stand alone onstage and recite a poem based only very loosely on one of my songs. He wondered if a poem to end the night would be too anticlimatic. I wasn't at all certain I was making the right call but decided to stick with my first impulse. The venue Ääniwalli was a skate park during the day that sometimes had concerts at night, and I remember all day skateboarders practicing jumps and tricks on the far side of the room as we sound-checked. Somehow Samuli's poem ended the Band Night perfectly. He spoke in Finnish, so I still don't know what he said, but the audience was so incredibly there with him, as I watched them, some of them even crying. He was riffing off my song "The Place & Time" and its chorus: "I used to be famous." And Samuli had actually been famous, had hit songs in Finland when he was younger, songs that everyone in the audience (except for me) knew and some knew by heart. Whatever he said in Finnish about having once been famous must have struck some chord of truth, reflected a reality of the situation, and of his life, that everyone present recognized. Or at least that's how it seemed to me at the time. But, then again, listening to languages I don't understand always creates a certain sense of imagination and possibility.

For the Band Night, the last band isn't actually the end of the show. We then call everyone back onstage to all play together, attempt a version of my song "The Broken Throat." Four different singers sing one verse and chorus each, their trading off reflecting a repeated line from the chorus: "I will be replaced, I will be replaced, I will be replaced." And in being generous enough to cover one of my old, unknown songs, each of these bands is also somehow replacing me, turning my entirely forgotten song into something else, into something I can fantasize I might have written if, when I was much younger, I'd had any real musical talent, instead of only a way with words.

\+ + + +

And then, just as *Every Song I've Ever Written* was beginning to build up steam, *The Project That Didn't Happen* (see next chapter) appeared in our lives and for a while took over everything. *Every Song I've Ever Written* was partly put on the backburner and when we returned to it in earnest, almost three years later, it felt like we'd lost considerable momentum. I think this is the major lesson I've learned over the past five years. Never put your own already-in-progress project aside in order to dedicate yourself to someone else's not-yet-begun project. However, I now think there was probably quite a bit more going on than that. I had been feeling ashamed to be onstage with my old songs, in a sense implicitly admitting the degree to which I had once wanted to be a rock star (of the singer/songwriter variety) and therefore somehow also admitting how completely I had failed. In fact, I hadn't even tried. When *The Project That Didn't Happen* came along, it represented an opportunity to put this shame aside for a while. Perhaps this was the real reason I jumped into the new project with such fervour. Jumping out of the (imagined) trap I was in, into another trap that of course turned out to be the (much more real) proverbial fire.

\+ + + +

So basically nothing for three years and then Austin and then Toronto. A strange, stressful gap in the middle of a project. The unnerving feeling of trying to pick it up again. Sylvie and Richard came with me to Austin. It was extremely rare to have them both on the road at the same time. We were put up in a gigantic guest house overlooking a river. Richard took someone else's suitcase from the airport conveyor belt, instead of his own, and had to go back to the airport to make the switch. Somehow the Austin Band Night (with Foot Patrol, the Octopus Project, Leticia Rodriguez, UME, and Francine Thirteen) and the Austin Karaoke are both a blur in my memory. I remember the bands were all really good. I remember feeling nervous again, wondering if I'd still remember how to do it after such a long break.

I thought Toronto would feel like a homecoming but it didn't. Two days before I get on the train to Toronto, I walk into a wall in my apartment and fracture my middle toe. I wonder if we should cancel the shows but don't really feel I have the right to cancel just because I've broken a toe. It's literally been years in the planning. I'm definitely not tough, but try to convince myself I'm tough enough to perform songs for five hours on a broken toe. In the days leading up to the Solo, I tell myself that this time I'll have to do it sitting down, but when the time comes, I can't. It's a performance I've always done standing and to do it seated feels wrong. I have no idea why. Is it only habit? But playing guitar seated feels like an old fogey in a coffee house. (My apologies to anyone out there playing seated for any reason and pulling it off.) *Every Song I've Ever Written* is definitely a project about getting older, but it seems I didn't want to hit that nail on the head too directly, even if – limping around on my broken toe at the Power Plant – I seemed to be portraying some kind of physicality of aging like never before.

Toronto didn't feel like a homecoming because there were so few people I knew in the audience. And the people I did know were people I had met more recently. And because the bands (Above Top Secret, Maylee Todd, Phèdre, Regina of Light Fires, and Snowblink) – expertly chosen by musical coordinator Victoria Cheong – somehow represented a new Toronto, a Toronto that began long after I left. The Toronto I grew up in doesn't exist anymore. Or perhaps it's still there, faded into the background. Or perhaps, when I fled twenty years ago, I simply didn't stay in touch, and as the years have rolled forward I've lost touch even more. Returning to the city where I wrote most of the songs, and playing them there again after all these years, on a broken toe, felt almost like I could have been performing anywhere. A full circle in which, by the time I get to the end, the beginning no longer remembers me.

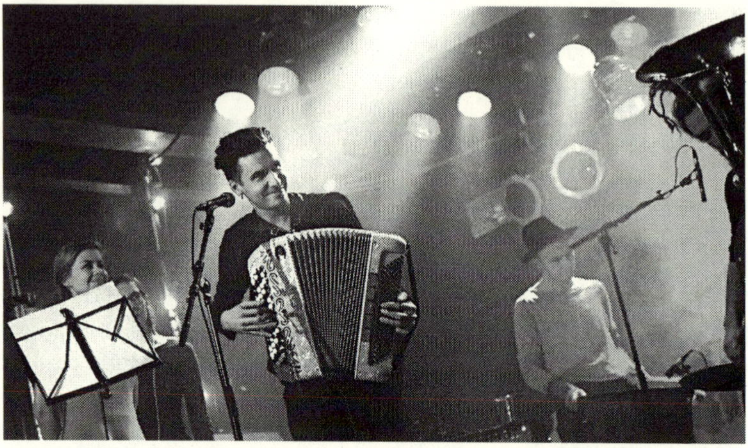

Kanerva, Tiiu Helinä, Janne Masalin, and Samuli Putro onstage together for the last song as part of the *Every Song I've Ever Written Band Night* at Baltic Circle in Helsinki. Photo: Tani Simberg

Because of *Every Song I've Ever Written*, there are now many pictures of me on the Internet playing, or simply holding, a guitar. And I really wish there weren't. Yet this embarrassment is also at the heart of the project. The other day someone told me they remembered something they'd heard me say on the radio a long time ago, that I had said I was into "an aesthetics of awkwardness." And they then asked me if this was still the case. This repeated image of a middle-aged man holding a guitar seems so horribly outmoded and misguided to me now. A few days ago I read this passage in an essay by Tegan O'Neil:

> Rock 'n' roll lingered because a powerful demographic decided it would accompany them through the world for the duration of their lives. It probably reached the end of its natural lifespan some time ago, but lingers in permanent attrition. The music now looks inward and tacitly accepts a senescence of diminished expectations juxtaposed against consistent technical refinement. It was born as the plaything of the boomers and it falls into eclipse just as the boomers' grip on cultural production has finally gone limp. Rock 'n'

roll is no longer quite so important as it had been, or perhaps more accurately, it is no longer quite so important as it had believed, and grows less important by the day.

That's how I feel when I see a photograph of myself holding a guitar, that I've turned into an image of myself "finally gone limp." But then I remember how much I still love to sing.

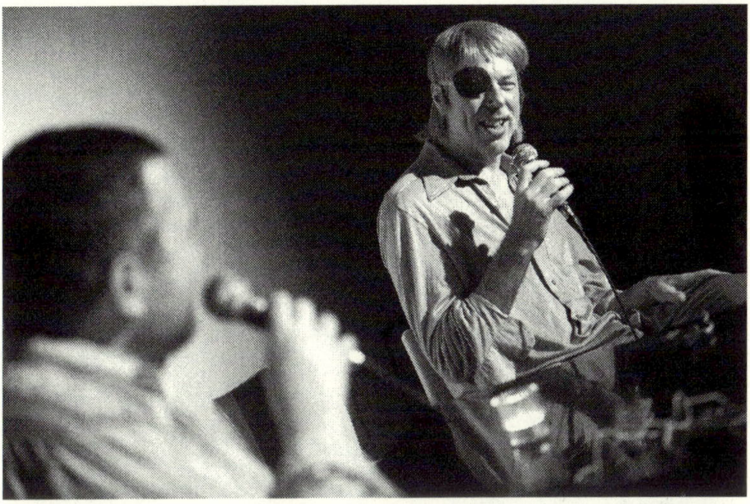

Jacob Wren interviewing Momus in the *Every Song I've Ever Written Band Night* at Sound Live Tokyo in Japan. Photo: Hideto Maezawa

By the time I'm in Japan for *Every Song I've Ever Written* I'm already more than halfway through writing this book, so as interesting things are happening to me, each time I find myself thinking: that's going in the book. The thing I still cannot completely believe is that I flew from Canada to Japan for only three days. That I was in Tokyo for only three days before I flew back. When I think back to having done this, I tell myself it's time to seriously rethink how I'm living. In Tokyo, much like my previous visits but this time considerably worse, I'm so jetlagged I can barely stand up. Tomoyuki Arai, who invited us to the festival Sound Live Tokyo, wanted to do the Band Night a little bit differently. Instead of five bands playing one song each, he wanted each band (Momus, Reiko Kudo, Maher Shalal Hash Baz, and the Hardy Rocks) to do a full set of my songs, to play for about forty-five minutes.

Another significant difference from other Band Nights is that, for the first time, I have history with three of the bands. This is what I wrote for the Sound Live Tokyo website:

> I can't remember how long ago it was now when I walked into the Montreal record store Phonopolis and, over the sound system, heard a record I absolutely loved. The album was *Rice Field Silently Riping in the Night* by Reiko Kudo. It is an album I have come back to again and again. Not a year goes by in which I don't listen to it at least a few times, and often many more.
>
> Around that time, I wrote to Hiromi Maruoka to ask her if she'd also heard it. I was surprised when she wrote back suggesting an artistic collaboration between Tori Kudo and myself. I was already in the process of listening to absolutely everything I could find by both Tori and Reiko. The owner of Phonopolis was also obsessed with their music so it was possible for me to get almost everything they'd put out.
>
> From January 24 to February 23, 2012, I went to Matsuyama and Kochi to begin working with Tori and figure out what we might do together. Tori suggested we begin by making pottery, something that not only had I never done but in fact had never even considered. Over a month I got to know Tori a little bit and we made some things. I have previously written that "all the artists I admire are such a strange combination of completely open and completely stubborn," and Tori might be the perfect example of this phenomenon. (Of course, the same might be said about me.)
>
> The music of Maher Shalal Hash Baz represents for me the perfect balance between structure and freedom, between pure music and impure anarchy. Tori's complex, and at times self-defeating, virtuosity meets the energizing non-virtuosity of so many different band members over such an expanse of years, each member twisting the project ever-so-slightly in their own direction. It is classical pottery full of spirited cracks, with the cracks built in, pushing forward and re-

treating against the pure timeless spirit of rock 'n' roll and glorious punk.

Reiko Kudo's music feels, to me, timeless in a different, perhaps deeper, sense. Timeless like dust. Like gold dust. Fragile melodies from multiple other worlds. You can hear Tori's anarchy informing the background and yet it is clear that Reiko is so precisely and delicately in charge. I of course don't understand Japanese so I often don't know what she's singing. But like the very best singers, somehow I do know what she's singing because I imagine I can feel it through and against the limits of language.

I do of course know what Momus is singing. More so than with most singers, because I have so many of his old songs memorized or almost memorized, like they have been with me from almost before I was born. There was a period of my life – the period I wrote many of the songs from *Every Song I've Ever Written* – when I listened to Momus every day. There were many, many days I listened to nothing else. With Momus I imagined the pop song as a literary novel, the pop song as a philosophical tract, the pop song as perverse *détournement* of everything else that wasn't a song by Momus.

And speaking of a perverse *détournement*: in Tokyo it is very possible we will have Momus performing the songs I wrote twenty-five years ago, which were, at the time, almost completely inspired by Momus. (But then again, he might also choose different songs.) My teenage self could have never imagined things coming full circle in quite this way. A story of time travel that is almost, but not quite, worthy of a Momus song.

I don't think I was able to do justice to just how obsessed I had been with Momus when I was a teenager. Or, for that matter, what it was really like to spend a month with Reiko and Tori doing pottery in Matsuyama. These are both such complex experiences they each almost require their own separate book. Momus did in fact choose songs other than the ones that were most inspired by him, which only made me realize how even the songs that weren't directly inspired by Momus were still very much inspired by him. Perhaps even, paradoxically, the songs I had written before I discovered his work.

I passed through the Tokyo Band Night in an exhausted, dreamlike haze. Watching these Japanese legends perform full sets of my songs was the kind of thing one might literally dream. And Momus doing so increased that feeling exponentially. Maher Shalal Hash Baz didn't actually play any of the songs. They projected all fifty-eight song titles on a screen behind them and did a one-minute performance for each. There were, I believe, over fifty of them onstage. I think we can agree this is also rather dreamlike. And then, during the interview, all fifty members repeated Tori's answers to each of my questions, sentence by sentence, in unison. By the end of the almost five-hour show, when it was finally time to interview my teenage idol Momus, I could barely keep my severely jetlagged eyes open. I think I did all right but I have no idea what I said.

\+ + + +

What I remember most about the weeks leading up to *Every Song I've Ever Written* in Montreal is that Nadia Ross won the Siminovitch Prize for directing, an annual Canadian prize worth $100,000. As I wrote at the time: things I never imagined would happen in a million years keep happening. It somehow undid so many of my assumptions about what was and was not possible in Canadian theatre. I still can't quite believe she won, but of course it was absolutely deserved. (Nonetheless, jealousy is a normal part of being an artist.)

Thinking about it now, I flashback to a conversation I had with Sven Åge Birkeland (in case you've lost track, the first person to invite me to Europe back in 1997). I might be misplacing it, but I think this conversation took place in Bergen while we were there performing *An Anthology of Optimism*, so that makes it sometime around 2009. And, as usual, I was in crisis, and I asked Sven for advice, if he had any advice for me about how I should proceed. Sven replied he thought we should find a way to merge PME-ART with STO Union, that the two companies should grow together and combine our respective artistic strengths. At the time, I found this advice almost offensive, since I read into it a subtext that my work should become more theatre. I suppose I had always thought of STO Union as similar to PME-ART, but a more "theatre" version, with scripts and actors. But a few months later I thought back and realized there was something petty about my reaction. I had asked Sven for advice and then felt resentful when he gave me an honest answer. Nonetheless, it was advice I was not able to take. Looking back on that moment I can see how, at times, black and white my thinking can be: there is theatre and not theatre, and everyone on the circuit is trying to drag my work toward the theatre side of the equation. And yet there is also a certain truth to this cartoon version, or at least that's what I tell myself and what keeps me pulling so hard in the opposite direction. At least when I'm feeling strong.

I no longer think of STO Union's work as being particularly more theatre than what I do, especially the work they've done after I stopped collaborating with them. Shows like *7 Important Things* and *What Happened to the Seeker*, made with people – non-actors – in Wakefield, have such a genuine sense of reality. But, paradoxically, I have a feeling that such reality couldn't have fully emerged until I left, that it came out of Nadia being unsure how to continue and then making full use of what was at hand. (She had long ago moved to the small Quebec town of Wakefield and has since moved to the even smaller town of Farrellton, where she makes work on a different basis from anyone else I know.)

+ + + +

The Karaoke at MAC Nocturne was also (positively) unexpected. The Nocturne is a monthly event in which the Musée d'art contemporain de Montréal stays open late into the night with DJs, drinking, and performances. We were one of the performances, and I was extremely surprised how many people got up to sing songs they had never heard before in their lives, and how every single person who did so basically got a standing ovation from the very packed room. As well, there were so many people getting up to sing who I felt had never been at a PME-ART show before, who felt to me like non-artists coming to the museum for a fun night out, and yet were completely game to join in, many of them genuinely beautiful singers. It felt like an experience of performing in Montreal unlike most of the others, a party made deeply uncanny by the bleak and philosophical nature of the songs and the "aesthetics of awkwardness" forced upon those generous enough to get up and sing them, an experience as new for them as it felt for me.

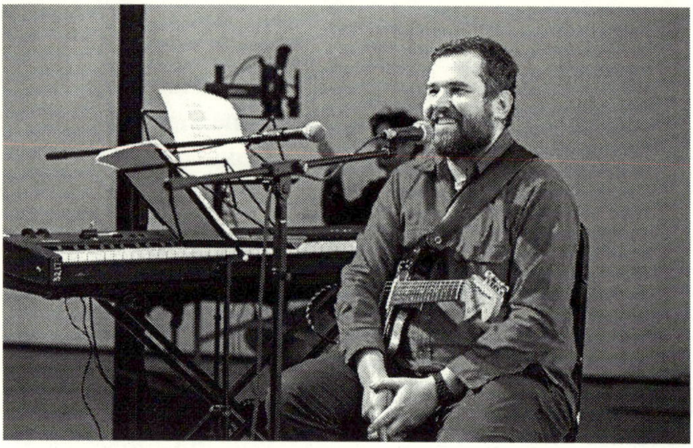

Jacob Wren in the *Every Song I've Ever Written Karaoke* at the Musée d'art contemporain Nocturne as part of at La Biennale de Montréal. Photo: Sébastien Roy

There was a full-page article about *Every Song I've Ever Written* in the Montreal newspaper *Le Devoir*. And in trying to describe how I was using my own songs as readymades, how I was using whatever I had around me in my work, I quipped: "Duchamp has his urinal and I have my songs." And I really regret saying this. Because just a few weeks previously I had been reading about how Marcel Duchamp actually didn't have his urinal at all. How *Fountain* was in fact a work that his friend, the artist Baroness Elsa von Freytag-Loringhoven, had sent to him as a gift, and how Duchamp then displayed it as his own. So the story of the urinal was yet another story of a more famous male taking credit, and therefore erasing, the work of a less famous female contemporary. It would have been so much better if I had mentioned these facts alongside my pithy Duchamp-related quip but unthinkingly I did not.

+ + + +

For the Band Nights in Montreal (with the Besnard Lakes, Mozart's Sister, Elena Stoodley, J. Ellise Barbara, and Catherine Valéry), it was the first time we had performed three nights in a row with the same bands. This wasn't my idea but I had agreed, agreed a bit too spontaneously during a meeting with the venue La Chapelle, still unsure if it would work. For me the Band Night had always been an event, gaining a certain intensity from the fact that these five bands would only be onstage together for one night and one night only. In Montreal, on each successive Band Night, during the interviews, the bands got more and more comfortable with me, grew more bold. Sylvie and Richard thought this was a good thing but I wasn't so sure.

During the second show, J. Ellise Barbara came over for the interview and started by announcing that Leonard Cohen had died. A friend who was in the audience later told me that the expression on my face, hearing that Leonard Cohen was gone, live in front of an audience, was one of the strangest things she had ever seen. It was strange how it struck me in that moment, that (all my talk of Momus aside) Leonard Cohen so was clearly at the root of my original desire to write songs. A poet who had become a songwriter, whose songs were so intensively about the words. An example that literature could be beloved. As one would expect, I had discovered Leonard Cohen years before I heard of Momus. And Cohen was Canadian. And was from Montreal. The fact that he existed had everything to do with my teenage sense of life, art, and possibility. The fact that I learned of his passing in the middle of *Every Song I've Ever Written* in Montreal once again brought the project magically full circle. It seems to be a project that takes me round and then around again, all the seeds of my later life all-too-intensely present in the words of the songs I wrote when I was just starting, when I had absolutely no idea what was to come.

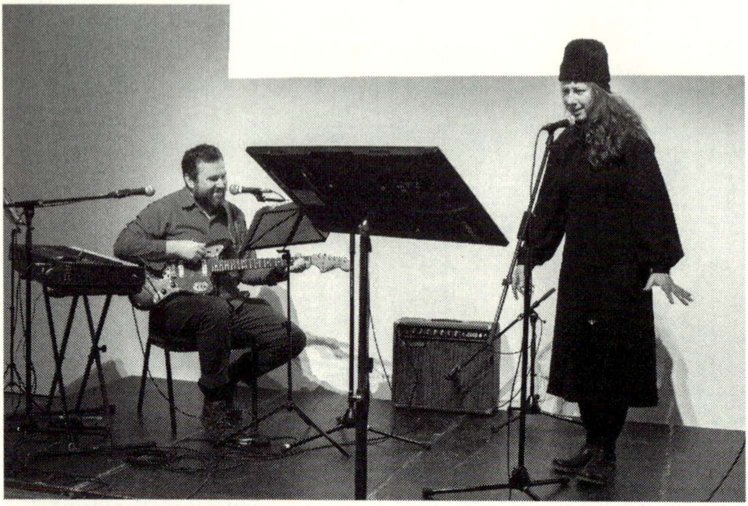

Jacob Wren and Sylvie Cotton in the *Every Song I've Ever Written Karaoke* at the Musée d'art contemporain Nocturne as part of at La Biennale de Montréal. Photo: Sébastien Roy

And now it's October 2017 and I'm on a plane from Norway back home to Montreal. It's been twenty years since I first went to Bergen and I've just been again. This should be the end of the book, ending more or less where it began (I'm supposed to deliver it in a little over a month), but because we're now doing at least three projects at the same time, all the timelines overlap and intersect, so events in the next chapter happened before what I'm writing about now. (In fact, the events in the next chapter happened almost four years ago. While what I'm writing about now happened over the past ten days.) In Stavanger and Bergen we performed *Every Song I've Ever Written*, and next year we'll perform *The DJ Who Gave Too Much Information* at the music festival Suoni Per Il Popolo (once again trying to do every single record and story, let's see if we actually make it this time) and shortly thereafter we'll premiere a new project, in some ways based on this very book, entitled *A User's Guide to Authenticity Is a Feeling*.

In Bergen I caught up with Forced Entertainment in the festival bar. They're still all working together, now for thirty years and counting. I think of the advice I took from them – to not keep working with only the same people, but instead regularly open the work up to new collaborators – and how such advice is actually the exact opposite of how they live and work, of who they are. They are like a family who have remained loyal to one another while I am now very far away from anything resembling such a model. Or perhaps Sylvie, Richard, and I are the family and others are simply fellow travellers that roll along with us for a while before getting on with their lives.

Performing the Solo twice in three days, first in Stavanger and then in Bergen, was, for obvious reasons, pretty much twice as exhausting as doing it only once. Completely exhausting. I notice now that each time I do it I build more of an overall narrative into the five hours. How at the beginning, starting at age fourteen, I was simply trying to teach myself to write songs, felt good if I managed to finish a song at all, often imitating other artists as I discovered them (Leonard Cohen, Nick Cave, Brecht/Weill, Momus, Will Oldham, Cat Power, Bill Callahan, Vic Chestnut, Pavement, Pulp, Serge Gainsbourg, Hefner, etc.). Then there was a period when I tried to break away from these influences and find my own thing, though in retrospect I can see the influences still dominated. Then a period when I realized I wasn't actually going to dedicate my life to writing and playing songs, when I tried to quit songwriting altogether but found I couldn't, writing songs in secret, not working on them very much. Then a period when I really gave up, when I barely wrote songs at all, only one or two slipped through the cracks because I somehow couldn't help myself. In this narrative, I have the feeling that my songs started to get better when I gave up, when I stopped trying. (Someone said this to me in Bergen.) I'm also not sure how true this narrative is. I don't think I saw things this way at the time. Surveying a period of my life that lasted about fifteen years, and doing so in five hours, compacts everything in ways that are bound to distort it.

Watching the show *Vive la Phrance* by Spreafico Eckly at the Meteor Festival, I started thinking again about the Norwegian performance group Baktruppen, who I also first met during that seminal first visit to Norway. In *Vive la Phrance*, Spreafico Eckly find different ways of re-enacting historical performances related to politics and/or audience participation. One of these re-enactments was of

Baktruppen's 1998 work *KVAKK*, in which Baktruppen turn their backs on the audience and instead perform for a field full of cows. The re-enactment was introduced by saying that Baktruppen, at the time, were having difficulty finding audiences for their work, so instead decided to perform for cows, which I believe is only part of the story. And suddenly I had such strong feelings of love for Baktruppen, for what they represented, a completely different way of making and thinking theatre, so eccentric and full of eccentric life. I also remembered that I had read the book *Performance Art by Baktruppen: First Part*, and wondered if I could even tell which of the many things I knew about them were told to me over the years and which things came from reading. (This of course relates to this book – will it begin to replace my real memories of PME-ART with things I have now written about those memories and experiences?) I felt sad thinking about how Baktruppen disbanded in 2011. When I first met them I had such a strong feeling they would keep going forever.

The Band Night in Bergen (with Kvit Skit, Johannes Fjeldstad, Rudi Valdersnes/Craig Wells, Elida Høgalmen, and Second Pest) was one of the best. Each of the bands was completely different from one another and each did something so committed and convincing. I was sitting onstage watching them, asking myself if I really understood what this project was. In each city it's been utterly different and yet the format is basically the same. These evenings where things come together in the moment in such surprising and unpredictable ways. I wonder if this is the direction our future work should take. Instead of touring with a group, I should arrive with a structure and fill it with local participants. There is such a freedom and unexpected spontaneity to these evenings, but, in comparison to all of my previous work, I feel noticeably less committed to those onstage with me. I meet them for one night and then we're done. But is a brief encounter, especially when it comes to art, necessarily less resonant than a more long-term one? For everything you gain there is also something lost.

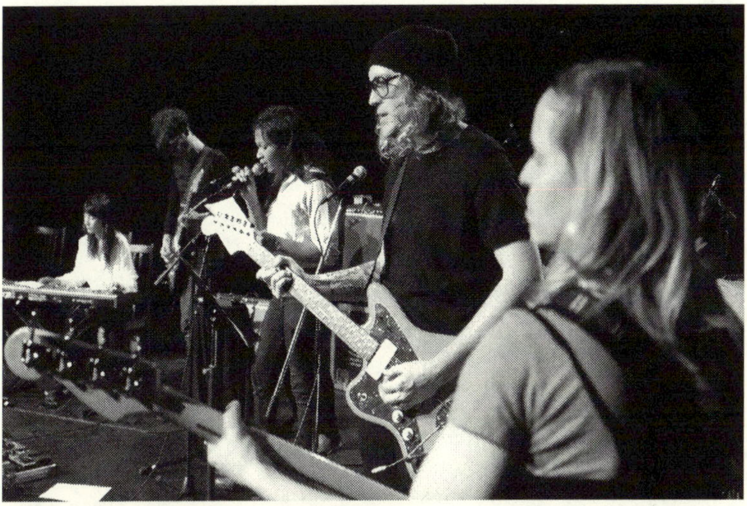

Sheenah Ko, Robbie MacArthur, J. Ellise Barbara, Jace Lasek and Olga Goreas onstage altogether for the last song as part of the *Every Song I've Ever Written Band Night* at La Chapelle Scènes Contemporaines in Montreal. Photo: Mathieu Chartrand

I was hoping to write so much more about all the bands who so graciously and beautifully participated. But there are already forty-three of them and, I believe, so many more still to come. How to do each of them justice, when music is so poorly described through words? And when you can so easily go online and listen to each of them for yourself? I have always been extremely bad at gratitude. Writing this book, I am slowly realizing that this lack of gratitude is my most grievous fault. Some of the bands I spent time with, but others I just barely met. And I was afraid to spend too much time with them, in the same way I am often afraid of strangers, but also I was nervous about influencing their cover versions, of accidentally saying something that might detract from the extra-freedom that makes the project thrive. These days I'm also feeling that my ability to make conversation with relative strangers, never great to begin with, is actually at an all-time low. And, come to think of it, it was my inability to more fully communicate and interact with musicians that made it so difficult for me to pursue music when I was young, to keep a band going or make it work, to figure out how we were going to play the songs together. Thinking about all of this now, I believe, as we continue to perform *Every Song I've Ever*

*Written*, I will try to leave more and more of this fear behind. This book started with projects very much in the distant past and ends with projects more and more within the struggle of the present. I am still learning how to do it. More gratitude and less fear might be a good place to start.

+ + + +

Projects come out of other projects. And while *Every Song I've Ever Written* was one kind of looking back over my life, this book you're holding in your hands is another kind. *Every Song I've Ever Written* was the first PME-ART project that was, in some sense, only me. But of course it wasn't only me by any stretch of the imagination, it was me and so many different bands in so many different cities, etc. And all the people who were kind enough to get up and sing the songs karaoke-style. Yet on the plane – going to Düsseldorf, Mannheim, Malmö, Tokyo, Stavanger, etc. – for the first time, I was often travelling alone. It marks some sort of noticeable change, in dialogue with my ongoing struggles with, and belief in, collaborative work.

*Every Song I've Ever Written* is a project about the songs I wrote when I was a teenager and in my twenties, about how music circulates on the Internet, and about how when we're young we think our life will be one way but later it so often turns out differently. And just exactly how has my life turned out? Julian Assange, Erykah Badu, Blevin Blectum, Mary J. Blige, Sofia Coppola, Snoop Dogg, MF Doom, Missy Elliott, Charlotte Gainsbourg, ?uestlove, Tupac Shakur, Renee Gladman, and Justin Trudeau were all born in 1971. That was also the year I was born. I looked up this list to try to get a better idea who my contemporaries are, what "my generation," if it can be said to exist, might look like or be about. First thought: my excitement around hip hop is most likely related to the fact that hip hop has happened entirely in my lifetime. I suppose this is mainly a digression. A singer/songwriter in the era of hip hop might be another aspect to this project that didn't occur to me at the time. (Which of course has to do with whiteness, something I've really only started understanding and thinking about in the past few years.)

I keep coming back to just how much I love music. How music for me is akin to a form of hope. Alan Mills writes: "I confuse music with happiness." And yet *Every Song I've Ever Written* places this hope (I don't think I can quite bring myself to call it happiness) mainly in the past. Or perhaps it takes this hope from my past and attempts to drag it into the present, in the process changing it so much more than my younger self would have ever believed. So many of the cover versions are so much more rich, full, and musical than anything I would or could have done on my own. A new lesson about what collaboration is for. Different ways to work together. I've always been amazed by the way musicians can get together and jam; without any preparation or plan they can start playing together immediately. I believe I will never completely understand just how that works.

Ten:

# Adventures can be found anywhere, même dans la mélancolie

[2014–]

Created/Performed by:
Claudia Fancello, Marie Claire Forté, Nadège Grebmeier Forget, Adam Kinner, Ashlea Watkin, and Jacob Wren

Continued/Performed by:
Julie Bernier, Anick Martel, and Étienne Provencher-Rousseau

We performed it in:
Montreal, Leonard & Bina Ellen Art Gallery • Chicoutimi, UQAC/Chaire de Dramaturgie sonore au théâtre/Conference Les pratiques contemporaines de l'écriture textuelle pour la scène/L'Œuvre de l'Autre Gallery

Before there was *Adventures can be found anywhere, même dans la mélancolie*, there was *The Project That Didn't Happen*. When I think of *The Project That Didn't Happen* I want to kill someone. I want to strangle someone with my bare hands. And when I think that after over twenty-five years of making work, after so many difficult professional experiences and trials and tribulations, to have this be the one that made me crack, that makes me lose faith in art in some way that I still can't even completely understand or fathom, I can't quite believe it. Since it actually wasn't *that* bad, just got to me in a way nothing else had. Ripped me in two. Perhaps it caught me on the upswing of a mid-life crisis and shone a bright light into the eyes of the dilemma. I'm still not sure.

As I was about to start writing this section, I found myself wondering: should I use real names? If I did, could some of those involved sue me for libel? (Or if one of them turned up dead, would I be a prime suspect?) I still have all this anger about it and nowhere to put it. No one particularly cares that the project you worked on for two years in the end didn't happen. One of the things that so struck me when I first read Chris Kraus all those years ago was the way she used people's real names. But that was a different situation, a different time (and Dick did actually threaten to sue her). So I've decided to just lightly run through it, leaving the real names aside. So many artists have had bad experiences much like this one. It's so common you're not even supposed to notice or mention it. Everyone has these stories because that's the way the art world works.

So there was an International Artist who was invited to do a project in Montreal. I had met her a few times in Brussels, and when she heard she was invited to Montreal she thought it would be a good opportunity for us to do something together. I had a meeting with The Curator and it sounded like something I wanted to do. We had a meeting with The Venue and it didn't go so well. We wanted to know how much money they were going to put into the project and they were reluctant to talk about it. I had heard bad stories about The Venue before, that especially with performance the conditions were poor. Why, I now ask myself, did knowing this not influence my actions more? I think I was blinded by the possibility of working with the International Artist. When I told people we were doing something together they often seemed so impressed. It made me feel like I was moving up in the world. I met with the International Artist in Cologne, then the next year followed her around a bit, to Granada and Bregenz, to see some of her exhibitions and continue meeting about our project together. The fact that I was following her around, that her busy schedule took precedence over mine, should have set off alarm bells. And maybe it did. By this point I was already starting to have reservations about the project but felt there was no turning back. Grants had been written and the results were positive. The Curator had met with Festival TransAmériques and had convinced them to join the project as a co-producer. During this time Sylvie and Richard were writing the budget over and over again, trying to get a budget everyone could agree on. Sylvie and Richard always try to pay the artists we work with as well as possible, and The Venue wanted to pay as little as possible in order to maximize their profits, so it was difficult to find common ground. Without a budget we couldn't have a contract with The Venue. Sylvie and Richard didn't want to move forward without a contract and yet the clock was ticking, the budget was being done and redone, and still The Venue would not agree. The Curator tried to intervene and it seemed for a while like we were making progress. We were scheduled to have a meeting with The Venue but instead were told that she was going away. We had a co-production contract from Festival TransAmériques, but Sylvie and Richard understandably didn't want to sign it before we had a contract from The Venue, because then we'd be caught, forced to pay for a project without any guaranteed financial input or working conditions from The Venue. As all this was happening the International Artist and I continued to develop the project and it was slowly becoming more concrete. I assembled the group of creator/performers and we began to have meetings, talk through the premise. But still no agreed-upon budget or contract from The Venue. (Sylvie reminds me that one of the points of contention was that they wanted the contract to impose things on the creator/performers without giving us time to consult with them first.) By this point all I felt was stress. I remember the morning I woke up early to go to the office, knowing that something was going to happen, suspecting it wouldn't be good. The Curator and The Venue had had a meeting in Paris. The Curator wrote to Festival TransAmériques (and cc'd us) to say the project was cancelled. The International Artist had agreed to redo a previous exhibition at The Venue during the same dates previously scheduled for our project. Sylvie and Richard went to see it but I never did.

For me this experience has so much to do with moving from the performing arts toward visual art. Over the past while there has been a significant trend of dance and performance in museums and galleries (exemplified by the work of Tino Sehgal). I have also somewhat been swept up in this trend. Since *The Project That Didn't Happen* I've had so many conversations with artists from dance or performance who have also had bad experiences in visual art that were considerably worse than anything they'd been through before. Well, not "so many" conversations. Maybe five or six. One thing is obvious. Not to generalize, but visual art doesn't want to pay for performance. It thinks it's something that should happen for cheap or free. (There are also now many fighting to change this situation, so it might be that my perspective on the question is already outdated. One can only hope.) Perhaps one of the reasons why I found *The Project That Didn't Happen* so devastating was because we had been taking our first careful steps into visual art, starting to feel it was the solution to some of our previous artistic problems, a place we could work and have our work more fully, critically received. For the time being I no longer feel that way. At the same time, I also feel I can't go back. We're an interdisciplinary group now, and therefore, it is most likely, the art gallery will continue to be one of our multiple sites of investigation.

And then I start thinking of all the other projects we started but, for one reason or another, didn't happen: *The Square and the Triangle*, *Extra-fin*, *It's A Sexist World LaLa LaLa La La*, *Do You Really Want to Hurt Me*, *Speaking These Lines for the First Time*, *Description of a Fight*. What if we had done all of these projects instead of the projects we did? It's like a whole other artistic trajectory that might have happened but didn't.

\+ + + +

*The Words in a Sentence* was another project that didn't happen around this time. PME-ART was one of three finalists for the first ever 1% for performance. (1% is a program in Quebec in which 1% of a new publicly supported building's total budget is put toward a public artwork.) The guidelines said the performance had to take place within the building-length windows of the 2-22 building, and had to happen at least once a year for five years. What we proposed was to take each of the words from the following sentence and print them individually on giant placards:

> Life is very short, and it ought not to be spent crawling at the feet of miserable scoundrels.

The sentence is a quote from Stendhal that I first encountered in Tarkovsky's diaries. We would find people from the neighbourhood, and in the window each person would hold one word from the sentence. The sentence would be large enough to take up all three floors of the building's windows. We would then go with microphones from person to person and interview them only about their word. So, for example, we would interview the person holding the word "life" about the word "life."

The 2-22 building is in the *Quartier des spectacles*, formerly the red-light district that has been rapidly transformed into a neighbourhood for festivals and especially for art and performance venues. I was most likely naive, but it didn't occur to me that our sentence would be read by the committee as a condemnation of the *Quartier des spectacles*, of which they were very much a part. I must have known this might be one possible reading, but felt the sentence was a considerably more open, humorous, ambiguous statement. A statement that applies to everything in life. However, in retrospect I believe some – I suspect especially the real-estate speculator on the committee – felt it was a condemnation of them. If you think you're a scoundrel that doesn't necessarily mean that I also think that about you. It apparently goes without saying we did not win (perhaps for this reason or simply because they liked Thierry Marceau's proposal better), and this response blurs together with *The Project That Didn't Happen* in my understanding of the art world.

+ + + +

Like a project rising from the ashes of another project, *Adventures can be found anywhere, même dans la mélancolie* rose from the ashes of *The Project That Didn't Happen*. There was an invitation from Michèle Thériault at the Leonard & Bina Ellen Art Gallery to propose something. Since we (Claudia Fancello, Marie Claire Forté, Nadège Grebmeier Forget, Adam Kinner, Ashlea Watkin, and I) had already started working, we thought we could take some of our collaborative research and begin to move it in a completely different direction. The first half of the title came from the novel *Artificial Respiration* by Ricardo Piglia:

> Once I was in a Warsaw hospital. Motionless, unable to use my body, accompanied by a pathetic series of invalids. Tedium, monotony, introspection. A long white hall, a row of beds – it was like being in jail. There was a single window, at the end of the room. One of the patients, a bony, feverish guy, consumed by cancer, named Guy by his French parents, had had the luck to be placed near that opening. From there, barely sitting up, he could look out, see the street. What a spectacle! A square, water, pigeons, people passing. Another world. He clung desperately to that place and told us what he saw. He was the lucky one. We detested him. We waited, to be frank, for him to die so as to take his place. We kept count. Finally he dies. After complicated manoeuvres and bribes I succeeded in being transferred to the bed at the end of the hall and was able to take his place. Well, I tell Renzi. Well. From the window all that could be seen was a gray wall and a bit of dirty sky. I too, of course, began telling them stories about the square and the pigeons and the traffic in the streets. Why do you laugh? It's funny, Renzi says. It's like a Polish version of Plato's cave. Why not, I tell him; it serves to prove that adventures can be found anywhere. Doesn't that seem like a beautiful practical lesson? A fable with a moral, he says to me. Exactly I say.

*The Project That Didn't Happen* was going to be in and around *Artificial Respiration*, one of my favourite books of all time (now somewhat ruined for me), but we were quickly moving away from it, toward the melancholy of *The Book of Disquiet*. I was asked to write a *dépliant*, a brochure in the gallery people could take home. This is what I wrote:

> The Book of Disquiet
>
> *The Book of Disquiet* was written as a series of interrelated fragments that Fernando Pessoa worked on between 1913 and his death in 1935. It was discovered in a trunk left behind in his small room, a trunk that also contained a lifetime of other writings: poetry, plays, philosophy, criticism, translations, linguistic theory, etc., variously typed, handwritten, or illegibly scrawled in Portuguese, English, and French. He wrote in notebooks, on loose sheets, on the backs of letters, advertisements, handbills, and in the margins of earlier texts. *The Book of Disquiet* was first published in Portuguese in 1982 and there have been many different versions since, as various editors and translators attempted to put the book together in whatever way seemed best to them at the time.
>
> Fernando Pessoa also continuously fragmented himself into other writers he famously called heteronyms: imaginary characters created to write in different styles. Some of his most fully developed heteronyms include: Alberto Caeiro, a shepherd, a humble man of little education who nonetheless wrote poems filled with philosophy and paganism; Ricardo Reis, a classicist, a monarchist, a doctor who wrote in an austere, cerebral manner, with particular attention paid to the correct use of the Portuguese language; and Álvaro de Campos, a world traveller, whose poems expressed a fervent wish to experience the entirety of the universe in himself. However, Bernardo Soares, the author of *The Book of Disquiet*, an accountant working on Rua dos Douradores in Lisbon, was merely a semi-heteronym. "He's a semi-heteronym," Pessoa wrote in the final year of his life, "because his personality, although not my own, doesn't differ from my own but is a mere mutilation of it."

Pessoa clearly planned to compile his fragments of disquietude into a finished manuscript, but never managed to do so. Based on the many notes he left behind, if he had been able to complete the book in his lifetime, it is likely he would have edited it down toward a shorter, more cohesive narrative. Like many authors, he might very well have edited out some of the most contentious, vulnerable, or revealing passages. Therefore, the ramshackle glory of *The Book of Disquiet* that we know today derives in no small part from the fact that it was assembled long after its original composition, and that this method of assembly implicitly acknowledges the work's deeply unfinished nature.

## Adventures can be found anywhere, même dans la mélancolie

> The only basis for truth is self-contradiction. The universe contradicts itself, for it passes on. Life contradicts itself, for it dies. Paradox is nature's norm. That's why all truth has a paradoxical form.
> – Fernando Pessoa

When you watch a film that makes you cry, do the tears come from within the film or from within you? This is a stupid question, since the answer must be something like: a bit of both. Another question might be: if you were to get together with your friends and remake the film not in order to imitate it, but in order to change it into something closer to your own life, would this new, remade version still make you cry?

The relation between art and emotion is a long and complicated one. With *Adventures can be found anywhere, même dans la mélancolie*, PME-ART rewrites *The Book of Disquiet* page by melancholy page, altering the emotional tenor of the book in many subtle and unsubtle ways. Of course, within any conventional view of literature, rewriting such a classic and deeply loved text is practically sacrilege. But the intention here is not to break any particular canonical rules, rather to see what happens when a door long assumed to be locked is partially reopened, when fragments left unfinished seventy-nine years ago are mischievously treated as if they still remained unfinished today, as if one could simply continue working on them.

Fernando Pessoa was a great writer and it is unlikely that PME-ART will be able to consistently match his eloquence or depth. They will give it their best shot, but clearly that cannot be the point. This is a more playful, democratic, collaborative notion of writing. Pessoa's virtuosity in turning his own compulsions and doubts into literature here meets a contemporary moment, the year 2014, in which compulsions and doubts are expressed in a multitude of old and new ways: online, in televised pseudo-reality, and in every kind of autobiographical literary expression. What might it mean to rewrite these fragments today? What shades of early twenty-first century emotion might be woven into Pessoa's unfinished twentieth-century elegy?

One joke we often tell: PME-ART is rewriting *The Book of Disquiet* to make it a little bit happier. But just a little bit. And then what kind of happiness could this possibly be? Is it the author or the reader whose mood will be lightened? The word *happiness* perhaps conjures an imaginary past-life America: "Life, Liberty and the pursuit of...," fantasies that in the harsh light of our current economic and ecological collapse might seem threadbare at best. At times, in artistic works, there is a kind of reverse psychology effect; extremely sad works can make you feel happy and vice versa. Sometimes simply expressing something socially taboo, for example extreme sadness or apathy, gives the viewer or reader a feeling of release, even elation. Pessoa's almost absolute melancholy has this effect on many readers, and therefore the happiness being sought of course already exists between the lines, in the affect of the original text.

One clue to the added happiness PME-ART is searching for might be found in the unfinished nature of the composition itself. While previous experts and translators sought to work toward some definitive version of *The Book of Disquiet*, here we clearly find ourselves drifting toward the distant other end of the finished/unfinished spectrum. (Emotions, one might suggest, are always left unfinished.) When nothing is finished, everything remains possible. At least for a while. Or at least within a work of art. This is one of the paradoxes that art can scratch away at and evoke: sometimes a job well done is a job left partially undone, to make room for the future. Pessoa never finished his masterpiece, *The Book of Disquiet*, and neither does *Adventures can be found anywhere, même dans la mélancolie*. One can gaze at a fragment and fear its implicit sense of failure. Or one can glance at a fragment and think: this is only the beginning.

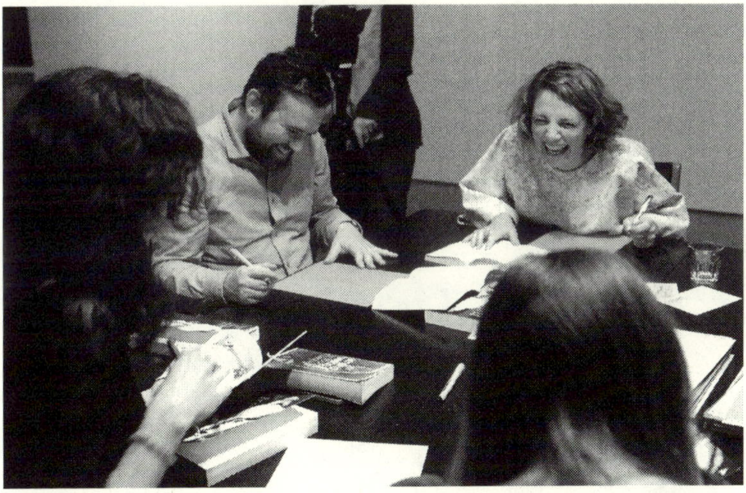

Marie Claire Forté, Jacob Wren, Claudia Fancello, and Nadège Grebmeier Forget in *Adventures can be found anywhere, même dans la mélancolie* at the Leonard & Bina Ellen Art Gallery in Montreal. Photo: Geneviève Perreault

Much like *HOSPITALITY 2: Gradually This Overview*, *Adventures can be found anywhere, même dans la mélancolie* was a project in which we were in the gallery all the time. But even more so than with the previous project, I had such a strong feeling that we were the art. Many who came in wanted to participate, to join in, to rewrite Pessoa alongside us. For some reason we had decided that, for this project, there would be no audience participation; it was the six of us who had dedicated ourselves to the task of rewriting *The Book of Disquiet*, not a free-for-all where anyone who wandered in could give it their best shot. This was a clear decision from the group, and I respect it, but also can't help but feel if we had made the opposite choice we would have ended up with a very different, but equally interesting, project.

When you finished rewriting your page, you went into the other room, placed your freshly rewritten page on a plinth underneath a video camera, the page now projected, taking up an entire wall, and read the page aloud. Often, in the two adjoining rooms, the reading of two pages would overlap, a background soundtrack to the concentration of rewriting, a reminder that literature is also about voice. When you finished reading you take not your page, but the previous page, which until then had been sitting under the video camera, to a long shelf that runs through every room in the gallery. Over the course of the performance/exhibition this shelf gradually fills up with pages, an in-progress book carefully spread out over many rooms.

+ + + +

The process for *Adventures can be found anywhere, même dans la mélancolie* was smooth and pleasurable. The creator/performers had been gathered together for *The Project That Didn't Happen*, and therefore, in a sense, had joined a project already underway. Together we took some of the preliminary rewriting exercises we had played with during our first meetings and pushed forward through trial and error, figuring out what we wanted to do with them, where we could take them. By the end, almost nothing from *The Project That Didn't Happen* remained, and perhaps it was this sense of transforming a first proposal into something so different, something considerably more our own, that energized the process.

On the last day of the performance/exhibition, for the finissage, we stapled all of the rewritten pages back into a copy of the original *Book of Disquiet*, reading each one aloud before we did so, creating what we called the Monster Book. I did not expect the finished

Monster Book to be so aesthetically compelling, so like an art object, the kind of physical object we had never really made before. All of the colourful pages jutting out at every possible, origami-like, unseemly angle. A record of our work together crammed into a somewhat unreadable package. Something I could imagine seeing in an art gallery, if the object in the gallery hadn't actually been us and our ongoing performative work.

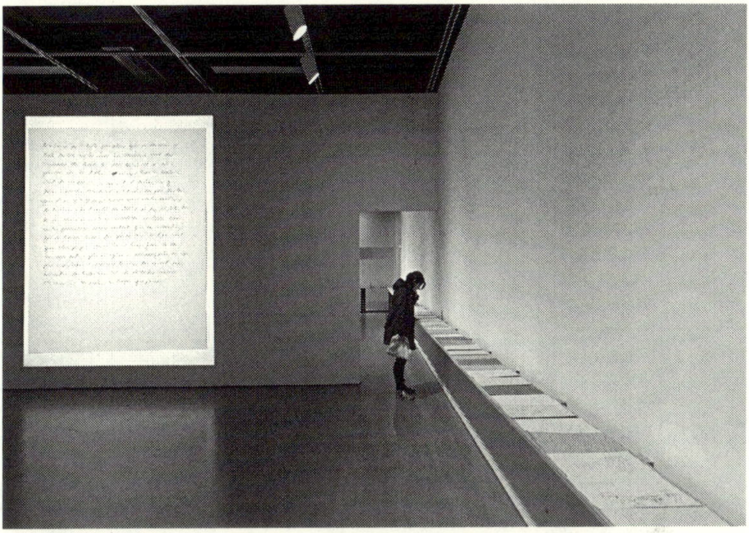

An audience member at *Adventures can be found anywhere, même dans la mélancolie*. Photo: Paul Litherland/Leonard & Bina Ellen Art Gallery

There was one moment during the process that I have absolutely continued to think about, that continues to perplex me. We were all sitting around the table, rewriting our individual pages, discussing how we should do so, that we could definitely ask the rest of the table any questions we had, that the rewriting was also part of an ongoing conversation between all of us that we were free to engage with at any time during the installation/performance. And Adam suggests, or more precisely asks the group, if instead we want to make the rewriting more collective, if there are ways we can move even further toward rewriting the pages all together. I believe Adam made some concrete suggestions as to how we could do so, though I can no longer remember exactly what they were, but what perplexed me so much about it was how negatively

I felt toward the suggestion. How clear it was to me that I wanted us to rewrite together, but to do so individually, and the idea of trying to do so more collectively made me feel almost a sense of dread. It really struck me that Adam had the opposite impulse, that he actually wanted everyone to be working together to a greater degree than we already were. I felt I should also be on his side of the argument and was frustrated with myself that I wasn't, at the same time feeling there was no way I could argue for something I so clearly didn't want to do. There was a short discussion about Adam's proposal and in general no one really got behind it, I feel more because it went against the way we had been working up until that point than because anyone had any strong arguments against it. And in the end I remember Adam saying: "Well, if no one wants to..." and thinking how strange it was that I didn't want to, or how strange it was that he did.

(Adam doesn't remember this incident and had no idea his comment affected me so much. However, he does remember wanting to bring the group toward clarifying the particular limitations we were putting on the word *collaboration*. He's noticed that the projects he's done with me outside of PME-ART and within PME-ART have been very different experiences. And *collaboration* is a word that is so often mischaracterized or misunderstood, a word that can refer to so many different kinds of "working together." Adam remembers that after this project, perhaps at a *The DJ Who Gave Too Much Information* rehearsal, Claudia and I began talking about collaboration and what it meant in all of these projects and that our conversation seemed especially charged. The "collaborator" talking to the "creator" about the project's future, a conversation full of the all-too-familiar micropolitics so often found in artistic creation.)

(One of the things that struck Ashlea reading this book were the conflicts and struggles that took place during earlier PME-ART projects and how the process for *Adventures can be found anywhere, même dans la mélancolie* was comparatively smooth. She feels this had something to do with how clear and decided the "rules" were from the beginning, and wonders what would have happened if everyone took more risks in rehearsal, for example trying Adam's proposal to collaborate on the writing, and also what would have happened if there had been more conflict during the process. It's possible that the intensity of *The Project That Never Happened* pacified us, that we needed to make the process "smooth and pleasurable" because the beginning had been so fraught with tension, conflict, and disappointment. This makes her a little sad, because she wonders if we missed an opportunity to push on the work. But also optimistic, because if/when we perform it again there will still be room try new things.)

Doing something alone and together at the same time seems to describe many of PME-ART's more recent projects: we all play records and tell stories about them, but do so only one at a time (Claudia reminds me that at regular intervals in *The DJ Who Gave Too Much Information* we also sing together, that this is one of our collective actions); each of the bands covers one of my songs, but they do so without any idea what the other bands on the same bill are working on; we all sit around a table rewriting Pessoa, but each working mainly on our own page. I feel there is something beautiful about all of this, that it gives each of us a much greater freedom to push in any eccentric, spontaneous direction we might choose. But there are also clearly limitations, and I believe it has been an ongoing struggle as to what things we can do even more together that don't undermine the fragile and energizing freedom of the work. When Adam brought his proposal to the table it troubled me because it made it so clear that what he was arguing with was something that I, in fact, am always bringing to the work. A desire to work with others but, at the same time, to keep doing my own thing. Another paradox or contradiction we embody in so much of what we do. And now, having realized this more fully, I also feel it might be time to turn around and go in the opposite direction for a while. Toward other paradoxes, more collective ones.

\+ + + +

*Adventures can be found anywhere, même dans la mélancolie* was our most recent project and also one of the projects we have done the least. (So far we have only done it in Montreal and Chicoutimi.) There has been interest in inviting it other places but I've been reluctant, partly because it would mean continuing to push our way into visual art, which I find myself increasingly unsure of, but mostly because it still reminds me too much of *The Project That Didn't Happen*. I know, keep telling myself, that this isn't a good reason. That I'm being short-sighted or petty, and what's worse doing so against the best interests of our work. *Adventures can be found anywhere, même dans la mélancolie* has such a playful, quiet integrity and intensity to it, unlike anything else we have done. I try to convince myself there is no reason not to continue.

In a way, this book started with my disillusionment (or pre-disillusionment) with theatre and is ending with my disillusionment with visual art. But is the problem really theatre or visual art? Or the fact that idealism shatters too easily? Back when I started reading heavily about visual art, I was amazed by how much of the well-received art writing was so intensely and effectively critical of art and the art world. I had the feeling that one of the things art and artists wanted from art writing was to be told all the things that were wrong about art. In this sense my criticisms don't cut very deep. I had a few bad experiences, as do all artists. In fact, most of the visual artists I spoke with had experiences similar to mine, one of the reasons I feel I should be writing about it, as we all should, so these things aren't happening only in the deep shadows of the background but instead are spoken about more openly on a continual basis. I feel like such a wimp that *The Project That Didn't Happen* affected me so negatively, even now, four years after the fact. I feel it should have been like water off a duck's back, a horse I could easily get back up on. But of course we survived, we're still going, I suppose we're still going strong. Such experiences will change how we work in the future, how we continue to think about what we're doing and enact such thinking, and will continue to remind us just how stubborn we are.

I have such a clear memory – when I was complaining about our project's collapse – of the International Artist telling me: "This is just the way things are in the art world." And then going on to tell me the story of a beloved curator who was unfairly fired from a museum, and how some artists started a petition to protest, to lobby for the curator's reinstatement, but while privately everyone they spoke with was against the firing, almost no artists would actually sign the petition for fear of being blacklisted by the museum. Her point was that artists are generally unwilling to work together to improve their long-term conditions. She said she had witnessed this again and again. Individualism was a mistake.

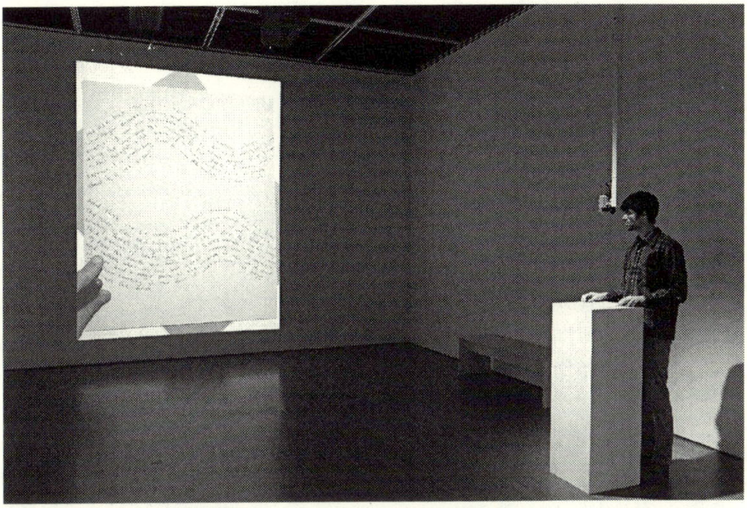

Adam Kinner in *Adventures can be found anywhere, même dans la mélancolie*. Photo: Paul Litherland/Leonard & Bina Ellen Art Gallery

In some ways this book – as required by the genre of memoir and perhaps also by the genre of an interdisciplinary performance group – can be seen as a journey. But when I try to articulate it as a journey from *what* to *what*, each of the terms I try on for size, each of the *what*s, seem to me to be more inaccurate than useful. If I could summarize it in a single sentence it's possible I wouldn't have felt the need to write an entire book trying to figure it out. But – and this is the closest I've come – let's say it's a journey from *trying to create a new kind of contemporary theatre* (unlike any I had seen before) and ending up – twenty years later – sitting around a table in an art gallery embodying *a kind of theatre so far away from theatre that I often suspect it is no longer recognizable as such*. Something I frequently ask myself is to what degree our work makes sense if it is no longer being viewed in relation and reaction to theatre. For me, much of the politics of what we do comes from its implicit critique of the hierarchies, roles, traditions, and limitations of theatre and its institutions (and how this critique can then also be transferred to other aspects of society-at-large), yet in an art gallery this critique often feels barely perceptible. And so the past twenty years might also be seen as a journey from critique toward something more constructive, from critiquing the things we're against toward trying to generate the things that we're for and that we want to see in the world, from *En français comme en anglais, it's easy to criticize* to *Adventures can be found anywhere, même dans la mélancolie*.

It is therefore fitting that this book ends with the act of rewriting, rewriting in contrast to critiquing (though this could also be said to be a false dichotomy). Rewriting as a way of changing the things you simply wish were a little bit different. Pessoa's melancholy makes for enticing and powerful literature, and yet, living with my own rather severe melancholy, I know all too well how painful it can be to live within such enticing and powerful emotions. What if we were to rewrite them just a little bit? What if we were to take the injustices and hierarchies of the world and rewrite them as well? Not just analyze and critique them but also rewrite them? In the world of our performances, this takes place mainly as representation, as an analogy, as metaphor. But I live in the hope that what is possible in art is also sometimes possible in life. And that by thinking about art and life together we begin to create new possibilities. I am definitely not an optimist. But I never thought PME-ART would last twenty years, and it has. So how can I help but end this book on an optimistic note. We are born into a world that is not of our making but there is always the possibility we might rewrite it. Just a little bit. For the moment. Hopefully not knowing what will happen next.

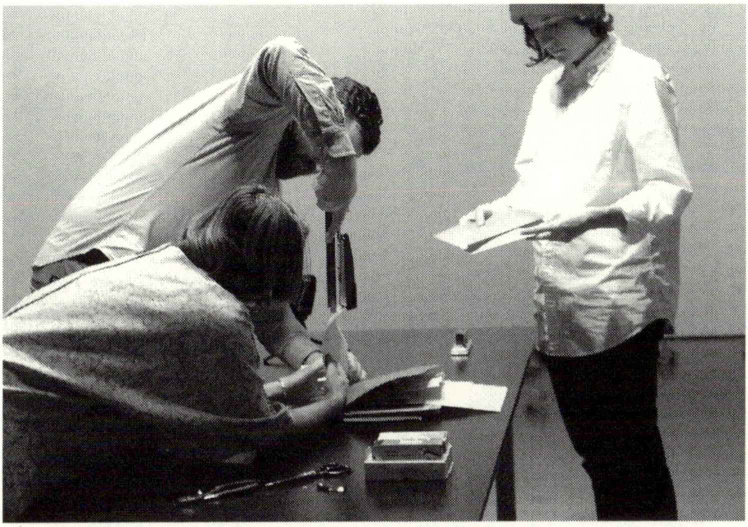

Claudia Fancello, Jacob Wren, and Ashlea Watkin putting together the "Monster Book" during the finissage for *Adventures can be found anywhere, même dans la mélancolie* at the Leonard & Bina Ellen Art Gallery in Montreal. Photo: Mathieu Chartrand

# Epilogue:
# Emotional Politics

> The artists I work with turn to emotion because this is where ideology does its most devastating work.
> – Jennifer Doyle, *Hold It Against Me*

Now we are at the very beginning of a new project. It hasn't quite started and I still very much don't know what it will be. Somehow I still have the feeling it could be absolutely anything. It is this moment of possibility, the moment before anything has started, that I've always found most energizing. I am not sure this is anything to be proud of. As we often do, we're starting with a title: *Emotional Politics*. And, as the title suggests, I am thinking the project will have something to do with the relationship between politics and emotion.

+ + + +

As I've moved forward through the years, I've often attempted to erase and undo my past. In some sense this book is a counter-attempt to not erase the past twenty years. I've always liked the idea of artists having "periods": Picasso with his rose period, his blue period, his cubist period, etc. I once again have the feeling I need to put recent work behind me, to enter into a new period, with little idea what this new period might actually become. I once tried to cordon my work into four decade-long periods (also including the *next* ten years):

| | |
|---|---|
| 1988–1998: | Theatre & Anti-theatre |
| 1998–2008: | Translation & Polemic |
| 2008–2018: | Books, Music & Hospitality |
| 2018–2028: | Emotion & Decolonization |

Because along with emotion and politics, all of the questions I find myself asking these days are around decolonization, around whiteness, white supremacy, white fragility, white saviourism, white guilt, structural inequality, anti-racism, intersectionality, and how all of these realities factor into the ways I live and work. My collaboration with PME-ART started by bringing anglophone and francophone artists to work together with *En français comme en anglais, it's easy to criticize*, a bringing together that wasn't happening so often and still doesn't happen nearly enough. This was a certain kind of bringing together that felt important to me at the time. But these days, like a lot of people, I'm feeling that art is simply too white and that it has to change.

+ + + +

I've always felt so strongly that there is something political about being yourself in a performance situation. But now, after twenty years, I say this with somewhat less confidence than I once did. I think it is political because it undoes some of the hierarchy between those onstage and those watching, and if those onstage and watching are more equal, then everyone can of course be onstage, can be involved, can be on the performance stage or the political one, can find a stage to speak out against injustice or get involved in whatever ways feel most vital. I still believe all of this is artistically true. However, saying a work of art is political is very different from saying that it's politically effective. Like many artists, or more precisely like a specific kind of artist who intensely desires the political, I'm always wondering if I'm doing enough. And of course I always know that I'm not.

+ + + +

People might think they're making rational decisions, but often, without even knowing it, they are essentially making emotional decisions. But where does emotion stop and thinking begin? Even to put it in these terms feels obnoxious and misguided. Such distinctions are artificial. Thinking and emotion are completely intertwined. To believe otherwise is to block so many genuine possibilities. In Western democratic politics the rational decision is supposed to rule the day. What could democracy possibly mean if people are unable to make rational decisions as to what is best for the society they are a part of? However, as we know, current electoral politics, much like advertising, often plays directly to the emotions of the voter. I'm not saying this is only a bad thing. What I'm getting at is how we all need to understand this process so much more. And how in further understanding it we might begin to change the ways it does and doesn't work on us.

But, then again, I'm not only, or even mainly, thinking about electoral politics. I'm thinking of politics as a question of how we treat each other, of caring and cruelty and how they relate to emotions such as love and anger. I'm also wondering if there's room for more emotion in PME-ART shows. In performance I associate emotion with acting, with being fake. With the opposite of what I'm searching for. However, if rejecting emotion in terms of how we are supposed to make political decisions is limiting and misguided, it might be even more so in relation to making art. I have absolutely no problem writing with great emotion, but in performance I generally find it to be more of a conundrum.

In PME-ART we perform as ourselves. In life, I rarely display much emotion. Like the good male child I was raised to be, I most often – without even realizing I am doing so – repress it. I often think my depression substantially consists of repressed anger and sadness. And, because I suspect I often set the tone for our work, I also wonder if there might be something emotionally repressed about how we create and perform. Or at the very least something straight and male (which others continuously undercut with their own contributions). In the past I didn't see it this way. I would have probably attributed this lack of expressed emotion to the fact of repetition. If I give a performance once, and some emotion arises in me as I am doing so, I am open to going with it. But how to do so over and over again without it feeling fake? How to do so in front of an audience without feeling I must deliver the emotions on cue? In *Emotional Politics* I mainly imagine us talking about emotions rather than embodying them. Yet I also find myself wondering what are the things I still haven't thought of that might allow us to go further (or explore in different registers from our previous work). At the moment I simply have no idea. It feels impossible to me. But that's also the feeling that makes me want to do it. Maybe it will be really bad, but is there a way to turn it inside out and make it good again. Is this the road we're really going to pursue or is it only a footpath to take us out onto the actual road we will eventually end up pursuing? At this early stage I still have no idea.

And then I wonder if some of our performances have contained far more emotion than I know or realize. And how the emotion comes from the encounter between us and the audience in ways that are difficult to pin down or describe, and in fact are even difficult to be certain of because they happen in the moment and then, just as quickly, are gone.

+ + + +

A few weeks ago I found myself thinking about the Wooster Group again. I believe I haven't seen a show by them in over fifteen years, but seeing their show *L.S.D. (...Just the High Points...)* at Harbourfront Centre in 1989, and reading a great deal about them during the same period, was probably the single most significant event in leading me to want to make the kind of performances I've dedicated my life to. And then when I started touring, about ten years later, I met or heard about many other groups and companies that were also catalyzed by their first experiences with the Wooster Group, and also next-generation companies who were later inspired by the companies that were first inspired by the Wooster Group. It reminds me of a story I once heard about the Ramones. The first time the Ramones toured the U.S. there were no punk bands to open for them. But the second time they toured, there was an opening band in every town, all consisting of young people who had seen the Ramones on their previous tour and then decided to form punk bands of their own.

Both the Ramones and the Wooster Group came out of a kind of New York City Lower East Side zeitgeist (which for me also has some relation to U.S. cultural imperialism). As I've already mentioned, I've always worried that we had no zeitgeist, though I suppose in many ways I've spent my life searching for one, all the while trying to tell myself that it's never too late. In a sense, zeitgeist is also a collective feeling of protest, and it has been argued that the past ten years plus have been a golden age of protest: the alter-globalization movement, the battle in Seattle, Occupy Wall Street, the Rolling Jubilee, Tahrir Square, Printemps érable, Idle No More, Black Lives Matter, Standing Rock, the Women's March, mass protests against Trump, etc. None of these protests have done as much they originally hoped but they all did something. I also realize I'm still romanticizing zeitgeists. If I were to actually experience one, I probably wouldn't like it.

+ + + +

The Ramones were white and the Wooster Group are white (as are many of the other artists and writers I've referenced in this book). Despite much work currently being done to change things, Western art and culture remain primarily white spaces. (Which is not to excuse myself, I really should have done better. But, at the same time, I didn't want to rewrite the past to make it sound like I was more woke than I was. Instead, I want to rewrite the future.) Much of my Internet reading over the past five or so years has been about feminism and anti-racism. For as long as I can remember, I've felt myself to be pro-feminist and anti-racist – which doesn't mean I've always lived up to my ideals – but more recently I've encountered concepts I didn't previously know about such as white fragility and white saviourism. These concepts have a lot to do with why white spaces remain so white, with how white people react when these spaces are challenged, and how such defensive reactions work to reinforce the status quo.

My Internet reading about feminism and anti-racism (alongside many real-life conversations on these topics) has had an enormous impact on my recent thinking and I'm still trying to figure out how to incorporate this thinking into my life and work. Many others I know are also currently trying to do the same. I think: PME-ART is about collaboration and therefore this collaborative spirit represents an opening through which to do something. I think: our work is about being yourself in a performance situation, so when the selves change, when new creator/performers are invited to join, then the work changes as well. And I want the work to change. But how much am I able to let it change, how much am I willing to let go? With each new collaborative project this is a primary question.

I can feel my reticence. How reluctant I am to write about these questions. The main thing is that it all remains in the future. We haven't actually tried anything yet and don't even know exactly what we plan to try. But also, in writing this, I can feel myself treading carefully, feel that I don't want to misstep. I have noticed that when white artists attempt to make anti-racist art they sometimes miss the mark and end up making racist art by mistake. They are too deeply entrenched within their own limited perspective, within their: "I'm an artist and therefore I can do whatever I want." (I think the artist has an ethical responsibility, but then again, I don't think there's any fixed way of understanding exactly what that responsibility is.) I hope collaboration and co-authorship is a way through and past this dilemma but I know from twenty years of experience that real collaboration is never easy. I feel the slogan "nothing about us without us" speaks to the matter most concisely. But still, we all have blind spots; it is always possible to get it wrong. And walking on eggshells has never produced the best art.

+ + + +

All of this is very much about me, and it is my hope that *Emotional Politics* is the PME-ART show we make that will be the most *not* about me. Is it possible to decentre myself within our work? What might this look or feel like? Some of our recent projects have been more about me, and now it's time to turn around, head in the opposite direction. To find ways for PME-ART to be more about others. I'm nervous to write this, worried that after *Emotional Politics* has been made and toured, I'll look back on these words and see how far away what we did was from my original hopes. And yet that is also the nature of our work. It starts somewhere, goes through an extensive, if rather imperfect, collaborative process, and ends up somewhere else, somewhere completely different, somewhere no one could predict.

The very beginning of a new project. Before the beginning. The pre-beginning. When everything is still possible. I want to hang on to this feeling for as long as I can, not to fix anything before it's absolutely necessary, be open to artistic possibilities that, as of yet, I am still unable to conceive. Is it really true that these things happen, that our work spins out in directions I am unable to imagine before they begin? Is this only a fantasy I have about the work, about the possibilities of art, or about the possibilities of collaborative art? I can see it both ways. And perhaps both ways can come together: such things might actually happen *because* they begin as fantasies, as searching, as curiosity, as openness. When something appears that you think you've never seen before, within your own work or the work of others, you can't let it slip by unnoticed, you need to be paying attention, follow it, see where it leads.

Epilogue:

# For Sylvie and Richard

The reason PME is called PME is because, long before I knew them, Sylvie and Richard had a company called La P.M.E. de l'art, a company that produced two shows: *La vie d'Eva* and *La Femme du 'Poète*. I believe *La vie d'Eva* was a kind of dada opera written by Richard, full of palindromes and nonsensical humour. I think I've seen a photograph of it. There are many stories I've been told about this time, but hearing them out of order, often in fragments, over many years, I'm never sure if I have any of it right. Sylvie and Richard were both members of the Quebec Communist Party and the Communist Party of Canada. They met when Sylvie went to the offices of the Party for the first time and Richard opened the door. Sylvie had gone there because she'd seen silkscreened posters, posters that Richard had made. Sylvie started doing youth theatre, I believe related to the Communist Party but I might be wrong, and eventually they decided they wanted to move from communism to art. (Sylvie says also to bring communism into art and to mix them.) Sometimes I feel this is actually all you need to know about PME (especially the communism part).

In the very early days, PME stood for Productions Madame Edgar. One story about it is that Richard was going to register the name, but when he got to the registration office the government official said he needed a signature from Madame Edgar in order to register a company under her name. And, of course, there was no Madame Edgar. Richard tried to explain this but the government official was adamant. Thinking on his feet, Richard asked for some liquid paper and erased the necessary letters on the registration form so it now read Productions M. E. and the name P.M.E. was born. In French, PME also stands for *Petites et moyennes entreprises* (Small and Medium Business), a standard term to categorize businesses that are of a certain size. Sylvie and Richard refer to these years as "the old PME," and I still know relatively little about it, and don't think I've met many of the other people who were involved. It was another era, before my time. By the time I met them, Sylvie and Richard had been doing their festival Les 20 jours du théâtre à risque for six years, so Productions Madame Edgar was already noticeably in the past. (Running a festival is so overwhelming that six years of doing so probably equals at least twenty years of normal living.)

+ + + +

When people now ask me what PME stands for, the question I most frequently get asked, I rarely tell them the Productions Madame Edgar liquid-paper story. At the beginning I told it a great deal but now it no longer feels right. It's not exactly my story. Instead, I tell them it stands for nothing. And then I say: as a fun game we make up things it could stand for. Some of my favourites include: Perfection Made Easy, Prisoners Murderers Entertainers, Pretty Much Everything. And in French: *Pour Mon Ego*. During *Families Are Formed Through Copulation* we joked that it stood for *Papa, Mama, Enfant*. I've never particularly related to the name PME-ART and it seems strange that I've been part of it for so long without the name ever really feeling like my own. In fact, I often think the name is evidence that what we're doing isn't actually mine, that it was something that already existed, that I joined, while at the same time my joining transformed it, and continues to transform it, in ways that, I believe, none of us originally expected or could foresee. Much of the time I feel that PME-ART is basically just Sylvie and Richard and I somehow work for them, or have joined them in something they would be doing anyway even if I wasn't there. (There is evidence supporting this theory in the fact that they co-sign my cheques.) But I know, objectively, this explanation doesn't work at all. It is unequivocally something we're all doing together. Something that would be completely different if any one of us weren't part of it.

+ + + +

Every day I go to the office. Some days there are a lot of things for me to do (most often writing emails) and other days I have the feeling that mainly I'm just watching Sylvie and Richard work. Sylvie is there every day but Richard is only there on Thursdays and Fridays. The other days of the week he works for the government as a tax collector. It is relatively new that Richard is with us Thursdays and Fridays. Previously he worked for the government five days a week and worked with PME-ART only evenings and weekends. (And yet now, as I'm writing this, Richard is preparing to retire from his government job and will soon be with us full-time.) Sylvie and Richard are married and Richard's government income is what has allowed them both to continue doing PME-ART in the selfless way that they do. For much of the past twenty years Sylvie has barely been paid in PME-ART. (We have recently been working to rectify that situation.) I don't think I have the words to express the degree to which, for Sylvie and Richard, PME-ART has been a labour of love. I don't know of any other stories like it. I want to write that they're saints, but know that, as atheists and communists, they wouldn't much like the religious imagery. Secular saints in service of being yourself in a performance situation. It has often crossed my mind that the real reason I'm writing this book is to give them the credit they so clearly deserve and have not received. They work behind the scenes, in the utterly thankless territory of arts admin, and yet their artistic input into what we do cannot be overstated, as ephemeral and difficult to put my finger on as these things so often are. Their thinking and understanding of the world permeates everything we do, the way we work, the way we understand art and life, the fact that we even still exist.

When I started writing this book, I decided beforehand it could not become a book about writing grant applications (and then later writing the final reports for those same grants). Nonetheless, that is what we spend a great deal of our time actually doing. Sylvie has said that, in the almost thirty years she's been doing this, the administrative burden of running an arts organization has gotten more and more strenuous, and often these days it feels like the administrative burden outweighs the artistic one by an absurd degree. The fact that so much of our life is now eaten up by the neo-liberal-arts-administration-bottomless-vortex definitely makes me feel that what we're doing is getting more difficult as the years progress (and I already felt this increasing difficulty on a purely artistic basis, that being an artist only gets harder over time). The grant forms are longer and more bureaucratic, with more and more questions about administration and increasingly fewer questions about art. Sylvie and Richard bear the brunt of these changes, most often protecting me from them. It is a strange dynamic. Once Richard said to me: "You might wonder why we're doing all of this for you. But there's no way to answer that question. There's no reason."

(And then I remind myself they're not doing this only for me. As Claudia says: throughout her many experiences working with companies, she has never felt more respected as an artist than during her time working with PME-ART. She is still astounded every time she thinks of Sylvie and Richard's dedication, and the fight that they both have taken on for all of us to have good working conditions. Claudia says she cannot stress this enough. Nor can she ever thank them enough.)

+ + + +

I've already mentioned that Sylvie and Richard are married. This also must be an important fact. (They also have an adult son named Denis.) Once, during a panel discussion in Toronto, someone asked: "How do you keep a show from going stale when you have to do it over and over again for years?" And I quoted Sylvie, who once said that it's a bit like keeping the spark alive in a relationship over time. The audience member then asked the obvious follow-up question: "How do you do that?" I of course have absolutely no idea. I think Sylvie and Richard know but perhaps they also don't. They're simply living it and dedicating themselves to the tasks at hand. I have now spent more time in the office with them than I have spent with anyone else I have ever met or known. So I probably should have great insights into the many complex dynamics between them. But I don't think I do. It's as mysterious to me as ever. I have since learned that one of the ways to keep a show from going stale is to always keep the possibility open you might surprise yourself or be surprised by others. This is easier said than done.

(Marie Claire says that, for her, the love in PME-ART is palpable. First of the all, the gorgeous, playful, generous, and open love between Sylvie and Richard, which is a constant source of energy. And the love between those in the room, working. She loves Sylvie, Richard, Jacob, Claudia, Caroline, Nadège, Ashlea, Adam. As artists and people. Perhaps this is just her experience, she loves quite easily, and brings it to everything and sustains it sometimes beyond functionality. But when she thinks of the first time she saw Claudia, Caroline, and me perform at Usine C, she remembers this feeling of love in the room. Between the three performers, but also a young girl, an audience member's child, dancing to some of the songs – on the stage, in the corner – and that it was normal and non-disruptive and loving.

It sounds trite that love be part of good work. Marie Claire says that I touch on it when I write about Tracy. And she wonders if I don't write about it more because my experience is so coloured by depression, which she is continually blown away by – how can I be so functional and generous with such an affliction? She also has a sense that she experiences love intensely and regularly and that I must have such a different – perhaps opposite – experience of it. She also wonders if I don't write about it because it isn't cool to talk about love, or worse, because "love is blind." But I honestly don't think that's the reason.)

+ + + +

One time I was walking down the street with Sylvie, I think it must have been five or six years ago, and I said something like: "Have you noticed that when we first met we always used to talk about the future, making plans for all the things we wanted to do, and now we mainly talk about the things we've already done, about the past?" And without missing a beat Sylvie replied: "That's because before we had no past, and now we have no future." I don't know exactly why, perhaps it simply appeals to my nihilistic streak, but for me this is still the funniest joke I've ever heard. (I've tried to tell it a few times and it seems no one else finds it particularly funny.) I rarely laugh at jokes, but when I do it's usually jokes of the blackest hue. The entire time we've been doing PME-ART, I've never been convinced it would last, I've never felt certain we had a future; like many small arts organizations, it often felt to me more precarious than precarious. And yet Sylvie and Richard always thought there was a way, that you keep something alive by continuously fighting for it. I know they're right but also know they have some sort of fight I don't quite have. It might be a generational thing, or might have something to do with class. (Sylvie and Richard are both Québécois working class and I grew up middle class in Toronto.) I look at them and continuously wonder where they get all their fight from. I know it's for a cause, to keep a certain kind of art alive, to create possibilities for art that weren't necessarily there before, but I don't think I have it. There is no question in my mind who it is keeping PME-ART alive.

+ + + +

Sylvie and Richard sometimes talk about being "naive on purpose." That this is something they choose, something they want, to try to be naive on purpose. What I think they mean by it is something like: knowing that what you believe in is not necessarily a clear route to success, and is definitely not the easy road, but doing it anyway because it's what you believe in. In some ways it might be related to Gramsci's famous "pessimism of the intellect, optimism of the will." In art, it's the opposite of cynically doing something just because it will sell. But being naive can of course also, at times, get you burnt. Being naive on purpose means not waiting to know everything before taking action. Rejecting the normal ways of doing things in favour of something more idealistic, more impossible, something that feels more right.

+ + + +

When I told Richard I was writing a book about PME-ART, his first reaction was to joke: "Is it going to be positive?" (And now that the book is almost done I still don't know. Is it?) This echoes another joke about me frequently made in the office: "Jacob is great. If only he could be just a little bit more positive." And it's true, when I let my defences down, which often happens within the day-in, day-out routine of running PME-ART, I seem to be a broken record of pure depression and negativity. Another PME-ART joke about me: "Jacob has a crystal ball that always says no," because so often, when predicting whether or not something we are attempting will work out or not, my prediction is most often that it won't. I've always had the ethical desire not to take my depression out on others. I have often fallen considerably short of this ethical desire.

+ + + +

When I started writing this book I also thought I would end up writing considerably more about my failure to learn French. But in the end I couldn't bring myself to. I'm too ashamed. From my perspective, it just won't stay in my head. People have frequently told me the problem is I'm unwilling to fully apply myself, and this may well be true. I don't know if I've ever actually been able to apply myself to anything other than art. They also say that the problem is I'm unwilling to look foolish by speaking badly. I can't quite believe this, I feel I've often looked foolish and don't particularly mind. But I also can't dismiss it as a factor. The grants we write are mostly in French. Very often French is spoken in the office and during our collaborative processes (though less than before). It's not true that I understand nothing. I understand about thirty per cent. (Sylvie wonders, since I don't understand, how I'm able to estimate the percentage.)

Sylvie suspects that all those years ago when they decided to start working with me, there were many Québécois artists who were irritated or even a bit angry. Why would they choose an anglophone artist from Toronto? What's worse, an anglophone who doesn't speak French, when there are so many amazing Québécois artists to choose from. When I start thinking about it too much I can't get over the degree to which it's a story that makes no sense. When I lived in Toronto I felt completely alienated. And now in Montreal I feel completely alienated and can give my lack of French as the reason for such alienation. But I know it's not the actual reason. It's only an alibi. It would be the same anywhere. At the heart of PME-ART is this cross-cultural act of curiosity, interest, and generosity on the part of Sylvie and Richard. An experiment in going outside of their comfort zones. An experiment that was only meant to last for one project but instead has lasted twenty years.

\+ + + +

Not as much now, but more when we first met, Sylvie would sometimes talk about the power of being the official opposition in theatre or in art. That the official opposition can sometimes do more to change things, both more to change the discourse and more to change concrete policies and actions, than those actually in power. The official opposition has the freedom to push as hard as they want, to act purely on principle, and by continually doing so they can keep things moving toward change. Other things I remember Sylvie saying over the years (most likely French expressions that have no specific equivalent in English): "One foot on the gas, the other foot on the brake." "Slippery like soap." (I'm sure there are so many others I can't remember at the moment.) "One foot on the gas, the other foot on the brake" has to do with how I'm always full of doubt about any given endeavour, how I'm pushing forward and pulling back at the exact same time. It goes without saying that this is an extremely frustrating way to run things. I believe Sylvie would prefer if I were to be this way considerably less often. However, she also says there's something universal about it, something about human nature, that it's a natural human desire to want to push forward and pull back at the same time, for these opposite desires to naturally intertwine. "Slippery like soap" is more like what we should be. We should be slippery like soap, impossible to pin down; as soon as you think you have our number, have us fixed, know exactly what we're about, we slip away, off toward something else. You can never quite get a grasp on what we're doing and there is something artistically energizing about always being able to slip away. We should be slippery like soap.

+ + + +

When young artists ask me for advice I always say the same thing: the only thing that works is persistence. I believe it is also Sylvie and Richard who have taught me this, not through their words but through their actions. There's nothing left to do but dedicate this book to them.

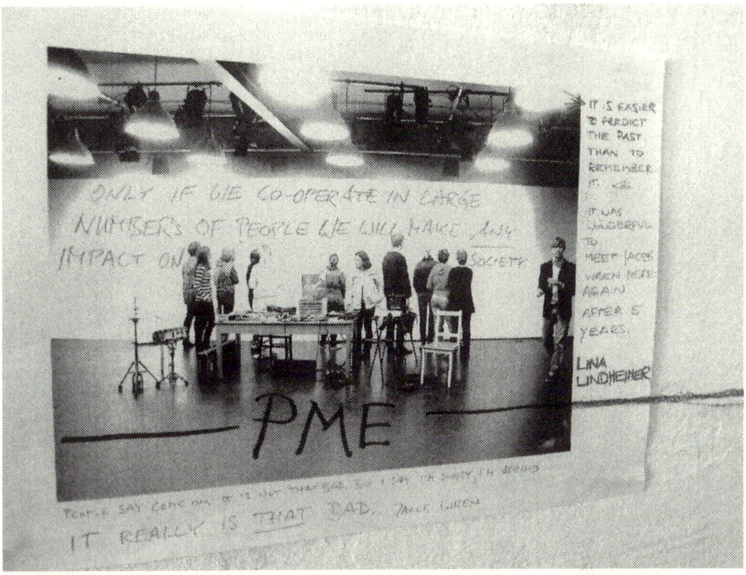


Detail from Jörn J. Burmester's *Vision Mapping* at Wunder der Prärie Festival in Mannheim. Photo: Jörn J. Burmester

Afterword:
## History in the Making
## Or Why 20 Years of PME-ART Aren't Enough

by Kathrin Tiedemann

We're at Podewil in Berlin, late 1990s, and it must have been one of the first editions of reich&berühmt. Jacob Wren had proposed doing a performance called *Every Song I Have Ever Written*. He is standing in a white room, which seems relatively large and empty, because there is nothing there except a microphone stand, a guitar amp, an electric guitar, and Jacob singing. One song after another. Songs written for a band that no longer exists or perhaps never existed in the first place. All in all, the performance runs for several hours, and the longer it takes, the weaker his voice becomes. Other performances are taking place elsewhere at the same time, and it's possible to wander through Podewil and hear the guitar and Jacob's voice in every hallway, no matter where you are in the building. Now and then, I go back and sit down in Jacob's room, listen for a while, and then go away again to watch something else. Then I return and listen to a few more songs.

Jacob later used this material to develop a cover-song project for the Internet and various live formats: a solo performance, a karaoke night, and a band night. Inviting bands to cover your songs may sound like a simple idea. Its charm lies in finding musicians willing to offer their skills to trace the work of another within a conceptual framework. Which, incidentally, contains a lot of parallels to the staging of work in theatre. In a music context, it requires a certain power of persuasion. Especially if you take into consideration that the project is actually an absurd twist on the cover-song idea. You can listen to the fifty-eight songs online at www.everysongiveeverwritten.com, record your own version of a song, send it to PME-ART, and so become part of the project. If you will, it's simultaneously a re-enactment and a pre-enactment – in the sense that these songs were never real hits, but nevertheless, there is still the possibility that they may become so someday. At the same time, the project reflects the ways in which the Internet has transformed how music is produced, disseminated, and consumed today. In the end, it's probably no longer about a song's or a band's success or lack of success, but rather about a collaborative practice and an autonomous artistic intervention, in a context in which it is increasingly difficult to offer alternatives to commercial interests. At any rate, it was brilliant to experience the actual realization of this ongoing project as an alternative to customary production conditions and to witness its continued survival.

Many groups are currently celebrating their twentieth anniversaries – She She Pop, Showcase Beat Le Mot, chelfitsch, theatercombinat – not just PME-ART. Twenty years in which an independent form of producing theatre outside of big institutions developed and successfully asserted itself. In a talk during a major cultural-politics conference at Podewil, She She Pop's Annemarie Matzke, who is also a professor at the University of Hildesheim, recently expressed her own awe at the continued existence of her artist collective and at the fact that the members of the group, now in their mid-forties, have not only managed to raise children, but are currently even thinking about developing their own form of pension plan.

One of the reasons why everyone is all still here, is probably that the story to be told is still in the making. The (hi)story of the interconnectedness of art and life is permanently being rewritten and extended by those whose artistic practice also simultaneously suggests an alternative approach to society. The history of the twentieth-century avant-garde movements may appear attractive and beautiful, dramatic and heroic. However, all those who began making art at the end of the twentieth century would probably no longer claim such things for themselves. Instead it's now all about carrying on and not giving up, about holding on to ideas or recycling them in the full knowledge of having to deal with conditions that aren't characterized by social transformation – quite the contrary.

And the question arises as to whether the desire to affirm one's own history also might have something to do with our currently somewhat obscured view of the future. I therefore consider Jacob Wren's book an invitation to think about the ways to possibly continue. When a performance maker writes a book, is that simultaneously a performative act? Is it possible to reflect one's own history, when it isn't over yet?

Why theatre? Of all things? I've often asked myself that. Over and over again. Why not literature or film or visual art? All that seemed so much more exciting and closer to the reality of my own life, when I began studying theatre in Berlin. The worst thing was that practically all the people who were important to me never felt like coming along when I once again had to go to the theatre. I couldn't even really blame them. I found most of it deadly dull myself. Once, a university professor of mine said that you need a lot of patience for the theatre. That you can only hope to see something really good every few years. But that it would become all the more exciting the longer you occupy yourself with theatre. When I recently brought this up with my former teacher at an event to mark her retirement, I was met with incredulous astonishment. She couldn't remember ever having said anything like it. Nevertheless, this thought has helped me cherish theatre as a space of possibilities. Forget "mirror of society" or "all the world's a stage!" It's about "spaces of becoming," as Ulrike Haß once called them, and about asserting, employing, and defending these spaces as fundamentally public property. In an age in which public spaces in cities are often no more than fakes, when the square in front of the theatre is already in private hands, none of this should be taken for granted.

My interest in theatre was awakened by a deep passion for the 1920s and the age of the Weimar Republic. Brecht and Benjamin, Piscator and the Russian avant-garde. As a teenager, I was fascinated by the era between the World Wars, and for a while I was convinced of having been born into the wrong time period. Theatre was easily accessible. It cost almost nothing for students and thus soon became a kind of alternative plan to school and to family life. In this respect, I just didn't want to believe it when one of my professors tried to convince us that we'd already missed the best, i.e., the 1960s. I skipped his classes and set out to explore the independent scene, which was quite lively in Berlin at that time. We read Brecht's *In the Jungle of Cities* and the *Fatzer Fragment*, together with the post-structural theories that were popular at the time, and attempted to imagine what the end of history could look like in theatre. "The chaos has been used up. And it was the best time." was our life motto, and it somewhat resembled the No Future of the punk age. Then the wall came down and suddenly chaos was within reach. And history was once again being made. Now, even my artist friends found some performances interesting. Müller's *Lohndrücker*; *Roy Cohn/Jack Smith* by Ron Vawters; the early works of Christoph Schlingensief and Frank Castorf at the Volksbühne – I went to see some pieces five times or more, simply because they were different every night and because I wanted to see once more how Herbert Fritsch lay down onstage in the middle of a performance, as if to sleep, and so forced his co-actors to invent something.

There is a wonderful collection of Roland Barthes's writings on theatre entitled: *I've always liked the theatre and yet I hardly go there anymore*. He refers to a divide between a "dreamt" theatre, theatre as a utopian space, and the actual reality of the theatre. Barthes is concerned with the role of the spectator, who wants to play an active "responsible" role in theatre and not be treated like a child, with its food already chewed for it. Barthes also speaks of an "adult" theatre, a theatre that does not attempt to live down or deny the mortality of humankind. Needless to say, this theatre would be a theatre that has overcome the supposed contradictions between popular/accessible and sophisticated/elitist.

The twentieth anniversary of a performance collective is a paradoxical success. Although it has nothing to do with PME-ART, the context reminds me of when Heiner Müller was awarded the European Theatre Prize in Taormina in Sicily. All his friends, renowned theatre scholars from France and Italy, had just delivered formidable speeches about specific aspects of his work. This lasted for several hours. At the end, Bob Wilson performed a charming salutation, for which the assembled flock of guests was very grateful, if only for not having to endure another academic lecture. Then Müller politely thanked the speakers and the sponsors of the prize. He had just been through a major operation and recently been released from the hospital and could hardly speak. Then he said that while listening he had felt much like the vampire in Carl Theodor Dreyer's eponymous horror film, who watches the gravediggers throw soil on his corpse, while lying in his coffin.

By now, the question of "Why theatre?" plays less and less a role for me. On the one hand, because the daily difficulties, the unbelievable inertia of tradition, the battles against windmills, can equally be found in other art forms, albeit in different, but comparable ways. On the other hand, because theatre as a place of assembly, where social interactions can be observed and reflected upon, where unfamiliar connections can be made and contingencies occur, leaves a lot of space for things to happen. Sometimes things are even possible that are not or not yet conceivable in reality. In this respect, theatre's potential as a laboratory or model seems far from being worn out. There are good reasons for the emergence of more and more experimental set-ups at the crossroads of multiple art forms. The desire to call a theatre group a band or think about a performance as an exhibition is also not least of all an indicator of this. You don't have to love theatre for its own sake to use it for certain purposes. You can skate round its representative character and "great art" and examine its practical value anew over and over again. A theatre, in which people do not pretend to be someone else in order to convince others of something, a theatre of non-pretending – which takes collaboration and the participation of spectators as equal players seriously – amounts to a political decision.

Once, Jacob and I went to a concert of the French band François & the Atlas Mountains at the Pudelclub in Hamburg. Before they turned famous. It was one of the most euphoric concerts I can remember. The musicians played their instruments at close quarters, in between the surrounding concertgoers. Afterwards, we talked endlessly about quitting. The theatre. The question has remained of how to realize concepts in theatre that aren't theatre. Usually, the conversations about quitting ended in a joke. For example, that PME-ART should emigrate south or finally do a project in Brazil. As a kind of compensation for the long, hard Canadian winters.

Perhaps then the world and the theatre would appear in a brighter light.

If I ask myself what the theatre of my dreams would look like, I realize that this form of theatre would simultaneously become redundant in the very moment of its emergence and that what we are yearning for is secretly the death of theatre. But just as utopian thinking will never totally be fulfilled, we know that this death is very unlikely to ever happen. It is not easy to comprehend what this realization means for one's own practice. As long as PME-ART exists, there will be no end to the doubt of whether it is right to continue, and I will probably no more likely be able to stop doubting, as I will not be able to stop carrying on.

Part Three:

# Supplementary Material

## **En français comme en anglais, it's easy to criticize** [1998 & 1999]

rough blueprint toward an eventual (never to be written) script

> For surely what is affecting the planet most at the moment has more to do with the movement of multinational capital than the issue of national differences.
> – Jonathan Rosenbaum

> The purpose of a provocation is to make people think.
> – Lars Von Trier

(What follows is only for the purpose of this grant application and is not by any stretch of the imagination meant to be read as a conventional script. The process we have created for *En français comme en anglais, it's easy to criticize* is one of continuous collaborative flux and requires that the show remain live and ever-changing. That means that we don't write it down and we never consider any section of the production "finished." As well, all of the dancing, which makes up the majority of the show, is basically beyond description. Nonetheless, experience has taught us that for members of a granting jury it is difficult to imagine just exactly what the show might look like and some sort of rough approximation in words often seems more effective than a badly made video. So here goes nothing...)

The show begins before the audience actually enters the theatre. On a small table near the front of the stage sits a small white ghetto blaster playing the *Wowee Zowee* CD by the American indie-rock band Pavement. Julie-Andrée is alone onstage wandering from chair to chair, listening to the music, not quite sure where to sit or what to do with herself. The audience slowly enters. While the audience is still entering, the record button loudly pops up on the tape deck of the small white ghetto blaster (there is a microphone placed directly over the record button) and Julie-Andrée goes to it, takes the tape out and turns it over, explains to the audience that she's just making a cassette dub of the Pavement CD for a close friend, and goes back to wandering from chair to chair.

After a while Alex enters. She doesn't know that Julie-Andrée is making a tape for a friend, goes to the small white ghetto blaster, pops open the CD lid, takes the CD out and places it in the second CD player, putting the first track on repeat. She then meanders toward the centre of the stage and does a slow, lonely dance, waiting for company. This is how the rest of the cast is introduced. First Tracy enters and does a slowly languorous dance with Alex. As each cast member dances with Alex, we see relationships form that will continue to develop and be fleshed out for the rest of the show. There are two microphones on stands side by side at the front of the stage. When Tracy is finished dancing she goes to the desk, picks up one of the hundreds of piles of white typing paper that litter the stage, and gloriously flings it up into the air. Paper falls everywhere. Among the carpet of paper that now covers the floor is a single sheet of text, the first piece of text of the show. Tracy gets down on her hands and knees and searches for it. When she finds it she goes to the first of the two microphones and says in French (a bit hesitantly):

TRACY: *Bonsoir, nous sommes très heureux de vous accueillir ici, ce soir. Nous sommes tous curieux de voir comment vous allez réagir à l'idée étrange de faire une pièce sur la critique.* Since this is a show about criticism and translation, we thought a good way to begin might be with a translation of a criticism of a translation.

She waits for Martin, who is now dancing with Alex. After a long and beautiful dance with Alex, Martin then joins Tracy at the microphone.

MARTIN: *Comme le spectacle est à propos de la critique et de la traduction, on a pensé qu'une bonne façon de commencer serait de faire la critique d'une traduction particulièrement mauvaise.*

TRACY: As well, since this show may well, by some, be perceived as being somewhat marginal, we've chosen to find such an example in the margins of Gilles Deleuze's last book before his suicide, *Essays Critical and Clinical*, or more specifically in footnote number 53, chapter 18: "The Exhausted," an essay that focuses on the works of

Samuel Beckett, I am sure you are all familiar with it. (Tracy walks to the back table to get the book.)

MARTIN: *Étant donné qu'on est marginalisé, on va assumer notre marginalité, en portant toute notre attention sur une petite note de bas de page du livre de Gilles Deleuze,* Critique et clinique *(Je m'explique mal la fascination des Anglos pour les auteurs français, à moins que ce soit par exotisme, et ce, d'autant plus qu'ils doivent comprendre tout de travers ou perdre la précision du style dans les traductions) note numéro 53, chapitre 18. L'essai en question est intitulé* "The Exhausted," *en français, « L'épuisé ».*

TRACY: The footnote reads as follows: "The second reference is to Jean-Luc Godard's famous formula"... Perhaps you should read the French:

MARTIN: *« pas une image juste, juste une image »*

TRACY: Which is then translated into English as: "not a correct image, just an image." This is an ineffective translation for several reasons.

MARTIN: *La citation « pas une image juste, juste une image » est traduite en anglais par « pas une image appropriée, juste une image ». Tracy pense que c'est une traduction inadéquate pour plusieurs raisons.*

TRACY: The translation we prefer would be "not a just image, just an image." This would maintain Godard's wordplay and also clarify that the theme he is addressing has something to do with morality. I realize this is only a small point, but within our show, the show that has already begun, morality, or more specifically ethics, are also at issue, also relatively "small points" – but simply because they are not highlighted does not mean that we wish them to be mistranslated.

MARTIN: *Je pense que ce que Tracy vient juste de dire n'est pas clair, même en anglais. Je vais donc essayer de traduire et de clarifier en même temps: une traduction plus efficace de la citation « pas une image juste, juste une image », en anglais, pourrait être "not a just image, just an image." En fait, c'est comme ça que ça a été traduit le plus souvent.*

*Cette traduction préserverait le jeu de mot de Godard. (C'est con, c'est un des rares cas où un jeu de mot peut traverser la barrière des langues et ils ont réussi à passer à côté.) Mais, chose plus importante, l'utilisation du mot « just » contrairement au mot* "correct" *sert à mettre en évidence que la citation de Godard renferme une composante morale. C'est peut-être un détail, mais dans notre spectacle, qui est d'ailleurs déjà commencé, les questions morales ou plus précisément éthiques sont abordées mais, comme dans la citation de Godard, elles demeurent à un niveau embryonnaire – elles restent des questions mineures.*

*Et j'en arrive au moment où les paroles de Tracy deviennent vraiment obscures, à savoir quand elle a dit: tout est effleuré, on ne souligne rien, mais ça ne veut pas dire qu'on cherche à être mal interprété.*

*Je pense que ce que ça signifie, c'est que le spectacle «* In both English and French, *C'est Facile De Critiquer » est de plus en plus un spectacle sur l'éthique, mais cette thématique se manifeste de manière extrêmement floue. Le manque de clarté laisse place à la confusion et au malentendu. Dans l'espace créé par cette confusion, il est possible de perdre tout sens éthique, de la même façon qu'on néglige la composante morale – la moralité – en traduisant le mot « juste » par le mot* "correct." *On perd non seulement le jeu de mot mais aussi quelque chose de beaucoup plus important. Je pense que ça clarifie un peu...*

While on the topic of ethics this might be a good time for another "small criticism." In this production I am replacing my good friend and colleague Benoît Lachambre, who was instrumental in the creation of this piece and who performed my role in the first production. Though I am more than happy to be here tonight, I also realize that my inclusion poses a number of ethical dilemmas. In the kind of "semi-collective" or "pseudo-collective" work this show represents performers are partially responsible for the creation of the material which they perform. They can claim a kind of ownership, a kind of authorship of their roles. Much of the material I will be performing tonight was created by me, but some of it was also created by Benoît. And a second, perhaps more important ethical question: can people be used interchangeably and of course it happens all the time, but are people really so interchangeable.

Julie-Andrée decides to forgive Alex for fucking up her cassette and they too begin a slow dance. Simultaneously, Tracy begins another text which Martin translates into French. As Martin tries to translate, Tracy continuously cuts him off.

TRACY: Criticism is always, to a certain extent, a utopian proposal. Because when one criticizes something one is simultaneously presupposing an imaginary alternative which, one assumes, is in some respects superior to the phenomenon or object currently on view. Because when things are going badly, it is important to have some vision of utopia in order to make life, at the very least, bearable. And if we wish to talk about the future we should speak not only about utopia but also about concrete political processes.

Martin is still having a difficult time translating, making mistakes, but Tracy goes on and on with the text.

TRACY: As Leszek Kołakowski writes: "We need a socialist tradition that is aware of its own limitations, since the dream of ultimate salvation on earth is despair disguised as hope – the will to power disguised as a craving for justice." I suppose the term "socialist" in that quotation is a little bit didactic but...well...you know...why not? All right, let's get started.

When Tracy is finished the text, having left Martin in the dust, she drops the sheet of paper onto the floor and returns to dance with Alex for a second time. Martin picks up the sheet of paper and speaks to the audience in French, more thoroughly translating what he was unable to properly translate the first time round.

MARTIN: *Je devrais peut-être reprendre les points saillants du texte, parce que je n'ai pas vraiment réussi à traduire (ni même à placer un mot).*

*Jusqu'à un certain point, la critique est toujours une proposition utopique. Quand on critique quelque chose, c'est qu'on présuppose une alternative imaginaire qu'on considère supérieure au phénomène ou à l'objet qu'on a critiqué.*

*Et quand les choses vont mal, c'est important d'avoir une vue sur l'utopie – une perspective en quelque sorte – qui puisse rendre la vie à tout le moins supportable.*

*Tant qu'à vouloir parler d'avenir, il faudrait parler non seulement de l'utopie, mais aussi d'intentions politiques concrètes.*

*Comme l'a dit Leszek Kołakowski: il nous faut une tradition socialiste, mais consciente de ses limites, car on sait bien que notre rêve d'un ultime « salut sur terre » est en fait du désespoir qu'on déguise en espoir, une soif de pouvoir déguisée en soif de justice.*

*Peut-être que le terme « socialiste » dans cette citation fait un peu didactique, mais bon. Pourquoi pas?*

He rushes to join the performers who have already started the show. Simultaneously, a drama is unfolding behind him. Tracy cuts into Alex and Julie-Andrée's slow dance and, in an act of subtle musical revenge, Alex puts on some rocking dance music ("Sounds Like Preset Rhythm" by the Laura Carbon Trio) at a volume loud enough to obliterate the previous slow-dance music. Tracy and Julie-Andrée adapt, morphing their slow dance into a frenetic, hyperkinetic twist. Soon everyone is in on the action, and a full-blown, partner-switching dance number is interrupted only by individual cast members casually walking to the front of the stage and placidly looking at the audience. The cast members watching the audience, against a background of frenetic dancing, has something very directly to do with criticism.

Moving on. Tracy returns to the first microphone, shutting off the music on the way. Moments later Martin joins her, having been interrupted from a particularly effective duet with Julie-Andrée.

At the microphones Tracy and Martin perform the following routine, with Tracy speaking English and Martin translating.

TRACY: This show was directed by Jacob Wren, who will be arriving onstage shortly. He has come all the way from Toronto to do so. And may I state from personal experience that he's been an absolute pleasure to work with.

MARTIN: *Le spectacle que vous voyez ce soir a été mis en scène par Jacob Wren, qui a fait tout ce chemin de Toronto pour venir à Montréal. Comme on sait, ils sont très conventionnels en danse et en théâtre à Toronto; ils ne sont pas super en mise en scène, ni en travail formel non plus. Je peux vous le dire parce que Jacob ne parle pas français, ne lit pas le français: il ne comprend pas un mot.*

TRACY: Did you just say that Jacob doesn't speak French?

MARTIN: *Oui.*

TRACY: Did you say it in an insulting way?

MARTIN: *Non.*

TRACY: All right. Next we will demonstrate how criticism actually works, in real life, using only an extremely frightening clown doll and a large glass jar with a somewhat garish pineapple motif.

MARTIN: *On va vous démontrer comment fonctionne la critique dans la vraie vie, en utilisant simplement un clown de chiffon (laid à faire peur) et une grosse jarre à motifs d'ananas (de très mauvais goût).*

TRACY: The clown doll represents the "work of art." The large glass jar represents criticism.

MARTIN: *Le clown de chiffon représente l'œuvre d'art et la jarre en verre, la critique.*

TRACY: The demonstration is as follows... (They demonstrate. The demonstration consists of stuffing the clown doll into the glass jar.) *Voilà.*

MARTIN: *La démonstration va comme suit.* That's it.

TRACY: I'm sorry. I forgot to put on my music cue. Just one minute.

Martin stops Tracy as she's walking back toward the third CD player.

MARTIN: As well as speaking about criticism I think it's important that we try and address some problems that we've been having with translation.

TRACY: Just let me get this CD.

Tracy continues toward the back table. When she gets there she finds something amounting to a minor war going on between Alex and Julie-Andrée. Julie-Andrée has taken the cassette which Alex ruined earlier in the show and is unwinding it all over the stage. Unwound cassette tapes from previous shows also litter the floor. Tracy breaks up the argument and gets the CD for her music cue. Simultaneously, Martin is talking to the audience in a strange mixture of English and French.

MARTIN: Translation was supposed to be one of the themes of this show. We started off with a quite good idea about how when someone was translating a text it would be a comic opportunity to insert some criticism.
*Je disais à Tracy qu'on ne devrait pas seulement parler de critique, mais aussi des problèmes de traduction qu'on a eus. On avait pensé que la traduction serait une façon comique d'insérer la critique dans le spectacle. Mais ça n'a pas été facile.*

Martin turns to Tracy, who is now putting on her music cue in the small white ghetto blaster.

MARTIN: *C'est l'idée qu'on avait mais on n'y est jamais arrivé. Sais-tu pourquoi le problème n'a pas été résolu, Tracy?*
And that idea never quite panned out. I think it would be interesting to discuss with the audience some of the reasons why that is.
*Ce qu'on aimerait, c'est de parler de la problématique avec les spectateurs.*

TRACY: Go ahead.

MARTIN: All right. (After a long pause of not being able to figure out what to say.) Fuck it. I have to go.

Martin storms off the stage as he will do many times over the course of the show. What follows is something we refer to as The Make-Up section or "the waiting section" or "the nothing section." Over and over again on the small white ghetto blaster plays the music cue Tracy put on: the intro to The Make-Up CD *Destination: Love - Live! at Cold Rice* - a short, incredibly funky, faux James Brown riff pumped out with manic energy as the band takes to the stage. Meanwhile the rest of the cast fill their time with various banal, but entrancingly performed, activities as they wait for Martin to return so the show can continue. Alex walks from chair to chair, ending each circuit with a violent, near-epileptic fit. Tracy tells a few jokes to the audience and then sets up a series of folding chairs for a later routine. Martin returns but for some reason "the nothing section" continues with Martin adding his walkie-talkie routine to the mix.

Martin's walkie-talkie routine involves his sitting on the desk near the front of the stage coyly waving at the audience, then picking one of the two walkie-talkies up off the table, walking to the back door of the stage with it, and reciting one of the following lines into the walkie-talkie - sometimes in English, sometimes in French.

MARTIN: This is my secret way of talking to the audience.
*Ça, c'est ma façon secrète de vous parler.*

When I have something secret to say this is the means by which you'll hear it.
*Si j'ai un secret à vous dire, ce sera le moyen par lequel vous pourrez m'entendre.*

I don't have anything secret to say right now. But when I do you'll hear it here first.
*Je n'ai pas de secret à vous dire pour le moment, mais quand j'en aurai un, vous allez être les premiers à le savoir.*

"The nothing section" slowly evolves into two simultaneous duets. The first duet is between Martin and Alex and involves a recap of their earlier slow dance, which rapidly degenerates into a sort of violent, very real and physical wrestling and then back into infinite tenderness. The second duet is between Tracy and Julie-Andrée and involves the folding chairs Tracy set up earlier. Tracy knocks over the chairs and Julie-Andrée scrambles to set them back up. While all this is going on, Jacob makes his first entrance. He puts a loud drum 'n' bass track on each of the three CD players, creating total cacophony to which he performs a completely spastic dance solo. At the same time the two duets have fallen into sync, mirroring the slow dance of the opening. Jacob finishes his spastic solo and, completely exhausted and out of breath, casually goes to the small white ghetto blaster and puts on the track "Censuré!" by the sixties French ya-ya singer Aline. Everyone runs as fast as they can to the back corner of the stage and performs the stupidest, most difficult to describe, unison group dance you have ever seen.

In the middle of the dance Martin storms offstage. He says something as he does so but we cannot really hear him. Tracy stops dancing as well and goes to the first microphone at the front of the stage.

TRACY: If there are any anglophones in the audience, what he said was that he couldn't, in good conscience, perform the dance because it was too cheap.

For the first time in the show there is a blackout. In the blackout Alex sits on a stool and turns on an electric heater. In the darkness, we see just the slightest outline of her face highlighted by the orange/red glow of the heater. Slowly, one by one, the cast members gather in a semicircle around her. Martin returns and as he opens the door we see only his silhouette against the white light of the outer hallway. When everyone is seated centre stage in a semicircle the lights slowly return and the discussion can begin. Each night the cast engages in a completely improvised discussion on a surprise topic. The discussion always begins in the same way, with Jacob explaining to the audience that one of the main ideas that hadn't yet found its way into the show is to be found in the second half of the title: "It's Easy To Criticize." And that this phrase is part of a larger idea that while it may well be easy to criticize, it's difficult in this age of Turbo-Capitalism to actually do anything that has any real effect on our lives or on the world. Then Jacob hits the cast with the surprise topic, which they are actually hearing for the first time. For example: one night the topic was "Have there been times in your life when money interfered with friendship?" and on another night the question was "Is sex important?"

Since the conversation is completely improvised it is never completely certain when or how it will end. Sometimes it would just end perfectly and spontaneously, effortlessly leading us into the next section. However, in case this didn't magically happen we came up with a number of different ways of getting out of it. One way was Jacob reading a quote from Susan Sontag's "Against Interpretation" in French translation. Since Jacob's French is so bad it's completely beyond recognition, this resulted in a comic effect. This would often lead to Julie-Andrée and Martin having their own French conversation in a rapid and fluent Québécois that would leave the rest of the cast completely behind.

At any rate, at some point in all of this Julie-Andrée would get up and put on the next piece of music ("The Emperor of Oranges" by Milky) and perform a lilting dance solo to it as the improvised conversation continued and slowly morphed into the following scripted conversation.

TRACY: We just thought now might be a good time to read you two short texts which relate directly to the topic of criticism. The first is rather well-known, a short except from the play *Waiting for Godot* by Samuel Beckett. During the following reading, I will be taking on the role of Vladimir while Alex will be reading the role of Estragon. Here we go.

Vladimir: Moron!

Estragon: That's the idea, let's abuse each other.

They turn, move apart, turn again, and face each other.

Vladimir: Moron!

Estragon: Vermin!

Vladimir: Abortion!

Estragon: Morpion!

ALEX: Actually, I'm not really familiar with that word: "morpion."

TRACY: No, I'm not really sure what it means either. I think maybe it's a made-up word.

ALEX: Sort of like a combination between a moron and a scorpion.

TRACY: Yeah, something like that.

Martin interrupts to explain that *morpion* is actually a French word meaning genital crabs.

ALEX: Thank you, Martin. Well, that certainly would be quite an insult. Maybe we should start again.

TRACY: Sure.

Vladimir: Moron!

Estragon: That's the idea, let's abuse each other.

They turn, move apart, turn again, and face each other.

Vladimir: Moron!

Estragon: Vermin!

Vladimir: Abortion!

Estragon: Morpion!

Vladimir: Sewer-rat!

Estragon: Curate!

Vladimir: Cretin!

Estragon: (with finality) Critic! (And that is of course the point. That critic is more or less the ultimate insult.)

Vladimir: Oh! (He wilts vanquished, and turns away.)

ALEX: Tracy, would you like to show us what that might look like, wilting vanquished and turning away.

TRACY: No, not really.

ALEX: Good, I didn't think so. What else? *Au début, on avait prévu vous lire le même petit extrait de* En attendant Godot *en anglais et en français. Mais dans la traduction française le passage a été complètement remplacé par une didascalie... L'as-tu avec toi?*

TRACY: What?

ALEX: Do you have it there?

TRACY: *Ah oui! Juste ici.* (Handing Alex the book.)

ALEX: *Didascalie: « Échange d'injures. Silence. »*

TRACY: *Vous pouvez vous imaginer à quel point nous sommes désappointées.*

ALEX: *Pourquoi tu penses?*

TRACY: *Pourquoi nous sommes désappointées?*

ALEX: *Non, pourquoi la série d'insultes dont le point culminant est le mot « critique » n'apparaît plus dans la version française.*

TRACY: *Je ne sais pas, c'est assez étrange. Même dans la version en anglais, les injures sont en français. Peut-être que le français se prête mieux à l'injure.*

ALEX: All right. Our second short text is from the book *Air Guitar* by American art critic Dave Hickey. It is from the title essay and it reads as follows. I'll just try and translate as I go along here.

*« Certains de mes collègues vous diront que les gens méprisent les critiques parce qu'ils craignent le pouvoir. Je dirais mieux. Les gens méprisent les critiques parce qu'ils méprisent la faiblesse et, vraiment, il n'y rien de plus faible - en matière d'écriture- que la critique. C'est l'équivalent littéraire du* "air guitar" *[lorsqu'on mime un solo, sans guitare,* Tracy would you please, show us...] *C'est l'équivalent littéraire du* "air guitar"*: rafales de silence et gestes attendrissants, mais qui ne reposent sur rien, sauf le souvenir de la musique. La critique ne génère pas de nouvelles connaissances, ne fait état d'aucun fait réel; elle ne se suffit pas à elle-même. Elle ne sauve pas non plus les démarches qu'elle affectionne (du moins, jamais comme on le souhaiterait), ni n'anéantit les choses qu'elle déteste.*
The Edinburgh Review *n'a pas réussi à détruire John Keats, ni Diderot, Boucher, ni Ruskin, Whistler; et c'est précisément ce que j'aime de la critique. C'est un jeu réservé aux perdants et ça, tout le monde le sait.*
*Même les gens ordinaires, quand ils découvrent que vous êtes critique, réagissent comme si vous étiez maquilleur pour un salon funéraire: ils sont un peu dégoûtés par votre travail, mais infiniment curieux de savoir ce qui vous a amené à faire ce boulot. ».*

Tracy, would you care to comment on that quotation?

TRACY: I don't think you read it very well.

While Tracy and Alex are performing the above text, Julie-Andrée and Martin are performing the string duet directly behind them.

The string duet begins with Julie-Andrée reaching into Martin's pocket and pulling out a length of string, one end still attached to the inside of the pocket. For the entirety of the duet the two dancers are connected by an umbilical cord of string. Martin places his hand in Julie-Andrée's mouth. Julie-Andrée looks mutely at the ground. Martin stretches out his arms. Julie-Andrée half walks away but then quietly decides to return. Martin bends over backwards. Julie-Andrée decides to walk away once and for all and as she does she accidentally pulls on the string and a spray of pocket change is scattered all over the stage. Martin, embarrassed, runs off the stage for a third time. Julie-Andrée gets down on her hands and knees and starts picking up the coins. All of this is danced intensively but also as if it were some sort of little story.

Then Jacob starts running as fast as he can back and forth across the length of the stage. While he does so, Alex asks him improvised questions in the microphone, which he attempts to answer, completely out of breath, as honestly as possible. Some sample questions: do you believe theatre still has the potential to change the world? Tell us about your shoes? Do you love your parents? Have you ever attempted suicide? The last question of this section always has something to do with Josephus, at which point Jacob stops running and, by this point completely out of breath, attempts to tell the story of Josephus.

MARTIN (into the walkie-talkie): So pay careful attention or you just might miss it.
*Je vous demanderais de rester attentifs. À plus tard.*

JACOB: Josephus was a Jewish historian who lived sometime around 73 BC and was one of a small number of survivors of the massacre at Masada. He survived through guile and a continuous stream of interlocking scams and he is often portrayed in Jewish history as a traitor but recently I came across two unrelated accounts, both of which portrayed him as a hero. In these accounts he was portrayed as a hero simply because he loved life, because he took enormous joy from simply being alive, and the moral of the Josephus story is that it's all right to find joy in simply being alive, it's nothing to feel guilty about. Life can be joyous.

At this point in Jacob's out-of-breath monologue he is interrupted by Martin, who re-enters with the walkie-talkie and speaks into it (in either English or in French).

MARTIN: This is my secret way of talking to the audience. And I have a secret....
*Ceci est ma façon secrète de vous parler. Et là, j'ai un secret à vous dire: « sans technique, un don n'est rien qu'une sale manie ».*

Martin then walks straight to the front of the stage and begins an extremely sloppy solo to the song "I Wish I Were Him" as sung by former Bikini Kill frontwoman Kathleen Hanna. At the same time Jacob wanders over to Tracy and they have the following conversation.

JACOB: So one of the things Josephus makes me think of is how real life is important. And how it's difficult to bring real life into a show like this one. So I thought now would be a good time to try and bring some real life into the show and the way I'd like to try and do that is by recounting some real-life stories that actually happened. Things that actually happened to us in real life. Let's see... The first story actually happened to you and me, we were getting on the subway and I saw a poster, an advertisement, for condoms. And I said that if I worked in advertising I also had an idea for an advertising campaign for condoms. And the slogan would be: "Condoms, The Best Thing About Sex!" And I told you this idea. Do you remember what you said?

TRACY: Yes, I said: I'm sure glad I haven't slept with you.

JACOB: Yes. And then I said that I also had an idea for a television commercial that would be part of this same advertising campaign. Just a little fifteen-second spot. And in this television commercial it would show a man and a woman having sex. And the woman would say: "Ouch, you're on my hair." And then it would cut to a black screen with the slogan in big white letters: "Condoms, The Best Thing About Sex!" Do you remember if I had any other ideas for television commercials?

TRACY: No, I don't remember if you had any other ideas for television commercials.

They are interrupted by Martin, who stops his solo to announce to the audience that he doesn't want to do the show anymore and that he's going to the bar of the venue. He asks Jacob if he understands (since he said it in French) and Jacob says he does. Martin then leaves the theatre and goes up to the bar. At the same time Alex has taken the flowers off of the back table and placed each one of them in the large water bottles the cast were using to drink out of during the improvised conversation. Jacob goes to get the second walkie-talkie so he can communicate with Martin at the bar and then resumes his conversation with Tracy:

JACOB (into the walkie-talkie): Martin? (No reply.) Martin?

MARTIN (from the bar, angrily): What?

JACOB: Just checking that you're there. Okay, now more real-life stories from the rest of the cast. One from Tracy maybe. Do you have a real-life story?

TRACY: No, I don't.

JACOB: Maybe I could request a real-life story that, once again, happened to both of us. We were sitting in the kitchen, I think this is quite relevant to the topic of criticism, and you were saying you were having difficulty reconciling yourself with being an actor. Maybe you could talk a bit about that?

TRACY: I don't really want to talk about that actually.

JACOB: I was just thinking we could each present a vulnerable real-life moment? I've done mine, maybe you could take one.

TRACY: Like the condom story?

JACOB: Yes, that really happened, didn't it?

TRACY: It really happened, but I don't think it made you very vulnerable.

JACOB: What interested me about what you were saying in the kitchen was that you were beginning to realize that actors were stupid. And that being an actor was starting to make you insecure about your own intelligence. And maybe you could speak a bit about that now.

TRACY: Fuck you, Jacob. You're an arrogant son-of-a-bitch. I've been sitting here doing nothing for half an hour. What about that? You know, you couldn't even make a traditional piece of theatre because you don't have the chops, actually. Has anyone ever told you that? And now I'm supposed to believe that Mr. I Hate Theatre is suddenly interested in what the actor has to say. Right, you're interested in my relationship to acting. That's bullshit. You're interested in finding someone to blame for this meaningless fiasco and I'm the easiest target. Besides, Alex is really busy over there putting some pussy willows in a jar. I'm so sorry, she's making art. Look at that, everyone, Alex is making art, isn't it beautiful. Shhh, we mustn't disturb her. Here I am talking over top of it like the stupid interpreter that I am. I have some mysterious talent. Where does it come from? Does it come from God? I don't know. I'm just a vessel. I'm not an artist. I'm not even a human being really. How can I be expected to understand this complex intellectual show with all these big ideas in it? Better I should humiliate myself now, that way you can breeze on out of here and get to the fucking bar and be the boy fucking genius. Just what the world needs, Jacob, another boy genius. Hey, maybe you'll get laid again, art boy. Be a fucking hero. So I come across looking like the Anglo of all Anglos. But you're so brave to cross cultures like that. Everyone will forget you can't speak a word of fucking French, you never will learn a word of French, because then you'd have to spend some time thinking about something other than yourself and your work. Everyone says that actors are supposed to be selfish but really actors are supposed to serve the piece. Well, I am fucking sick of hearing men talk about what they're trying to do with their work, I'm sick of it...

They are interrupted by Julie-Andrée, who has gone to the back of the stage and is making a strange, comical purring noise. Tracy sees her, stops arguing, and goes to the back of the stage and joins her. They both stand at the back of the stage making a strange purring noise.

MARTIN: *Trop de discussions et d'analyse, c'est emmerdant et ça mène nulle part, sinon à la paralysie du processus.*

And then the show is basically over. We're still not completely sure how to end it, but the way we ended it in Montreal was with a timid group dance to the extremely relevant French song "Mourir pour des idées" by Georges Brassens. Halfway through the song Jacob walks to the front of the stage and puts his foot on the wah-wah pedal, making the entire song warble charmingly. Julie comes frontstage and continues the same dance and then, as the lights are fading for the final time, we hear Martin over the walkie-talkie (still at the bar): asking what's going on onstage, asking if the show was over yet, and inviting us for a drink.

## Theatre Reminds Me of Politics (2009)

It makes me sad that there is no convincing term to describe the kinds of theatre I love. Over the years there have been many attempts to coin such a term and make it stick: experimental, radical, theatre of cruelty, the alienation effect, post-mainstream, post-modern, ontological-hysterical, conceptual, contemporary, devised, iconoclastic, post-dramatic, etc. However, none of these terms feel particularly compelling to me.

Theatre reminds me of politics. The fate of the kind of theatre I love reminds me of the fate of the radical left over the course of the past century. One way or another, the conservative bloc always finds a way to suppress or absorb all more adventurous paths. In theatre, when I hear someone speak of the need for a "return to the classics," it reminds me of fascism. This might be unfair, but it is how I honestly feel.

The radical left certainly had its share of problems, but without an effective left-wing presence everything simply drifts further and further to the right. Without anything concrete to back it up, critique gradually becomes meaningless.

There are many formal, structural, and process-based qualities that characterize the kind of theatre I love:

- a rejection of artifice as the basis for theatre
- a foregrounding of the human dimension of the performer and the human dimension of the performance situation
- performance as a vulnerable activity
- treatment of the physical space of performance as a real, shared space
- theoretical and philosophical thematic content and research
- an ongoing, long-term collaborative creation process with the wisdom to avoid stasis
- room for imperfection

- constantly starting from scratch
- attempting to significantly push beyond what one already knows
- etc.

However, none of these qualities particularly define what I actually most love about it.

Sometimes I suspect what I love about it is how improbable it is that something so compelling and alive can potentially, perhaps only momentarily, exist within the structurally conservative world of theatre, a world in which there is always this intense pressure to sell tickets, to please people, always the fear that when you walk onstage the audience will see too much of you, will see things about you that you don't want them to see. Sometimes it seems to me that the process of rehearsal is simply a process of emotional armouring: we will make everything absolutely perfect so no one will ever see who or what we really are.

Everything about the theatre setting conspires toward something manageable and safe: the fact that onstage one is exposed, the fact that you have to repeat it over and over and over again, the fact that if no one comes the work is considered a failure, the fact that it is ephemeral and does not last, that its history is in a constant state of evaporation, the fact that it is collaborative, the fact that it is funded by the government, the fact that tradition hangs over it like a blood-soaked sword, all the various spoken and unspoken levels of hierarchy, administration, and authority.

How can one possibly create something alive and vital within such a deadened and deadening space? How might the radical left reinvent itself in a manner that might, even in a small way, begin to make the world more humane and people more emancipated? I have no idea if this analogy between theatre and politics is fair, but if it is not, that makes it only one of the many unfair things that, day after day, somehow keep me going.

## **A short text on certain aspects of collaboration** [2014]

All of my performance work has been in (some sort of) collaboration and yet I've always found these experiences of working together difficult, often unpleasant, and continue mainly because I have some ideological belief in it: that in working together with other people it is possible to make something more compelling, more tender, more unexpected, more vulnerable than it is possible to make alone. I don't know if I genuinely believe this (anymore) in reality, but I continue to believe it in some other sense: as an ideal or fantasy. Then the question becomes: how does this ideal or fantasy interact with the difficulty of the reality? What do I do with my frustrations and disappointments? How do I lower my expectations while at the same time working toward something worthwhile?

Or a different kind of question: how does one live and take energy from one's own loneliness? I know, as a teenager, I thought it perfectly reasonable to assume that working with others would make me feel less alienated, less isolated. For the most part it has not. I now fear I pinned my teenage hopes on the wrong misguided solution. I now wonder if there was some other question: how to be alienated together (from both each other and the world). I associate being in a group with talking. What would it mean for me to associate it with silence? Or music? In a conversation about working in collectives, someone once told me there was a Colombian (I think it was Colombian) expression: "He with the most spit wins." This made me laugh out loud in recognition. But am I even thinking about collectives anymore? What about leadership? What kind of leadership allows all members to flourish? Or a model where, for different things, at different times, we each take turns being in charge?

In a completely different text, I recently wrote: "I keep circling round and round this idea that what politics needs today is a different way of thinking about time, that the problem with Marxism is it was working toward victory in the future, while what we need is more like a victory of living together in mutual loneliness, a victory-in-the-present-as-future-that-will-never-come, which sounds frustrating, and probably is. But how to imagine this impossible present-future hybrid as not frustrating, as something good, something desirable, a struggle and strength worth having, as possible. Trying to imagine the things I am not yet able to imagine."

A short text should end with a fantasy and the fantasy is as follows: I have an idea for how we should do it and you have an idea for how we should do it. I don't much care for your idea and you don't much care for mine. But we respect each other enough. So we try to think together what aspects of your idea are most important to you and what aspects of my idea are most important to me, to come up with a third idea that is so much more remarkable than anything either of us could ever come up with on our own. And we realize we have made a breakthrough, cherish this fact, want to keep going so it might someday happen again. And perhaps such things happen every day. Or perhaps togetherness really becomes magical when we leave, once and for all, the realm of ideas behind.

## Credits for performances created and produced by PME and PME-ART (1998–2018)

Artistic direction: Sylvie Lachance and Jacob Wren.
Administrative direction: Richard Ducharme.

**En français comme en anglais, it's easy to criticize** (1998)

Created and performed by Alexandra Rockingham Gill, Benoît Lachambre, replaced by Martin Bélanger, Julie Andrée T., Tracy Wright (once replaced by Shannon Cochrane), and Jacob Wren. Translation of the texts by Carrie Loffree, Sylvie Lachance, Caroline Dionne, and the cast. Translators/cameo performers on tour: Ondřej Hrab (Prague), Detlef Skowronek (Dresden), Sven Åge Birkeland (Bergen and Stockholm), Sven Medvesek (Zagreb), Nikolai Francke (Berlin), and Veit Sprenger (Hamburg). Lighting: Robert Gauthier and Lee Anholt. Production support: Catherine Bisaillon. Technical Direction: Lee Anholt and Paul Caskey. Touring agents/advisors: Menno Plukker and Sherrie Johnson.

A co-presentation with Tangente and Les 20 jours du théâtre à risque Festival (Montreal). With the support of the Canada Council for the Arts, Heritage Canada, the Department of Foreign Affairs and International Trade of Canada, the Conseil des arts et des lettres du Québec, the Toronto Arts Council, Laidlaw Foundation and Laoun, opticien, as part of Québec in Motion-UK 2000 and Québec in New York 2001.

**Unrehearsed Beauty / Le Génie des autres** (2002)

Created and performed by Martin Bélanger, Alexandra Rockingham Gill, Simone Moir, Samuel Roy-Bois, Julie Andrée T., Tracy Wright (once replaced by Shannon Cochrane), and Jacob Wren. Translators/cameo performers on tour: Thomas Lehman (Hamburg and Berlin), Vladimir Javorksý and Ewan McLaren (Prague), Ayako Kuwabara and Adam Broinowski (Tokyo). Technical support: Mathieu Chartrand. Additional production and touring: Virginia Preston and Martin Bélanger.

A co-production with Kampnagel (Hamburg), BIT Teatergarasjen (Bergen), MAI (Montréal, arts interculturels), Carrefour international de théâtre de Québec, and Les Productions Recto-Verso / Méduse (Quebec City). With the support of the Canada Council for the Arts, Heritage Canada, the Department of Foreign Affairs and International Trade of Canada, the

Conseil des arts et des lettres du Québec, the Conseil de Arts de Montréal, as part of Quebec Focus in the UK 2003 and the Canadian Season-Prague 2003.

**Families Are Formed Through Copulation** (2005)

Written and directed by Jacob Wren. Created and performed by Gaétan Nadeau, Laure Ottmann, and Tracy Wright. Translation by Eva Labarias (in French), Nikolai Francke (in German), and Tomoyuki Arai (in Japanese). Visual art installation by Jean-Pierre Gauthier. Choreography by Martin Bélanger. Technical direction: Mathieu Chartrand. Stage managers: Keri Strobl and Isabelle Beaudry.

A co-production with Forum Freies Theater (Düsseldorf). Residency: Usine C (Montreal). With the support of the Canada Council for the Arts, the Department of Foreign Affairs and International Trade of Canada, the Conseil des arts et des lettres du Québec, and the Kunststiftung NRW (Arts Foundation of North Rhine-Westphalia, Germany).

## HOSPITALITÉ/HOSPITALITY PROJECT

**HOSPITALITY 1: The Title Is Constantly Changing** (2008)

Created and performed by Caroline Dubois, Claudia Fancello, and Jacob Wren.
A co-presentation with Studio 303. Residencies: Studio 303 and Usine C (Montreal).

**HOSPITALITY 3: Individualism Was A Mistake** (2008)

Created and performed by Caroline Dubois, Claudia Fancello, and Jacob Wren. Sound: Radwan Ghazi Moumneh. Lighting: Philippe Dupeyroux. Technical direction: Mathieu Chartrand. Interns: Chélanie Beaudin-Quintin and Amélie Lapointe.

A co-production with Forum Freies Theater (Düsseldorf), in collaboration with Usine C (Montreal), Studio 303, Playwrights' Workshop (Montreal) and Harbourfront Centre World Stage (Toronto). With the support of the Canada Council for the Arts, the Conseil des arts et des lettres du Québec, the Ministère de la culture, des communications et de la condition féminine du Québec, the Conseil des arts de Montréal, and the Kunststiftung NRW.

**The Title Is the Question** (2009)

Video installation created and performed by Caroline Dubois, Claudia Fancello, and Jacob Wren. Video editing: Julie Favreau. Technical direction: Mathieu Chartrand.

As part of the group exhibition *Making It Work*, curated by Susannah Wesley, a joint-production with the Leonard & Bina Ellen Art Gallery (Montreal).

**HOSPITALITY 2: Gradually This Overview** (2010)

Installation-performance created and performed by Caroline Dubois, Claudia Fancello and Jacob Wren. Technical direction: Mathieu Chartrand.

A joint-production with Articule (Montreal). With the support the Conseil des arts et des lettres du Québec and the Conseil des arts de Montréal.

**The DJ Who Gave Too Much Information (Hospitality 5)** (2011)

Created and performed by Caroline Dubois, Claudia Fancello, and Jacob Wren, continued and performed by Marie Claire Forté and Adam Kinner. Technical Direction: Mathieu Chartrand. Interns: Mélanie Cadieux and Séléné Caron.

A co-production with Forum Freies Theater (Düsseldorf), in collaboration with Studio 303 (Montreal) and Noorderzon Festival (Groningen). With the support of the Canada Council for the Arts (touring), the Conseil des arts et des lettres du Québec, the Conseil des arts de Montréal, and the Kunststiftung NRW, as part of Tallinn 2011, European Capital of Culture.

**Bring Your Own Record/Listening Party** (2012)

Public encounter created and animated by Caroline Dubois, Claudia Fancello, and Jacob Wren, on a suggestion by Jasmine Catudal/OFFTA (Montreal).

**Party vinyles** (2012)

Hospitable DJing by Caroline Dubois, Claudia Fancello, and Jacob Wren at a OFFTA/Festival TransAmériques party (Montreal).

**MIXOFF 2.0: Big Brother Where Art Thou?** (2011)

Facebook collaboration by Jacob Wren and Lene Berg.
A co-production with OFFTA (Montreal).

**Evey Song I've Ever Written** (2012)

(Website, Solo, Karaoké, and Band Night Versions)

Concept, songwriting, and performances by Jacob Wren. Website Design: Uniform. Website programming: Bruno Cloutier. Website recordings: Radwan Ghazi Moumneh (hotel2tango). Website translation: Christophe Bernard and Sylvie Lachance. Karaoké assistant: Adam Kinner (Montreal) and Satu Herrala (Helsinki). Artistic Consultants: Patricia Boushel (Montreal), Janne Masalin (Helsinki), Victoria Cheong (Toronto), and the artistic directors of the festivals and venues. With the participation of local bands: the Besnard Lakes, Mozart's Sister, J. Ellise Barbara, Catherine Valéry, Elena Stoodley (Montreal), Kvit Skit, Johannes Fjeldstad, Craig Wells & Rudi Valdersnes, Elida Høgalmen, Second Pest (Bergen), Momus, Reiko Kudo, Maher Shalal Hash Baz, the Hardy Rocks (Tokyo), Above Top Secret, Maylee Todd, Phèdre, Regina of Light Fires, Snowblink (Toronto), the Octopus Project, Leticia Rodriguez, Ume, Foot Patrol, Francine Thirteen (Austin), Christine Owman, Mathias Kristersson, Sandra Mujinga & Linda Spjut, Octopus Ride (Malmö), Tiiu Helinä, Kanerva, Kap Kap, Samuli Putro, Tundramatiks (Helsinki), Ape Diem, the Alicka Problem, Betina, callahaan, Hans Reffert (Mannheim), Fragil, Kreidler, Niobe, and PDR/ex Punk'd Royal (Düsseldorf). Technical Advisor: Mathieu Chartrand.

A co-production with Forum Freies Theater (Düsseldorf), Wunder der Prärie Festival-Zeitraumexit (Mannheim), Baltic Circle International Theatre Festival (Helsinki), and Inkonst (Malmö); in collaboration with Usine C (Montreal). With the support of the Canada Council for the Arts (touring), the Conseil des arts et des lettres du Québec, the Conseil des arts de Montréal, and the Kunststiftung NRW.

**MIXOFF 2** (2014)

Performance-installation by Jacob Wren and Raphaëlle de Groot.
A co-production with OFFTA (Montreal).

**Adventures can be found anywhere, même dans la mélancolie** (2014)

Performance-installation by Claudia Fancello, Marie Claire Forté, Nadège Grebmeier Forget, Adam Kinner, Ashlea Watkin, and Jacob Wren, continued by Julie Bernier, Claudia Fancello, Marie Claire Forté, Anick Martel, and Étienne Provencher-Rousseau.

A joint production with the Leonard & Bina Ellen Art Gallery (Montreal), on an invitation from Michèle Thériault, remounted at Galerie L'Œuvre de l'Autre for the international conference Les pratiques contemporaines de l'écriture textuelle pour la scène, organized by the UQAC's Chaire de recherche en dramaturgie sonore (Saguenay). With the support of the Conseil des arts et des lettres du Québec and the Conseil des arts de Montréal.

**A User's Guide to Authenticity Is a Feeling** (2017)

Created and performed by Jacob Wren. Translation: Christophe Bernard and Marie Claire Forté. Light: Paul Chambers. Technical direction: Mathieu Chartrand.

Residency, co-production, and collaboration: Forum Freies Theater (Düsseldorf), Inkonst (Malmö), and La Chapelle Scènes Contemporaines (Montreal). With the support of the Canada Council for the Arts, the Conseil des arts et des lettres du Québec, and the Conseil des arts de Montréal.

## Acknowledgements

The review on page 77 was translated from French to English by Marie Claire Forté. It was originally published as "*L'art en questions*" by Solange Lévesque in *Le Devoir* on November 21, 2002.

The text "Theatre Reminds Me of Politics" (2009) was originally commissioned by the Perfect Performance festival in Stockholm.

The afterword by Kathrin Tiedemann was translated from German to English by Elena Polzer.

A substantial portion of this book was written during an artist residency at Centre Bang in Saguenay, Quebec. I thank them for their hospitality, support, and the time they gave me to write.

PME-ART acknowledges the support of the Conseil des arts de Montréal.

## Thanks

I say somewhere in this book that gratitude is not my strong suit and yet gratitude is what I'm here to express. Infinite thanks to everyone who appears in this book. I of course especially want to thank everyone who has worked with us to create a PME or PME-ART show – Mathieu, Martin, Tracy, Julie-Andrée, Alex, Benoît, Simone, Samuel, Gaétan, Laure, Jean-Pierre, Adam, Marie Claire, Nadège, Ashlea, Lene, Raphaëlle, Julie, Anick, etc. – I wish I could have done greater justice to how remarkable you all are. And then Caroline and Claudia get an extra-special thanks for their brilliant work, dedication, insight, and hospitality. And just as much thanks to everyone who has presented us. Who took a risk, invited us somewhere, gave us the space, time, and support that truly makes performance thrive. And to our co-producers, who made things possible when all seemed lost. And, of course, to our funders. And then it seems even more important to thank everyone who has come see us perform. When no one comes, there is not much of a performance situation to be yourself within. Thanks for taking a chance on us. Like the Bauhaus song says: "We Love Our Audience." I would also very much like to thank everyone who has served on our board over the years: Catherine Bodmer, Karine Denault, Yves Sheriff, Marilou Craft, Fabien Marcil, and Robin Simpson. Finally, I need to thank Sylvie and Richard at least one more time each. For better and worse you have saved my life and kept me alive these past twenty years. Lachance and Ducharme. May there be so much more luck and charm to come. To anyone who should but doesn't appear in this book, we love you as well. It's only I ran out of pages. I wish I could have included everything. Twenty years simply doesn't fit into a single book. I tried.

## Colophon

Distributed in Canada by the Literary Press Group:
www.lpg.ca

Distributed in the United States by Small Press Distribution:
www.spdbooks.org

Shop online at www.bookthug.ca

BOOK PRODUCTION WAR ECONOMY STANDARD

Designed by Malcolm Sutton
Edited for the press by Malcolm Sutton
Copy-edited by Stuart Ross